The Jewish Community
in British Politics

The Jewish Community in British Politics

Geoffrey Alderman

Clarendon Press · Oxford
1983

Oxford University Press, Walton Street, Oxford OX2 6DP
London Glasgow New York Toronto
Delhi Bombay Calcutta Madras Karachi
Kuala Lumpur Singapore Hong Kong Tokyo
Nairobi Dar es Salaam Cape Town
Melbourne Auckland
and associates in
Beirut Berlin Ibadan Mexico City Nicosia

Oxford is a trademark
of Oxford University Press

Published in the United States by
Oxford University Press, New York

British Library Cataloguing in Publication Data
Alderman, Geoffrey
The Jewish community in British politics.
1. Jews—Great Britain—Political
activity—History   2. Great Britain
—Politics and government—1837-
1901   3. Great Britain—Politics and
government—20th century
I. Title
322.1'0941   DA560
ISBN 0-19-827436-X

Typeset by
DMB (Typesetting), Oxford
Printed in Great Britain
at the University Press, Oxford
by Eric Buckley
Printer to the University

For Naomi Alicia
and
Eliot Daniel

Preface

The work which follows is neither a history of Anglo-Jewry in the nineteenth and twentieth centuries, nor an account of the Jewish contribution to British political life; nor is it an examination of British Zionism, or even of Jewish involvement in the English trade union movement, or of the part played by Jews in the House of Commons. All these matters are themselves worthy of full-scale treatment and all of them, and more besides, play an important part in the story which I have set out to tell. My book, however, is concerned merely with one particular aspect of Anglo-Jewish and British political history, namely the relationship between the political system and those British voters who were or are Jewish.

The term 'Jewish vote' is commonly used in two distinct senses. As 'the Jewish vote' it is a shorthand way of referring to Jewish voters in a particular constituency or locality, or throughout the land. As 'a Jewish vote' it refers to any recognizable tendency on the part of Jewish electors to react in a uniform way or as a distinct bloc, or both, to political issues, or perhaps just one political issue. I employ the term 'Jewish vote' in both these senses; the use of the definite or indefinite article will indicate which meaning is intended in the text.

Unless stated to the contrary, I apply the word 'Jew', and its derivatives, to anyone who considered or considers himself to be Jewish, or who was or is so regarded by his contemporaries. I do not import to the word 'Jew' any exclusively religious or communal connotation.

The politics of Anglo-Jewry has always been something of a taboo subject within the Jewish community. Any talk of the Jewish vote or, worse still, of a Jewish vote, has been actively discouraged in official Anglo-Jewish circles. In the United States of America, by contrast, thanks to the seminal work of Professor Lawrence Fuchs (*The Political Behaviour of American Jews*, The Free Press of Glencoe, Illinois, 1956) the subject of Jewish political behaviour has deservedly received wide scholarly attention, and Jewish political attitudes in other countries of the Diaspora have also attracted academic interest

(See P. J. Medding, 'Towards a General Theory of Jewish Political Interests and Behaviour', *Jewish Journal of Sociology*, xix (1977), 115-44). An examination of the British experience seems long overdue.

My treatment of this subject is largely historical. In the first chapter I trace the politics of Anglo-Jewry in the period before emancipation, and in the second I attempt to show how the dynamics of the emancipation struggle, in the 1840s and 1850s, led to the appearance of distinct attitudes among Jewish voters; a major feature of this period was the alliance between Jewish voters and the mid-Victorian Liberal party. The collapse of this alliance is charted in Chapter Three. In the following chapter I attempt to explain the impact of socialism among Jews in Britain, and Chapter Five describes the effect upon Anglo-Jewish political attitudes of the 'aliens' question in the early years of the present century. The subject-matter of Chapter Six is the relationship between Anglo-Jewry and the Zionist movement. In my view, Zionism was exploited by the Labour party in the mid-twentieth century in order to win the allegiance of Jewish voters; but there were, in fact, a variety of reasons behind the attraction of left-wing politics for many British Jews in the period 1918-45, and these are explored in Chapter Seven. In Chapter Eight I try to explain why the 'special relationship' between Anglo-Jewry and Labour broke down in the thirty years following the end of the Second World War.

This explanation is only partly to be found in the creeping hostility of the post-war Labour party to the State of Israel. It lies also in the profound social and demographic changes which have affected and are still affecting the Anglo-Jewish community. After 1945 an upwardly mobile but still working-class Jewish electorate became disenchanted with Labour politics. Conservative politicians were quick to exploit this alienation. In the 1960s and 1970s Jewish voters became substantially middle class and also substantially Conservative in outlook. Chapter Nine explores these changes and suggests reasons for them. It relies not only upon documentary evidence but also upon my own surveys of Jewish voting intentions in London, carried out between 1974 and 1979.

I am well aware that my work in researching and writing this book has not found favour with those who lead and articulate the opinions of Anglo-Jewry. The major conclusion of this research—that, far from being totally assimilated within British political culture, Jewish voters in Britain have always been capable of independent political behaviour, sometimes in marked contrast to national or regional trends—is also one which runs counter to the most cherished beliefs of Anglo-Jewish leaders. For this I make no apology. In writing this book I have deliberately set out to expose some of the most sensitive areas of Jewish life in Britain. And I believe that the book itself is a contribution towards the intellectual and moral freedom of Anglo-Jewry.

This book could not have been written without a great deal of help from individuals, institutions and libraries, and I am happy to be able, on another page to acknowledge such assistance. Here, however, I must thank The Royal Holloway College for having granted me two terms sabbatical leave, which enabled me to research and write unencumbered by teaching duties. One of these terms was spent gathering material in Israel. This journey would not have been possible without a generous grant from the British Academy (Small Grants Research Fund in the Humanities), supplemented by an award from the Central Research Funds Committee of the University of London. In addition, a specific piece of research in Israel was financed by The Royal Holloway College. To all these bodies I wish to place on record my most sincere thanks.

My wife has lived with this book from the time I began the research for it, in the autumn of 1973, shortly after our marriage. Nine years and two children later I can only marvel at her patience and good humour in tolerating it, and me, for so long.

Finally, I should like to thank here the many Jewish voters who have given of their time to take part in my surveys and answer my questions. They and their forebears are, after all, the central characters in the story I have to tell, and it is to them that my gratitude must surely be most profound.

GEOFFREY ALDERMAN

The Royal Holloway College,
University of London

Acknowledgements

I should like to acknowledge the help of the following institutions, archives, and libraries in making available to me manuscript and printed sources in their possession, and in generally and courteously assisting me with my research: *Beit Lohamei Hagetaot* [Ghetto Fighters' House], near Nahariya, Israel; Research Unit of the Board of Deputies of British Jews; The British Library, London; The Central Zionist Archives of The World Zionist Organization, Jerusalem, Israel; Conservative Friends of Israel; Guildhall Library, London; House of Lords Record Office; Institute of Historical Research, London; Library of the *Jewish Chronicle*, London; Library of Jews' College, London; Labour Friends of Israel; Mocatta Library, University College, London; National Front; National Library of Israel at the Hebrew University, Jerusalem; Plaid Cymru; Library of Royal Holloway College, Egham, Surrey; Scottish National Party; Tower Hamlets Central Library, Stepney, London; Weizmann Archives, Rehovot, Israel.

I also wish to thank the undermentioned individuals for generously placing their time and knowledge at my disposal: The Reverend Saul Amias, MBE; David Carrington; Rabbi A. S. Chaitowitz; Mrs Nehama Chalom; Martin Cohen; Rabbi D. Cooper; Ivor Crewe; Patricia Crimmin; Rabbi S. P. Cutler; Samuel Daly; Mrs Winifred Ewing; Albert Elder; Michael Fidler; Dr David Fisher; Rabbi S. Franses; Leslie Glenville; John Gorst, MP; The Reverend Leslie Hardman; Dr Michael Heymann; M. Howard; Tom Iremonger; Raymond Kalman; A. Kinzley; Dr Barry Kosmin; Mark Lavine; Trude Levi; Harold I. Lightstone; Heinz J. Lobenstein; Abraham J. Marks; Lord Mancroft; Ian Mikardo, MP; Dr Lesley Morgan; Maurice S. Owen; Geoffrey D. Paul; Phil Piratin; Malcolm Rifkind, MP; Moshe (Maurice) Rosetté; John M. Shaftesley, OBE; The Rt. Hon. Lord Shinwell; Dennis Signy; Trevor Skeet, MP; Gerald Viner; Bill Williams; Dafydd Williams.

In addition, a number of party workers and other individuals were kind enough to supply me with information on a non-attributable basis.

Contents

Tables

Manuscript Sources

The British Library, London
Dilke Papers
Gladstone Papers
Peel Papers

The Central Zionist Archives, Jerusalem
Records of the Central Zionist Office, Vienna
Papers of the Zionist Organization, London
Files of the Zionist Federation of the United Kingdom
Papers of Herbert Bentwich
Papers of Philip Guedalla
Papers of S. Kaplansky
Papers of Samuel Landman
Papers of David Wolffsohn

The House of Lords Record Office, London
Lloyd George Papers

The Mocatta Library, University College London
Gaster Papers
Neville Laski Papers
Lucien Wolf Archives

1. The Politics of Pre-Emancipation Jewry

A Jewish dimension has rarely been absent from British political life. This is true irrespective of the part Jews themselves have played in politics. The Jewish minority in medieval England depended utterly upon the protection of the monarch and the support of his local officials. Consequently, the Jews tended to suffer from popular hostility to corrupt sheriffs and rapacious tax-collectors. The Jews existed outside the framework of English politics in the twelfth and thirteenth centuries. Yet they were part of it. A department of state, the Exchequer of the Jews, regulated not merely the financial affairs of the Jewish community but also, to a considerable extent, its relationship with the Gentile majority. The Exchequer and the Wardens, or Justices, of the Jews, associated with it, constituted a Ministry of Jewish Affairs. This apparatus was of tangible benefit to the Jews and they helped administer it. But they did not make policy. When, towards the end of the thirteenth century, political and economic as well as religious factors combined against them, they were helpless to prevent, in 1290, their own expulsion.[1]

Between the Expulsion and the so-called Readmission of 1656, Jews played no part in English political life because there was no recognized Jewish community in the country. That is not to say that England was bereft of Jews. Individual Jews could always be found in England, particularly after the expulsion of the Jewish communities from Spain, Portugal, and Navarre at the end of the fifteenth century. A colony of Marranos—Iberian crypto-Jews who had outwardly espoused Catholicism to escape persecution—had already established itself in London by 1536. Its existence was precarious, to say the least, and was perhaps made possible only by a deliberate resemblance to Protestant refugees. The accession of the Catholic Mary I was the signal for the colony to disperse itself abroad.

Under Elizabeth I, Marranos returned to England. Henceforth, fear of Catholicism, and of the consequences of the return of a Catholic monarchy in England, remained among the basic political tenets of English Jews. What they desired was a stable Protestant government, and this desire was not diminished by the important events of the Civil War and Interregnum.

These events, and the philo-Semitic manifestations which preceded them, have been painstakingly chronicled by the late Dr Cecil Roth.[2] Briefly, in 1651 Rabbi Menasseh ben Israel of the Jewish community in Amsterdam was persuaded—perhaps by Cromwell's Secretary of State, John Thurloe—to make a formal application to the Council of State in England begging that the Jews be allowed to re-enter the country. The matter was to be the subject of heated controversy within the Council, and beyond it, for the next five years. Cromwell himself was sympathetic to Menasseh's request, not on religious grounds, but because, as Lord Protector, he believed that Jewish commercial talents would serve England well. But he underestimated the strength of popular feeling against Jews, and could not bring the Council of State to support him.

As we have seen, Jews were already resident in England. But the Marrano community (of about twenty households) in London, whom Menasseh had never consulted before making his approach, now became thoroughly alarmed. In a manner reminiscent of attitudes adopted by succeeding generations of Anglo-Jewish leaders, the Marranos reacted against the attempt to emancipate them. They wanted only to be left alone, in obscurity; they certainly did not want more Jews coming into the country, perhaps because they knew, and were fearful of, the ease with which anti-Jewish prejudices could be aroused. But Menasseh had pushed them into the political arena. The situation was doubly dangerous, because England was now at war with Spain, and the Marranos were threatened with persecution as Spaniards. So, playing on English hatred of Spain as well as on Puritan hatred of Catholicism, they boldly revealed themselves as Jewish refugees from the Spanish Inquisition. In association with Menasseh, they presented a petition to Cromwell for written permission to meet for private worship as Jews. On 25 June 1656 the Council of State granted their request.

The 'Readmission' did not, however, convert the infant Anglo-Jewish community to Republicanism. The safety of the community was grounded largely in the person of Oliver Cromwell as absolute ruler of the country. When he died, popular reaction against the Jews became much stronger, and when Charles II was restored to the throne the community feared that its end was in sight. In fact Charles turned out to be its saviour. Personally inclined to religious toleration, while in exile he had unsuccessfully attempted to extract a loan from the Jews of Amsterdam.[3] Menasseh ben Israel, though he had addressed himself to Cromwell, was, in common with most of his co-religionists in Holland, sympathetic to the Stuart cause, regarding the Civil War as a divine punishment for the expulsion of the Jews from England.[4]. The early years of the Restoration were ones of great anxiety for Anglo-Jewry. But its position, and the attitude of Charles II, were made clear in 1664 when the Privy Council, with royal approval, gave the Jews what amounted to a dispensation freeing them from the penalties of the Conventicle Act, which prohibited religious assemblies not held in accordance with the liturgy of the Church of England.

Thereafter, the politics of the Jews of the Resettlement may be summarized as strong support for the Stuart succession, but an equally strong aversion to a Catholic ascendancy in England. And this position, dictated by the facts of their existence in England, necessarily forced the Jews to take sides in domestic political struggles, which always had religious overtones and implications. Thus in 1670 there were 'various expenses on solicitors and goings and comings to the Parliament and bottles of wine were presented' as part of a campaign to win friends at Westminster during a popular outcry against Popery.[5] Four years later the community had to appeal to the Privy Council once more, to prevent legal proceedings being taken against the Jews on account of their exercise of their religion.

But this reliance on the royal prerogative had obvious dangers. In November 1685 the community had to throw itself on the mercy of the Catholic James II to prevent a prosecution (under the Elizabethan recusancy laws) for failure to attend

church; the Attorney-General was instructed to stop all proceedings. By thus relying on the absolute powers of the Crown
the Jews threatened to involve themselves in the constitutional
struggle between James and his subjects. And few Jews could
have relished the prospect of living indefinitely under a
Catholic monarchy. Whether the Jews of England played any
part in the overthrow of James, and his replacement by his
Dutch Calvinist brother-in-law, William of Orange, is not
known. But it is certain that William's English and Irish ex-
peditions were financed by Dutch Jewish army contractors and
that, as king, William embarked upon a deliberate policy of encouraging wealthy Dutch Jews to settle in his new realm.

So it was that under William, and then under Queen Anne,
the precariousness of the existence of Anglo-Jewry melted away.
Alongside the growing Sephardi community there grew up an
Ashkenazi community from Germany. In 1685 Anglo-Jewry
numbered about 400 souls, but by the end of the seventeenth
century the number had doubled.[6] By the early years of the
eighteenth century Jews were firmly established in English
commercial life. Several prominent members of the community
were sworn brokers on the Royal Exchange; the twelve 'Jew
Brokers' were, indeed, the only brokers allowed to practise on
the Exchange without being Freemen of the City of London.

This commercial toleration has also brought with it certain
religious benefits. In 1698, when Parliament passed a bill 'for
the more effective suppressing of Blasphemy and Pro-
phaneness', a clause was included specifically exempting Jews
from the bill's provisions. The practice of Judaism in England
thus, at last, acquired parliamentary approval, and this helped
pave the way for the enormous expansion of the Anglo-Jewish
community during the Hanoverian period.

As a corollary, however, the Jews had to become the staunchest supporters of the Glorious Revolution of 1688, the most
forthright opponents of the Stuart Pretenders (James II and his
son Bonny Prince Charlie, the Young Pretender), and the most
vigorous upholders of the Protestant Hanoverian succession.
Economic as well as political considerations dictated this position. As shareholders in the National Debt, the richer sections
of the community risked financial ruin had there been a Stuart
restoration; for such an event would certainly have been

followed by a repudiation of government debts. So the Jews
became Whigs. During the Jacobite Rebellion of 1745 Jewish
merchants and brokers closed ranks behind the government.
They accepted bank notes at par and helped minimize a run on
the banks. Samson Gideon, the most prominent Anglo-Jewish
financier, advised the government on money matters and
helped raise the loan of £1,700,000 floated to meet the crisis.
Other Jewish brokers were equally ostentatious in their support, financial and moral, for the Hanoverian cause. Services
of intercession were held in synagogues.[7] Gideon, in particular,
became the confidant of successive Prime Ministers and
Chancellors of the Exchequer, and raised a number of government loans during the War of the Austrian Succession and the
Seven Years War. In 1757, the most critical year of the Seven
Years War, the government implemented the suggestion of the
enigmatic Jewish dealer in lottery tickets, Jacob Henriques,
that a guinea lottery be instituted to help balance the budget.

Nor were the Whig magnates slow to repay the political
debts they owed to the Jews. But they could only do this to the
extent that public opinion would allow. In 1744 George II and
his government responded warmly to the petition of Moses
Hart and Aaron Franks, the leading members of the
(Ashkenazi) Great Synagogue in London, and successfully persuaded the Empress Maria Theresa to reverse her banishment
of the Jews from Bohemia. Two years later emboldened, no
doubt, by the alacrity with which the government had accepted
Jewish support during the Jacobite uprising, the Spanish and
Portuguese congregation determined to ask Parliament to ease
the process of naturalization of foreign-born Jews. This question was to dominate the political activities of the Anglo-Jewish
leaders for the next eight years. No instance shows more clearly
the extent of Whig support for the Jews in the eighteenth century, nor more forcefully the latent xenophobia of the common
people.

The naturalization question was in essence a simple one.[8]
Foreign-born merchants resident in England, and who were not
naturalized, had to pay various extraordinary charges called
'alien duties'. Naturalization was a difficult and costly process,
necessitating private Acts of Parliament. Moreover it was not
a method open to professing Jews, for Parliament required

those who became naturalized in this way to have received the Sacrament within the past month according to the rites of the Church of England, and to take the Protestant Oaths of Supremacy and Allegiance. In 1746 the Spanish and Por-tuguese community appointed a standing 'committee of deputies' to lobby for a change in the naturalization laws. On 14 January 1753 Joseph Salvador, a wealthy and prominent member of the community, sent a memorandum to the Duke of Newcastle, Secretary of State in the ministry headed by his brother, Henry Pelham, requesting the passage of a Jewish Naturalization bill. At the same time Philip Carteret Webb, a solicitor who had acted for a number of years on behalf of the community in naturalization cases, was engaged as legal ad-viser and, as it turned out, public relations expert.

The Pelham brothers, thankful for continued Jewish finan-cial co-operation, were personally sympathetic to the Jewish case. They knew, however, that the bill was sure to meet with popular hostility, which was just as likely to be exploited by their political opponents. So, though they gave the bill their blessing, it was not formally adopted as a government measure. A modest reform, merely exempting Jews naturalized by private Act from the obligation of taking the Sacrament, and allowing them to omit the words 'on the true faith of a Christian' from the Oaths of Supremacy and Allegiance, the bill had an easy passage through the House of Lords, a somewhat less easy passage through the House of Commons, and became law on 22 May 1753.

The passage of the Jewish Naturalization Act was the signal for a country-wide agitation against it. With a general election due the following year, the Act served as a rallying point for the disaffected, amongst whom were powerful vested interests in the City of London, High Churchmen, disgruntled Whigs, and, above all, implacable Tories. In general the propaganda against the Act was of a crude religious kind. But the Tories determined to make political capital out of it. Newcastle and Pelham were accused of having accepted Jewish bribes to see that the legislation was passed.[9] In the political rhetoric of 1753-4, the words 'Jew' and 'Whig' were used synonymously. One Tory newspaper alleged that the Act would attract hordes of Jews to England; 'they will make money, buy land, and therby secure votes'.[10] Here, for the first time in English history, the spectre was raised, and the possibility (however remote or far-fetched at the time) discussed, of a 'Jewish Vote', and of a substantial Jewish (and therefore 'foreign') dimension being introduced into English political life.

Against this tide of abuse Anglo-Jewry was helpless. Webb wrote an anonymous pamphlet attacking City opposition to the Act, but to little effect. During the summer of 1753 the Pelhams decided that the Act would have to be sacrificed if a Whig majority were to be assured in the elections the following year. On 15 November Newcastle himself moved the repeal in the House of Lords, and on 20 December the repeal received the Royal Assent.

Were the Pelhams justified in believing that the Act was a political liability? Professor John Owen writes of Henry Pelham's 'exaggerated fear of unfavourable repercussions in the forthcoming general election'.[11] But, during the passage of the Act, the number of Government supporters in the Commons remained virtually static at ninety-six, while the opposition, on the third reading of the bill, was able to increase its strength from sixteen to fifty-five. And, as Dr Roth has pointed out, the Government lost a number of supporters in the 1754 election directly as a result of the Naturalization Act: in particular, General James Oglethorpe, who had supported the bill, was turned out at Haslemere after thirty-two years as its MP, and Sir William Calvert was unseated in the City of London.[12]

It is probable, therefore, that the Jewish Naturalization Act was a political liability at the time, and that the Pelhams suffered politically from identification with religious liberalism in an age when (as the Sacheverell case of 1710 had shown, and the Gordon Riots of 1780 were to show) religious bigotry was still very much alive, waiting to be used by unscrupulous political malcontents. For that reason, if for no other, the Jews had become a not unimportant fact of English domestic politics.

For a community so small—there were probably less than 8,000 Jews in Great Britain in 1753—and so dependent on being allowed to engage unhindered in commercial activity, the dangers were obvious. There was, on the one hand, a clear need for a permanent organization to deal with any future political contingencies. From time to time during the first half of the eighteenth century the Spanish and Portuguese congregation had appointed *Deputados*—Deputies—to deal with political matters as and when they arose. Thus, in 1702, *ad hoc* Deputies had been appointed when a bill was passed by Parliament compelling Jewish parents to support such of their children as were (perhaps through adulterous unions) Protestants. And in 1746 a 'Committee of Diligence' was set up to see if anything could be done to facilitate the passing of a Naturalization Act for Jews in Ireland; a minute book was kept but has not survived.[13] The activities of Philip Webb, both before and during the 1753 crisis, suggest that, as Attorney to the Spanish and Portuguese community, he acted also as its political agent.

But the rapid expansion of the Ashkenazi congregation made such unilateral political activity by the Spanish and Portuguese Jews both anachronistic and devoid of realism. A crisis was reached in 1760 when the Elders of the Spanish and Portuguese congregation appointed a standing committee to convey suitable expressions of devotion to the new King, George III, and to deal thereafter with any urgent political matters. The Ashkenazi leaders protested against their exclusion from the delegation, and set up their own 'German Secret Committee for Public Affairs'. Both sides, however, soon saw the absurdity, and danger, of having two separate political organizations. So, towards the end of the year, it was decided to hold joint meetings, and it was out of these that the London Committee of Deputies of British Jews, now known as the Board of Deputies, evolved.[14]

On the other hand, there was felt to be a need, just as great, for Anglo-Jewry to maintain a low profile. The naturalization question was not raised again during the eighteenth century nor, indeed, for much of the nineteenth. The object of the ill-fated 1753 Act was achieved, quite incidentally, in 1826, when Parliament reformed the naturalization laws without so much as mentioning the Jews. Throughout the long reign of George III Anglo-Jewry asked nothing of the British political establishment. Continually augmented by Jews from abroad, the community maintained its foreign character, and this was a powerful incentive for it to keep well away from the public limelight.

In social and economic terms the late eighteenth century was a period of growth for Anglo-Jewry. At the end of the Napoleonic Wars its numbers had swollen to somewhere between 20,000 and 30,000. Jewish communities were firmly established in the major provincial centres, though the majority of Jews lived (as they have always lived) in London. At the top of the social scale were the wealthy Jews, engaged in wholesale commerce, stockbroking, and the diamond trade. Below them were to be found shopkeepers, silversmiths, watchmakers, and, in the seaports, ships' agents, and below them a class of Jewish artisans. At the bottom of the social scale were the Jewish pedlars and old-clothes dealers, who became familiar sights both in the cities and in the countryside.[15]

Communal growth and social diversity thus brought with it, for the first time, the problem of a Jewish pauper class, among which was inevitably to be found a criminal element. Owing to the character of Jewish immigration to Britain in the eighteenth century, this problem affected the Ashkenazim much more than the wealthier but, by now, smaller Sephardi community. The Ashkenazi leaders hoped at first that the tide of immigration could be stemmed. The authorities of the Great Synagogue decided to refuse poor relief to foreign Jews who had left their country without good cause.[16] But deteriorating conditions for Jews in eastern Europe meant that the immigrant flow was maintained. Above all else, therefore, was the desire to prevent the Jewish poor from becoming a burden on the English public purse, even though Jewish parishioners, like their Gentile counterparts, contributed to the poor rate. Thus, when the Ashkenazi leaders were discussing with the Government a scheme for the statutory establishment of a Jewish Poor Fund (in 1795) they were quite happy that the fund should be financed by a special tax on Jews, not instead of payment of the poor rate but in addition to it. The scheme failed because the community feared that, if successful, it would attract even greater numbers of poor Jews from abroad.[17]

One factor which certainly encouraged this ultra-cautious attitude was the outbreak of war with revolutionary France.

The Jews, like other 'foreign' elements, were under constant popular suspicion of harbouring Jacobin sympathies. The Aliens Act of 1793, designed to control foreigners in England, resulted in sporadic harassment of Jewish traders and the deportation of some Jews. From time to time mobs attacked Jews and Jewish property, including at least one synagogue (at Birmingham, in 1813). The government of William Pitt the Younger did not take seriously the wilder accusations against Anglo-Jewry. The synagogues themselves were entrusted with the registration of Jews born abroad, and the Seditious Meetings bill of 1795 was specially modified to meet Jewish objections.[18]

None the less, the temper of the times demanded every show of loyalty from the Jewish community. At one extreme, Jews enlisted in unprecedented numbers for service in the army. At the other, Jewish financiers took upon themselves the task of finding for the Treasury the money to pay for the military operations. Two names stand out in this field, those of the Goldsmid brothers, Benjamin and Abraham.[19] Towards the end of the French wars a third name rose to prominence, that of Nathan Mayer Rothschild, whose unrivalled contacts made it possible for him to forward, via Paris, the bullion needed to pay Wellington's forces in Spain.

Just as the political realities of the early and mid-eighteenth century had turned the Jews into loyal Whigs, so those of the late eighteenth and very early nineteenth centuries made of them unswerving champions of the Younger Pitt. This was to have important repercussions upon the political complexion of Anglo-Jewry in the 'Age of Emacipation' and, in particular, must surely account in some measure for the phenomenon of Jewish Tories during the great emancipation struggle of the nineteenth century. The process took place at different but interconnecting levels. How many Jews had votes during the period of the Napoleonic Wars is simply not ascertainable. Theoretically no professing Jew could vote, for the returning officers at elections had the power to demand the swearing of a Christian Oath of Abjuration by all prospective voters at the polls. The law on this subject was not changed until 1835; thereafter voters were not required to take any oath before voting. But this reform merely brought the law into line with current practice, for the oath was often regarded as a tiresome preliminary and was simply not administered. Thus in December 1832 Rabbi Asher Ansell of Liverpool was able to vote in the general election without hindrance.[20] Certainly by the 1780s many Jews—and not just the very wealthy—possessed the property qualifications necessary for the franchise. A Gillray cartoon of 1788, showing 'Election-Troops bringing in their accounts to the Pay-Table', depicts one account 'for perjury and procuring Jew voters'. And it is beyond doubt that the Jewish electorate of the period cast their votes for the Government of the Younger Pitt.

Pitt was a Whig politician, brought up in the ways of his father, the Earl of Chatham, and his political mentor, the Earl of Shelburne. But his personal following in the Commons was very small and his Government, in fact, included a variety of Whig groups, King's Friends, and Tories. The repressive measures which he introduced during the French wars were welcomed by Tory and Whig factions alike; indeed, by 1797 Pitt's government had been significantly strengthened by the support of most of the Whig groups in Parliament. Though foreign-born Jews were inconvenienced by some of the repressive measures, there is certainly no evidence that the Jewish community was alienated by them. After Pitt's death, in 1806, and especially in the period of social unrest and political repression associated with the Tory Government of Lord Liverpool (1812-27), Government supporters professed to be merely following the policies of the late Mr Pitt. The period was not one of strongly defined political groupings. So it must have been easy for some Jews to transfer their political loyalty from William Pitt to Tory politicians. Thus in June 1818 the famous Jewish quack doctor of Liverpool, Samuel Solomons, occupied himself in canvassing on behalf of George Canning, President of the Board of Control in Lord Liverpool's 'Ministry of Mediocrities'.[21] Thus, too, did Sir Menasseh Lopes, a baptized Jewish MP, support Pitt between 1804 and 1806 and Liverpool from 1812 to 1819.[22]

The Wars of the French Revolution had practically cut off the flow into Britain of poor Jews from the Continent. Relieved of this embarrassment the Jewish community had seized the opportunity to merge into its British background. Many of its

members were now British-born, so the problem of naturalization was no longer pressing. The pedlars and old-clothes
men were becoming shopkeepers and tailors, and, as such,
they helped augment a growing Jewish middle class. The
wealthiest Jewish financiers rubbed shoulders with the cream
of the English aristocracy, and even with members of the Royal
Family. Socially, popular attitudes to the Jews became notice-
ably more liberal after Waterloo. In 1818, for instance, a London vestry allowed Jews to vote by proxy when parish elections
were held on Jewish holy days.[23] Most remarkable of all, the
former hostility to adopting men of Jewish origin as parliamentary candidates had become much less fierce. In 1758 William
Villareal, a baptized Sephardi, had been rebuffed in his attempt
to become Government candidate at Nottingham.[24] But in
1770 Samson Gideon the younger—'Pitt's Jew'—the son of the
famous financier (who had married out of the faith), was elected
for Cambridge. In 1802 the notorious borough-monger Sir
Menasseh Lopes was returned for Romney; in 1814 his sister's
son, Ralph Franco, became MP for Westbury (a Lopes
borough). In 1818 Ralph Bernal was elected at Lincoln, and
the following year David Ricardo, the famous political econ-
omist, became MP for Portarlington.

But Lopes, Franco, Bernal, and Ricardo were not professing
Jews. All had abandoned the Jewish faith. Their political success underlined the disabilities under which Anglo-Jewry still
laboured.[25] For though in commerce Jews suffered little, in
public life all avenues were barred to them. These barriers
could only be lifted by baptism and, hence, religious assimilation. In politics, government, the law, the universities, and a
wide range of professional callings, the Test and Corporation
Acts stood in the way, and required of all who sought advancement in these fields the taking of the Sacrament in accordance
with the rites of the Church of England and the swearing of the
Oaths of Supremacy and Allegiance 'on the true faith of a
Christian'.

When peace returned to the country, in 1815, wealthy Jews
who aspired to public life, themselves or for their children,
therefore faced practically insurmountable obstacles. But these
were not obstacles which confronted Jews alone. Roman Catholics and even Dissenters—indeed any who were not prepared

to enter into the bosom of the Established Church—were the victims of similar discrimination. There could be no question of Jewish claims for emancipation being satisfied ahead of those of Christians. The one ray of hope lay in the fact that not every Tory was a die-hard opponent of liberality in these matters. Canning himself, though he opposed the repeal of the Test and Corporation Acts, favoured Catholic emancipation. Both reforms were eventually carried, in 1828 and 1829 respectively, by the Conservative government of the Duke of Wellington. It seemed, therefore, that Jewish emancipation could not be far distant, and there were those within the Anglo-Jewish community who looked to the Tory party to grant it.

2. The Jewish Vote is Born

The story of Jewish emancipation in Britain has been told many times and with a variety of emphases.[1] Inevitably, during the struggle and after it, myths developed about the friends and foes in the contest, the quarters from which the Jews received most help, and hence to which they were supposed to be most beholden, and even about the way in which emancipation had been won. These myths were themselves part of the struggle, and they in turn became the foundation stones of subsequent political attitudes on the part of Anglo-Jewry.

The basic narrative of events is well known. What needs to be stressed at the outset is that the campaign for emancipation (or, more correctly, for the removal of the remaining civil disabilities, affecting British-born professing Jews, of which the bar to a parliamentary career was but the most obvious) was not a campaign undertaken by Anglo-Jewry *en masse*. Only a handful of very wealthy Jews could possibly have afforded a career in public life, at municipal or parliamentary level. Emancipation was not likely to be of much benefit to most British Jews in the immediate future. Researching in the 1850s, Henry Mayhew, the great chronicler of London life, had this to say about the attitude of the Jewish 'man in the street' to the emancipation battle:

Perhaps there is no people in the world, possessing the average amount of intelligence in busy communities, who care so little for politics as the general body of the Jews....

I was told by a Hebrew gentleman (a professional man) that so little did the Jews themselves care for 'Jewish emancipation', that he questioned if one man in ten, activated solely by his own feelings, would trouble himself to walk the length of the street in which he lived to secure Baron Rothschild's admission into the House of Commons....

When such is the feeling of the comparatively wealthier Jews, no one can wonder that I found among the Jew street-sellers and old-clothes men with whom I talked on the subject ... a perfect indifference to, and nearly as perfect an ignorance of, politics. Perhaps no men buy so few newspapers, and read them so little, as the Jews generally.[2]

This indifference was, moreover, bolstered by tensions within the Anglo-Jewish community. Not only were the wealthy families who fought for emancipation remote from the mass of the community. Some of them were at odds with its religious leaders. This dispute had its origins in the cloying exclusivity of the Spanish and Portuguese congregation, which refused to allow any of its members to hold services within six miles of the congregation's synagogue, at Bevis Marks in the City of London. But the dispute was soon affected by the reverberations of the Reform Movement in Germany. The English dissidents demanded drastic revision of synagogue services and, ultimately, of orthodox doctrine. In particular like their German counterparts they held that emancipation would only come when Judaism had discarded its nationalistic elements and its 'foreign' overtones. Battle-lines were drawn, and in 1840 eighteen Sephardim and six Ashkenazim resolved to establish a place of worship in west London which would be neither Ashkenazi nor Sephardi, but 'British'; two years later the first English Reformed Synagogue, the West London Synagogue of British Jews, opened its doors.

Sir Moses Montefiore, the banker and philanthropist who became President of the Board of Deputies in 1835, refused to admit to membership of the Board any Jew who was an adherent of the Reform movement. In 1853, when four provincial congregations elected reformers as their deputies, Montefiore (some of whose relations had been among the original Reform dissidents) used his casting vote to keep them out. And from 1845 Montefiore had a staunch ally in Nathan Marcus Adler, elected that year as Chief Rabbi in succession to Solomon Hirschel. Adler, who came from Hanover, could claim an allegiance which his predecessors could not, for his was the first election in which provincial communities had participated as well as the London congregations. He believed that the orthodox structure in England was too weak to permit the growth of self-governing communities, as existed in Germany and Poland, and that what was needed was strong centralization of religious institutions, under his aegis.[3] In this work he could count on the backing of Montefiore while Montefiore could count on his unswerving support in dealing with the Reformers.

The Reform controversy was bound to affect the campaign

for political emancipation. Thus in 1845, for instance, when Sir Robert Peel's Government was faced with demands to legislate to enable Jews to hold municipal office, a cautious approach to the Government by the Board of Deputies was countered by a demand for 'the rights of British subjects' by a group of thirty-five Reform Jews, headed by Isaac Lyon Goldsmid.[4] The founders of the English Reformed Synagogue, and in particular the Mocattas and the Goldsmids, were among the most energetic workers for emancipation; for them the two movements went hand in hand. Other leading emancipationists, such as the Lloyds underwriter and banker David Salomons, were at odds with the orthodox establishment because they viewed the rift within Anglo-Jewry as a hindrance to the removal of civil disabilities; Salomons argued that the Jews could not demand equality with the Gentiles while denying it to their fellow Jews who happened to be Reformers. Salomons did not regard the Reform controversy as being by any means the most pressing problem facing the community, and he resented Adler's attempts to assert rabbinical authority in this matter and others, such as education.[5]

This attitude in turn convinced some religious leaders that political emancipation would lead to assimilation and the complete loss of religious identity. So they rejected the quest for political equality, and were not afraid to identify themselves with Christian opponents of emancipation in this regard.[6] Adler, it must be said, was not of this view. But he had no enthusiasm for the emancipation campaign. Montefiore viewed emancipation as a desirable object, but not one to be pushed to extremes. Moreover, he was highly critical of the attempts of the leading emancipationists to bypass the Board of Deputies in their dealings with the Government on this issue. Little wonder, therefore, that under these influences the Board did not stir itself until the very last stages of the emancipation struggle.

The movement for emancipation was not, therefore, a straightforward one. At the time it was fashionable to see it as a clash—one of a series of clashes—between the forces of reaction (the landed aristocracy, the House of Lords, the Church of England), embodied in the Conservative party, and the forces of enlightenment (Benthamism, evangelicanism, the *nouveaux riches* of the industrial revolution), represented by radicals, Whigs, and Liberals. Two of the staunchest defenders of Jewish rights, Robert Grant and T. B. Macaulay, were the sons of two of the best-known early nineteenth-century evangelicals, Charles Grant and Zachary Macaulay. Whereas the Tory *Quarterly Review* ignored the Jewish question until after 1846, the radical *Westminster Review* and the Whig *Edinburgh Review* had championed the Jewish cause from the first.[7] To Jews of the next generation the strength of Conservative hostility to emancipation, and the warmth of Whig/Liberal support for it, were axiomatic:

It may seem an absurd thing to say, [Lucien Wolf wrote in 1885] but it is nevertheless true, that if anyone will read the Pentateuch carefully ... and then read that admirable book, 'The Radical Programme' ... he will find a close relationship between the two works, with the one difference, that he will be bound to award the palm for consistent and thorough Radicalism to the Pentateuch.[8]

And in 1908 the Revd A. A. Green, of the Hampstead Synagogue, could say:

When I was a boy, [he was born in 1860] the first thing that I was taught was that the principles of the Liberal party had given Jews their equal rights with other Englishmen, and that the principles of the Conservative party had opposed the removal of Jewish disabilities ... I remember going to the election meetings in 1874 and regarding as traitors to Judaism coreligionists prepared to vote against Baron Rothschild.[9]

But in reality all was not black and white during the emancipation period. Popular anti-Semitism was not something which Whigs and radicals could ignore, even assuming they wanted to. The crude religious bigotry of William Cobbett, in and out of Parliament, and his seemingly endless tirades against 'blaspheming Jews', were not the exception which proved the rule. Although Chartist newspapers protested indignantly against persecution of Jews, there was little sympathy for Jews as a people; they were regarded as wealthy parasites, and bracketed, along with 'jobbers, oppressors and murderers', as enemies of the working classes.[10]

Other opponents of emancipation (on religious grounds) included the factory reformer Lord Ashley (later Lord Shaftesbury) and the future Liberal leader, W. E. Gladstone. Gladstone opposed Jewish emancipation for nearly twenty years, both in Parliament and in his book on *The State in its Relation with the Church*,[11] and though he eventually changed his mind his antipathy towards Jews was something which remained with him throughout his long political career. Supporters of emancipation included the Tory peer (and anti-Catholic pamphleteer) Lord Bexley[12], the future Conservative Prime Minister Benjamin Disraeli, and his predecessor as Conservative leader in the Commons, Lord George Bentinck. Lord Grey, the Whig Prime Minister beetween 1830 and 1834, consistently refused to give his or his government's support to Jewish emancipation.[13] But the bill which eventually became law in 1858 was a Conservative measure, passed owing to the benevolent neutrality of a Conservative Government.

Why, then, did the impression gain ground that the Conservatives were, *en bloc*, the enemies of emancipation, and the Liberals its champions, and that, as a consequence, the Jews rightly delivered their political strength into the hands of the Liberal party? The answer lies partly in the tactics of Liberal politicians and their Jewish allies in the late 1840s, and partly in a series of accidental circumstances and personal friendships.

The granting of Catholic emancipation by Wellington's Government made Jewish emancipation for the first time a practical possibility. The 1828 repeal of the Test and Corporation Acts would have benefited Jews and Dissenters alike. But an amendment, introduced in the Lords by the Bishop of Llandaff, inserted the words 'on the true faith of a Christian' in the declaration henceforth required of those taking up public office. Lord Holland moved that Jews be permitted to omit these words, but his amendment was lost. The position of Jews wishing to enter public life was, indeed, materially worse after 1828 for the Indemnity Act, previously passed annually to benefit dissenters of all sorts, now lapsed. With the enactment of Catholic emancipation the following year, Jews and atheists alone were henceforth subject to political disabilities because of their religious faith.

It seemed natural that those Jews interested in pursuing the emancipation question should turn to Wellington's Government for support. Foremost among these Jews were Nathan Mayer Rothschild, the orthodox head of the celebrated banking firm, and Isaac Lyon Goldsmid, nephew of the deceased Goldsmid brothers, a financier and philanthropist in his own right, and eventually to become a founder of the Reform Synagogue. Goldsmid was a close personal friend of Lord Holland, the nephew and political devotee of Charles James Fox. He was anxious to obtain Holland's support and advice in the campaign he intended to launch, and offered to put his constituency interest in Surrey at the disposal of the Whig peer to help launch his son on a parliamentary career.[14]

In the spring of 1829 Holland advised Goldsmid to approach Wellington's Government on the Jewish question. Discussions took place between Rothschild and leading members of the Government, including the Prime Minister. As a result, Rothschild advised the Board of Deputies to draw up a petition to the House of Lords. Lord Bexley and the Duke of Sussex, a younger brother of George IV, were brought into the deliberations, a petition was actually presented, and a bill prepared. But Wellington was not enthusiastic. Catholic emancipation had split the Tory party badly; he did not want a similarly controversial bill for the Jews introduced in the same session. So the matter was postponed.

Meanwhile steps were taken to elicit wider support. There was a more systematic collection of signatures for another petition which was presented in February 1830 by Lord Bexley in the Lords and Robert Grant in the Commons.[15] Then, in April, Grant introduced the first Jewish Relief bill. Though it did not have Government support it is possible that its promoters expected some show of sympathy from Wellington's Administration. In the event the Duke and Duchess of Gloucester prevailed upon George IV to let it be known that the King opposed the bill.[16] This sealed the fate of the proposed reform, for against royal influence neither Wellington nor Peel was prepared to act. The bill's second reading, on 17 May 1830, was defeated by 228 votes to 165.

In November Wellington's Government fell. The Whigs came to power, and in the general election of 1831 they secured a majority in the Commons. But this did not bring Jewish emancipation any nearer. In May 1833 a Jews' Civil Disabilities bill passed the Commons only to be defeated in the Lords. This happened again the following year. In 1836 the second reading in the Lords was never moved.

At this point the parliamentary struggle was, temporarily, brought to a halt. But although this first phase of the battle had not been successful, some compensating advantages had been derived from the campaign. A great number of influential persons had been won over to the cause: the socialist Robert Owen, the Irish leader Daniel O'Connell, David Ricardo, Joseph Hume, T. B. Macaulay, and a host of others. More striking still was a perceptible shifting of ground by opponents of the cause. A distinction was drawn between the admission of Jews to Parliament and the removal of other civil disabilities, and many Tories who opposed admission to Parliament were none the less prepared to concede reform in other directions.[17] Thus in 1830 the Mayor and other members of the unreformed Corporation of Liverpool signed a petition in support of Grant's bill; they were joined by the most important sections of the Liverpool business fraternity, and by several clergymen of the Church of England.[18] The 1830 bill was also supported in a petition from 14,000 bankers, merchants, and traders of the unreformed City of London. It was also in 1830 that Jews obtained entry to the freedom of the City of London by special oath; in 1835 David Salomons was elected Sheriff (necessitating special legislation for Jews taking up this office) and, two years later, Moses Montefiore received the same honour. In 1835, too, as was pointed out in the previous chapter, Jews were granted the franchise. The following year the Board of Deputies itself received statutory recognition in the Marriage Registration Act.

The tide of political opinion, and especially of Conservative opinion, was thus not all in one direction. Of the many reasons for the lack of success in the first phase of the struggle for emancipation, two stand out as of supreme importance. Firstly, the Jewish community was itself divided over both issues and tactics. It was not only that a section of Anglo-Jewry was hostile and the bulk of the community indifferent. More damaging was the fact that some Jewish merchants made no secret of their willingness to settle for half a loaf. Lewis Levy, for instance, petitioned the Commons in 1830 in favour of a declaratory law on the right of Jews to own land, but insisted that he desired neither the franchise nor the right of election to Parliament, and he informed the Commons that his Jewish acquaintances were of a similar opinion.[19] Views such as these undoubtedly gave comfort to many Conservatives in their belief that some reforms, falling short of entry to Parliament, would be acceptable. Indeed, after the failure of the 1830 bill the faint-hearted Deputies refused to finance further parliamentary adventures. In 1838 the Deputies broke with Goldsmid, and he with them; henceforth those who wished to continue the campaign had to fight on alone, without official communal support.[20]

Secondly, although Conservative and ecclesiastical opinion in the House of Lords was undoubtedly the major obstacle to reform, it would have been less formidable had the Whigs presented a united front to the forces of reaction. But they did no such thing. Grey refused to give Goldsmid the assurance he desired so much, that the Whig Government would support the removal of Jewish disabilities.[21] Rothschild continued to believe that the key to Jewish emancipation lay with the Tories and, in 1834, he urged Wellington to form a government 'and consent to some reforms; saying to His Grace that he must go with the world, for the world would not go with him'.[22] Lord Melbourne's Whig Administration, dismissed by William IV, was restored the following year and agreed to support the 1836 Disabilities bill, but evidently with little enthusiasm: the second reading was passed in a near-empty House, thirty-nine voting for and twenty-two against.[23] The Tory die-hards and the bishops in the upper House could have wished for no better indication that there existed a great deal of apathy over the reform, which they might therefore reject without fear of repercussion. The Whigs' lack of enthusiasm for Jewish emancipation was made perfectly plain in 1837 when an amendment to extend the Municipal Corporations Declaration bill to all citizens, which was moved by the radical George Grote, was defeated in the Commons by 172 votes to 156.

For the moment, therefore, the movement had reached a political impasse. Those Jewish individuals intent on pursuing the question had to do so largely outside the parliamentary arena. The outstanding figure of the period was David Salomons, whose persistent efforts to obtain election, as a professing Jew, to the Court of Aldermen of the City of London, were rewarded in 1845 with the passage of Lord Lyndhurst's Jewish Municipal Relief Act, which allowed professing Jews to hold any and every municipal office. Also noteworthy was the Religious Opinions Relief Act of 1846 which, *inter alia*, placed Jews in exactly the same position as Protestant dissenters so far as places of worship, schools, and charities were concerned. Lyndhurst was a devout Tory and both Acts were made possible only by Conservative support and approval in both Houses.

With the passage of these Acts the inability of professing Jews to enter Parliament became ever more prominent as the last and highest peak to be conquered. But the achievement of this object required several acts of political will. In particular, it required a change of attitude on the part of the major political groupings of the early Victorian period. The political emancipation of Anglo-Jewry might have come about, eventually, through the most altruistic of motives on the part of those active in political life. But politicians will always act more rapidly when it can be demonstrated to them that it is in their own interests that a particular policy or course of action be followed. So it was with Jewish emancipation. The Whig/Liberal connection wanted votes, and allowed itself to be seduced by the allure of Jewish voters.

It is difficult to pinpoint exactly the emergence of the idea of there being 'a Jewish vote', that is, a recognizable tendency on the part of Jewish voters to react in a particular way to political (though not necessarily Jewish) issues. That there were Jewish *votes* in the early nineteenth century, to say nothing of Jewish money with which to buy votes, was well known. Individual Jewish voters might bring pressure to bear on Gentile voters. But they were also important in their own right. In 1831 Francis Goldsmid, Isaac's son, noted that although Robert Grant's bill of the previous year had been defeated, every one of the twelve MPs who represented those London constituencies in which the majority of British Jews resided had supported the measure.[24] In June 1841 Isaac urged the Jewish electors of the City of London to vote for Lord John Russell, the Whig statesman, because he was a supporter of Jewish emancipation.[25] By 1841 both Rothschild and Salomons were also active in encouraging a Jewish vote in the City, where 'Hebrew Committees' (based on Isaac Goldsmid's earlier 'Jewish Association for Obtaining Civil Rights and Privileges') came into existence to issue propaganda and to marshal Jews to the hustings.[26]

Contemporary observers reckoned that the City of London contained several hundred Jewish electors, concentrated mainly in the Aldgate, Portsoken, Billingsgate, and Tower wards.[27] Since the City, the commercial centre of the Empire, returned four MPs to Westminster, these Jewish votes were highly valuable prizes, the more so because the constituency was highly marginal. In 1841, when two Tories and two Whigs had been returned there, the Jews had assured Russell of his nine-vote victory in the seat, and they helped the Liberal James Pattison to a by-election success there two years later. In his novel *Coningsby*, published in 1844, Disraeli warned the Tory party that the Jewish vote was something they could not afford to ignore: 'The Tories lose an important election at a critical moment; 'tis the Jews come forward to vote against them.'[28]

Russell could certainly have been found a safer seat, but not one so prestigious; in any case, to have deserted the City would have been interpreted as an act of political defeatism. His 1841 victory demonstrated that the Jewish vote could be tapped. Now the Liberals prepared to raise the stakes. David Salomons had been adopted as the unsuccessful Liberal candidate for New Shoreham (1837) and Maidstone (1841). In 1847 the Liberals pulled off a *coup*. Five Jews were adopted as Liberal candidates: Salomons at Greenwich, Isaac Goldsmid at Beverley, his son Francis Henry at Great Yarmouth, Baron Mayer de Rothschild at Hythe, and Mayer's brother, Baron Lionel de Rothschild, at the City of London. Lionel's candidature succeeded brilliantly in focusing the minds of the Jewish electors upon the Liberal party and upon the importance of the City contest. In December 1846, for instance, the *Jewish Chronicle* called upon its 'Brother Israelites' not to vote for the Peelite John Masterman, who had declared himself against Jewish emancipation.[29] More importantly, there was a great deal of canvassing of Jews to support the Liberals and hence secure the election of Rothschild and Russell.[30] Liberal

propaganda sought unashamedly to identify Liberalism and
Jewish rights in the minds of the Jewish voters.

The outcome was a double victory. Rothschild was elected,
as was his running-mate, Russell, the Prime Minister. It was
widely and probably correctly asserted that Russell himself,
once again, owed his success to Jewish votes.[31] When, in
December 1847, Rothschild declared his objection to the forms
of oath required of him before he could take his seat in the
Commons, Russell moved that the House should resolve itself
into a committee on the removal of the civil and religious
disabilities of the Jews. The resolution was agreed to by 257
votes to 186. The overwhelming majority of MPs who represented constituencies with substantial Jewish populations
voted in its favour.[32]

A Jewish Disabilities bill was introduced by Russell the
following session. It was defeated, predictably, in the Lords,
but its passage through the Commons was a remarkable event.
Peel and Gladstone voted in favour of it, as did four anti-
Peelite Conservatives: James Milnes Gaskell, Thomas Baring,
Lord George Bentinck (leader of the Conservatives in the Commons), and Disraeli.[33] Bentinck, who was forced to resign the
leadership as a result of his boldness, realized that Jewish
emancipation could only be delayed, not prevented. He had
already explained to John Wilson Croker:

The city of London having elected Lionel Rothschild one of her
representatives, it is such a pronounciation of public opinion that I do
not think the [Conservative] party, as a party, would do themselves
any good by taking up the question against the Jews.

It is like Clare electing O'Connell, Yorkshire Wilberforce. Clare
settled the Catholic question, Yorkshire the slave trade, and now the
city of London has settled the Jew question.[34]

The Jewish vote had indeed arrived!

The final phase of the Jewish emancipation struggle thus
opened in circumstances very different from those which had
pertained twenty years before. However little the Jewish community as a whole might have cared for the matter, Liberal
politicians appeared as suppliants before it, forcing it to sit up
and take notice. Even the Board of Deputies was roused, and

resolved in January 1848 to petition Parliament in favour of Russell's bill.[35] The *Morning Advertiser* warned that though in the past, Anglo-Jewry had never, 'as a body, taken any prominent part in political matters', the public was 'about to meet with an exception to this'.[36] Jews, whether they liked it or not, had become the subject of party politics.

A Parliamentary Oaths bill, passed by the Commons in 1849, was again rejected by the Lords. Rothschild resigned his seat and successfully fought a by-election in the City, but was still unable to take his place in the Commons. An Oath of Abjuration bill, approved by the lower House, was thrown out by the peers in July 1851. At this point Rothschild was joined in the struggle by Salomons, who had won the Greenwich by-election the same month. Salomons did not refuse to take the Oath of Abjuration; he merely omitted the words that offended him, took his seat, voted in three divisions during the debate which followed, and only then agreed to withdraw. Salomons thus saw to it that he, not Rothschild, was the first professing Jew to sit in Parliament. This magnificent gesture—for which he subsequently suffered severe statutory fines in the courts, as well as various civil penalties—brought the matter to the forefront of political debate. Though Salomons lost his seat at the general election of 1852, the minority Conservative Government of February to December that year, headed by the Earl of Derby and Disraeli thought enough of the controversy to pass an Act relieving Salomons of the civil disabilities the courts had imposed upon him. This was itself an admission by the Conservative leadership that Salomons, though legally in the wrong, was morally somewhat less worthy of condemnation.

Lionel de Rothschild had, however, been re-elected in 1852. A Jewish Disabilities bill introduced by Russell (now Foreign Secretary) the following year was again rejected by the peers, and a Parliamentary Oaths bill in 1854 was actually lost in the Commons because it sought to abolish the special oath prescribed for Roman Catholics. In 1856 a private bill to do away with the Oath of Abjuration altogether passed the Commons but was automatically rejected in the Lords.[37] Matters thus again appeared to have reached an impasse. Not even Palmerston's support for Jewish emancipation could move the

upper House to agree to the reform. It was clear, however, that
the obstinacy of the peers was bringing Jewish electors and the
Liberal party closer together. In 1855 a leading article in the
Jewish Chronicle called for some restriction of the Lords' powers
of veto.[38] This was, by any name, Liberal politics. And the
general election of April 1857 provided further evidence of this
trend.

That election was the first in which the Jewish vote gained
general prominence, not just in 'Jewish' constituencies, but
wherever Jewish electors, however few, happened to live. In
the City of London the invocation to Jewish voters was passionate and intense. Rothschild was standing, of course. But
the poll had been fixed for 4 April, which was a Saturday and
hence the Jewish sabbath, upon which all work, including
writing, is forbidden. Before the secret ballot (1872) the poll
was a public one; electors did not have to write anything down.
But could Jews attend public assemblies and meetings of Gentiles on the sabbath? The *Jewish Chronicle* thought so, and
quoted the medieval Jewish scholar Maimonides in support of
its contention that the Jewish vote was so important in the City,
and the cause—'the sacred principle of civil and religious liberty'—so vital, that the sabbath would be 'hallowed, not
desecrated' by a full turnout of Jews at the hustings; even the
Chief Rabbi, it pointed out, 'the appointed interpreter of your
religious convictions', had not ruled against such action.[39] In
the event, the Jews 'rushed to the polling booths' and
Rothschild was re-elected again.[40]

The repercussions of the City campaign were felt in places
remote from the metropolis. At Plymouth, which could not
have numbered more than a handful of Jews in an electorate of
2,482, one of the Liberal candidates, James White, was quick
to point out that, as a citizen of London, he had always given
his vote to Rothschild and his support to the removal of Jewish
disabilities; to make sure that there could be no doubt where
his support lay, he gave ten pounds 'for distribution among the
poor Hebrews'. 'Our Hebrew brethren, with only the singular
exception of Mr Woolf', the *Plymouth Journal* recorded, voted to
a man for White and his running-mate, R. P. Collier.[41]

The summoning of the Jewish vote in 1857 was not, in the
main, the work of Jewish interests. Even Rothschild was

careful to avoid any special public appeal to his Jewish voters, though behind the scenes, in the Rothschild headquarters at New Court, a great deal of lobbying did take place.[42] The main thrust in the appeal to Jewish electors came from Liberal politicians, who had now a decade of experience behind them in meeting and making friends with Jewish audiences.[43] The Board of Deputies worked in a rather different way. It did not intervene in the election, but after the poll (which had resulted in the return of Palmerston's government with a large majority) the Board orchestrated a campaign of petitions from synagogues and communities throughout Great Britain, and from sympathetic Gentiles.[44] The Government introduced an Oaths bill which passed the Commons comfortably but was killed in the Lords. Rothschild resigned his seat, but was re-elected; this time there was no need to have a poll, for the Conservatives did not oppose him. Russell, though no longer in office, introduced a new Oaths bill, but by the time it reached the Lords Palmerston's government, defeated on its Conspiracy to Murder bill, had fallen.

The Earl of Derby was once again head of a minority Conservative Administration, with Disraeli as Chancellor of the Exchequer and leader of the party in the Commons. Derby was a confirmed opponent of Jewish emancipation, as was Lord Chelmsford, the Lord Chancellor. On Chelmsford's motion the central clause of Russell's bill was struck out. When the Lords' amendments were reported to the Commons, a committee was appointed to draw up reasons for disagreeing with them. An unsworn member of the Commons was debarred merely from sitting or voting in the lower House; so Rothschild, though unsworn, was appointed to the Commons' committee. And though the conference of both Houses which followed was without agreement, a gauntlet had been thrown down which the Conservative party could not ignore.

The key to the solution of the problem clearly lay with Conservative politicians. The conflict between the two Houses had become an embarrassment for the party, and was symptomatic of the reactionary streak which had deprived it of a majority in the Commons for twelve years. Wider considerations of political strategy, therefore, seemed to call for some form of compromise. Appropriately, it was a Tory peer, and a

consistent anti-emancipationist, who put one forward. The Earl
of Lucan, the Crimean War veteran, suggested the simple expedient that each House be left to determine for itself the form of
oath to be administered to a Jew.[45] The bill which was introduced to give effect to this compromise passed the Lords by
33 votes to 12 and the Commons by 129 votes to 55. In the
Commons four Conservative front-benchers voted for its second reading: Disraeli, Lord Stanley, Sir John Pakington, and
Sir F. Kelly. At the same time the amended Oaths bill was also
given parliamentary approval. On 23 July 1858 both bills passed into law. Neither of them could be said to have been a par-
tisan Liberal measure. More significant than the small number
of active and leading Conservatives who supported the bill was
the much larger number of Conservatives who, perhaps
through constituency pressures, abstained. The crucial point
was that the face of the Conservative party had been saved.

How important was this for the development of the Anglo-
Jewish approach to mid-Victorian party politics? The evidence
of poll books suggests that throughout the period of the emancipation struggle there was a significant Jewish Conservative
vote.[46] Unfortunately, no poll books for the City of London in
this period have survived. But at Westminster, in 1837, 12 out
of 36 Jewish voters supported the Conservative Sir George
Murray; and in the same constituency in 1841 the Conservative candidate, Captain H. J. Rous, attracted the votes of 26
of the 62 Jewish voters. Of the 17 identifiable Jewish electors of
Liverpool in 1832, 3 gave their votes to the Conservative candidate, Viscount Sandon; in 1835, of 16 Jewish voters, Sandon
picked up the votes of 4, and 2 supported the other Conservative candidate, Sir Howard Douglas. At Birmingham, in
1841, 12 voters known to be Jewish supported the Liberal candidates, but a further 2 plumped for the Conservatives. Even in
Manchester Conservatism had its Jewish admirers. In 1839
Jewish support for the Conservative candidate there amounted
to 2 voters out of 15; at Salford, in 1841, it amounted to 1 voter
out of 8.[47]

This evidence, admittedly sporadic, suggests none the less
that in the late 1830s and early 1840s Jewish support for the
Conservative party could vary from one-eighth in the north-
west to a third or more in London. No doubt such support was

adversely affected by the emancipation controversy, and had Conservative opposition to emancipation continued beyond the 1860s it might have disappeared altogether. But this did not happen. The party had no official policy on the matter, and there was no collective Conservative view of Anglo-Jewry. At Beverley in 1847 Isaac Goldsmid, though standing as a Liberal, had the support of some prominent Tories; George Liddell, an influential Tory banker from Hull, canvassed for him.[48]

Likewise, Jewish reaction to Conservative candidates depended to a great extent on their individual views. Sir Moses Montefiore called himself a Tory.[49] The Reform controversy within Anglo-Jewry may itself have alienated some religious Jews from supporting Liberalism; Eleazer Moses, who voted Conservative at Salford in 1841, was a strictly orthodox Jew who had moved from London in the mid-1830s and who, in the 1850s, was to lead the anti-Reformist faction in Manchester. Even in 1859, when Jewish entry to the House of Commons still depended upon a special resolution passed pursuant to the 1858 legislation and hence upon there being a sympathetic majority in the lower House, Jews had no qualms about supporting Conservative candidates. Abraham Levi Bensusan defended such a vote at the Bedfordshire poll by explaining that he had ascertained that the Conservative candidate there, Richard Gilpin, had abstained from voting in the Commons on the emancipation question.[50] A 'Consistent Jewish Conservative' in Southampton assured the readers of the *Jewish Chronicle* in 1865 that Jews had voted Conservative there and had 'for upwards of thirty years' supported the Conservatives in Portsmouth and Salisbury.[51] It seems, too, that there was very heavy Jewish support for the Conservatives at Newcastle in 1868 and 1874.[52] And it is worth noting that Baron Henry de Worms actually stood as the first Jewish Conservative parliamentary candidate in 1868, barely a decade after the emancipation victory and only eight years after the resolution of the Commons which allowed professing Jews to take a modified oath had been converted into a Standing Order by Act of Parliament (1860).[53]

Jewish Conservatism thus had a continuous history, unbroken even in the era of emancipation. In 1866, without fuss, a Parliamentary Oaths Act was passed which prescribed for

both Houses a simplified oath to which professing Jews could
have no objection; the way was thus paved for the creation of a
Jewish peerage. It cannot be denied that the bulk of Anglo-
Jewry inclined to the Liberal party during the emancipation
era (if they inclined to any party at all). But the community was
never in the pocket of that party. Later on, Liberal publicists,
especially Jewish Liberal publicists, were fond of urging that
Anglo-Jewry owed a debt to Liberalism and was under some
kind of moral obligation to it. The fact is that by the end of the
1860s there were people on both sides who were ready to
forgive and forget, and that the wounds quickly healed. The
sympathetic stance of leading Conservatives, pre-eminently
Disraeli, undoubtedly helped. So did the expansion of the
Jewish middle classes. The continental revolutions of 1848
brought renewed immigration of foreign Jewish exiles to
England. Jewish destitution, not only in London, 'grew alarm-
ingly'.[54] The community turned in once more upon itself and
its problems. Harbouring political grudges was a luxury its
leaders could not afford.

The very fact of emancipation brought a further worry.
Lionel de Rothschild's brother, Mayer, was returned for
Hythe at a by-election in 1859. At the general election later
that year they were joined in the Commons by David Salomons
and, in 1860, by Francis Goldsmid. The appearance of a
'Jewish lobby' in the Commons was not viewed with unqualified joy:

Every movement and every vote of theirs [the *Jewish Chronicle* explain-
ed] will be identified with the community, and the latter morally held
responsible for their public acts. ...
   What if it should be our misfortune to be represented by men only
nominally Jews ... without Jewish feeling, and without Jewish conviction ... Would it not be better for the Jewish community not to have
any of its members in Parliament than to be represented by men of
this kind?[55]

Emancipation was a fine thing. So was politics. The question
now was whether Anglo-Jewry could reconcile itself to both.

3. The Eclipse of Jewish Liberalism

Emancipation replaced the anomaly of underprivilege with the anxiety of political responsibility. For the man at the centre of the battle the yoke he had won for himself proved too heavy. Baron Lionel de Rothschild took his seat in the Commons on 26 July 1858, but he did not speak once in debates in the chamber during his membership of it.[1] By the late 1860s the number of Jewish MPs had grown to six, a figure already so grossly disproportionate to the size of the Jewish population of the UK that it was in itself a source of worry in some communal quarters.[2] Without exception all the Jewish MPs at this period were Liberals. The first Jewish Conservative MP, the obscure Nottinghamshire coal-owner Saul Isaac, did not make his appearance at Westminster till 1874.[3] Until then the parliamentary Jewish lobby was a Liberal lobby, one which had, moreover, developed during the decade (1859-68) when the Liberal party had taken on a definite form and substance, under the leadership of, first, Lord John Russell and then Gladstone. The triumphs of Liberalism and Jewish emancipation thus seemed to go hand in hand, as products of the same political ethos. On Saturday, 28 April 1866 there was a remarkable demonstration of this fact, when Russell's Parliamentary Reform bill passed its second reading in the Commons by a majority of five votes; all six Jewish MPs voted for it, the sabbath notwithstanding.[4]

These early Jewish MPs were not, however, a particularly inspiring group. The most notable of them, George Jessel, elected for Dover in 1868, became Solicitor-General three years later, on the strength of an accomplished speech on the Bankruptcy bill. Later he became Master of the Rolls. But Jessel's undoubted talents were not employed in the ambit of Jewish communal affairs.[5] The three Rothschilds (Lionel, his brother Mayer, and his eldest son Nathan Mayer, MP for Anglesey 1865-85 and later the first Lord Rothschild) were communal leaders of the highest rank, but they were in no sense gifted parliamentarians. Frederick Goldsmid, Isaac Lyon's second surviving son, died within a year of his election for Honiton (also 1865) and was succeeded in the seat by his son, Julian, who eventually became Deputy Speaker of the House.

The three Jewish MPs who stood out as unashamed advocates of Jewish interests in Parliament were David Salomons, Francis Goldsmid, and John Simon. None of them sat for Jewish constituencies. Salomons, who represented Greenwich from 1859 to his death in 1873, came into the House with a ready-made reputation. He was not a frequent speaker, but commanded respect on account of his financial expertise, and made it his business to watch over Jewish interests, especially in connection with the Factory Acts; he secured legislation enabling Jews who closed their factories or workshops on Saturdays to open them on Sundays for members of their own faith.[6]

Salomons's contemporary, Francis Henry Goldsmid, returned for Reading in 1860, was a founder-member of the West London Reform Synagogue, and a staunch defender of Jewish rights. Some of his greatest parliamentary speeches were made in outrage at the attacks on Jews in the Danubian provinces and in Russia and Poland between 1862 and 1872.[7] In 1868 Goldsmid—dubbed 'the member for Jewry'—was provided with an ally in the person of John Simon. When Goldsmid was killed in a railway accident, in 1878, Simon assumed the role of senior Jewish member of Parliament.

John Simon, a lifelong devotee of the Reform movement, personified the late Victorian emancipated Jew, tied to the Liberal party by bonds which were more emotional than rational. Born at Montego Bay, Jamaica, in 1818, he had settled in Liverpool, where he practised as a barrister, eventually becoming a deputy County Court judge. He also became a close friend of John Bright. As one of Liverpool's leading Jews Simon played a key role (whose details may never be completely unearthed) in making Jewish emancipation a test question at all parliamentary elections there in the 1840s and 1850s, and in inducing Liverpool Jewry to vote heavily for the Liberal party. As MP for Dewsbury, 1868-88, he was never afraid of taking up radical causes; he spoke, for example, against capital punishment, was a fervent Irish Home-Ruler, and a pro-Boer. In 1872 he organized a Mansion House meeting to protest against the treatment of Jews in Serbia and Romania, and spared no effort in persuading Gentile MPs to join Goldsmid and himself in speaking on their behalf in the Commons. He had already, during the debate on W. E. Forster's Elementary Education bill (1870), defended the right of Jewish children to absent themselves from school on the Jewish sabbath and festivals and had, significantly, defended no less strongly the parallel right of Roman Catholic children in relation to Saints' Days.

Inevitably, John Simon was one of the moving spirits behind the great Mansion House meeting in 1882 to protest against the Russian pogroms. In March 1888 he intervened in the anti-Jewish agitation in Cork, wrote to *The Times*, and got the Irish nationalist leader Parnell to support him. Later that year he intervened in the Holborn by-election in order to urge Jewish voters there to continue voting Liberal because, he said, the Liberals had emancipated them. He was also, it must be added, a founder of the Anglo-Jewish Association (1871), a self-elected club representing the ruling circles of the Anglo-Jewish community, and shared with the Association's élitist membership a profound distrust of Jewish nationalist movements.[8]

In the closing decades of the nineteenth century Simon provided a link with the past: a Jewish progressive Liberal whose political attitudes had been formed during the era of emancipation, and who stood, apparently, as a living witness to the identity of Liberal interests and Jewish interests. In 1868 it had seemed impossible that such interests could ever diverge. The Conservative party, it is true, had reconciled itself to emancipation. Jews did vote for the Conservative party; with the passage of the second Reform Act (1867), which enfranchised most urban male heads of household, more of them could no doubt be expected to do so. This, indeed, was one reason given by Conservatives for the necessity of a more agreeable attitude towards the seed of Abraham. But the idea that Liberalism might ever be inimical to Jewish interests seemed absurd, and the possibility of the emergence of a Jewish Conservative lobby appeared as 'a sort of political treason'.[9] Yet within a couple of decades such a lobby had emerged, and its growth did not seem the least bit unreasonable.

There were a number of reasons for this remarkable turn of

events. One element was to be found in the very nature of the emancipation struggle. Jewish emancipation had been won partly on the grounds that Jews differed from their fellow-citizens only in their religion. The campaign had never had the promotion or furtherance of Jewish interests in Parliament as one of its aims, less still the creation of a Jewish faction or party. Even the idea that there might now develop a specifically Jewish dimension to British political life was quickly discounted. When Parliament assembled in 1860 the *Jewish Chronicle* declared 'We are interested in it as citizens, not as Jews.'[10] A correspondent in 1865, describing himself as an 'English Jew', echoed these sentiments when he wrote that he considered 'that our right to vote on political matters should only be exercised by us as Englishmen, and not as Jews'.[11]

This was a theme to which communal leaders were to return again and again in their search for social integration. Now it was one thing to be grateful to Liberals for their support during the emancipation era but when Liberals began to put it about that the Jewish vote throughout the land was 'a sort of appanage which belonged to them by prescriptive right', a line had to be drawn.[12] 'There is nothing whatever in the faith of a Jew', one writer pointed out, 'that need, of itself, influence his political proclivities.'[13] In August 1865 the *Jewish Chronicle* had waxed lyrical, in its leader column, on the Liberal victory at the general election earlier in the summer.[14] And in 1867 its Bohemian-born editor and proprietor, Dr Abraham Benisch, had written:

It is true that the overwhelming majority of the Jewish community are Liberals; but Liberalism is not forced upon them from without. It is not only a product of a feeling of gratitude for the triumph which the Liberal party has achieved for the Jewish cause, but also the firm conviction that it is the vital principle upon which rests the Revelation of Sinai and the indispensable condition of all progress. The Jew feels instinctively that, politically, he is nothing if he is not a Liberal.[15]

But in 1869 the paper had been bought by the three communal leaders, Lionel Louis Cohen (a founder of the Jewish Board of Guardians and—in 1870—of the United Synagogue and a future Conservative MP), his brother-in-law Samuel

Montagu (later Lord Swaythling and a future Liberal MP), and their close friend Lionel Van Oven, and they had installed as editor an English-born patent agent and poet, Michael Henry.[16] In a long editorial on 'The Political Future of the Jews' Henry, as if to reassure his Gentile readers and his employers, announced:

The ethics of Judaism constitute a kind of moral guarantee that the Jewish vote will ever be given to uphold the Monarchy, to disseminate morality and education, to advance social and sanitary reforms, and to preserve peace ... the political and social status of the Jew has so far altered since his enfranchisement that he is now in a position to give a free and independent expression to the opinions he holds.[17]

He had already declared:

The House [of Commons] may have its Roman Catholic party, its Presbyterian party, its Evangelical party; but if of the six hundred and fifty-six gentlemen who compose the House of Commons, one third were members of the Jewish community, there would be no such section as a Jewish party.[18]

From expressions such as these it was but a short step to argue that Anglo-Jewry, in its own interest, should not be seen as a one-party group within the body politic. Rather Jews should be seen as favouring both major political parties.[19] Otherwise, as the young Lionel Cohen had already pointed out in 1865, Anglo-Jewry would obtain for itself a bad name as a selfish and 'separatist' collection of citizens.[20]

Such issues of principle were reinforced by pragmatic considerations. One was the undeniable fact that some Liberals were anti-Jewish. When Henry de Worms, a member of one of the leading Jewish families, and closely connected with the houses of Goldsmid, Rothschild, and Montefiore, put himself up as the Conservative candidate at Sandwich in 1868, his Liberal opponent, Knatchbull-Hugessen, attacked him as a Jew, and one local Liberal newspaper descended to the depths by suggesting that if Jews 'give one shilling they generally expect two in return for it'.[21] At Manchester the remarks of Jacob

Bright (John's son) on the subject of the Jews were less than flattering.[22] At Tower Hamlets the considerable Jewish electorate—about 5,000—was embarrassed to find that the Liberal candidate there was a Jewish convert to Christianity, Joseph d'Aguilar Samuda. To bolster Samuda's reputation local Liberals obtained for him the patronage of Lionel de Rothschild. Samuda was victorious, but orthodox Jewish opinion in the City was not pleased, and this may have cost Rothschild his own parliamentary seat.[23]

But it was the attitude of Gladstone himself that finally broke the spell which the Liberal party had cast upon Anglo-Jewry. Gladstone knew little about Jewish people, other than the few in high society with whom he mixed socially and politically. His odyssey towards support for Jewish emancipation had been an intellectual exercise, and a slow and painful process at that. Its completion did not mean that he liked Jews as individuals or particularly sympathized with their plight. He was, and remained, a Christian militant. As such he had first opposed emancipation, and as such he had found it expedient to change his mind.

This deep sense of Christian purpose was uppermost in his mind at all times. When, in the summer of 1876, news reached England of the atrocities perpetrated by the Turks upon Bulgarian Christians, Gladstone emerged from his first retirement to lead a crusade against the Ottoman Empire in the Balkans. It did not for one moment occur to him to consider the position of Balkan Jews or the likely reaction of Anglo-Jewry to his demands. But the policy of Disraeli, the Prime Minister, was very different. Whilst wanting to see drastic changes in the way the Turks governed their Balkan provinces, he was not prepared to allow the Tsar to use the Bulgarian Horrors as an excuse to extend Russian influence in south-east Europe. In April 1877 Russia declared war on Turkey, and in March 1878 forced her to submit to the humiliating Treaty of San Stefano, by which Serbia, Romania, and the Montenegro became independent, and Bulgaria virtually so. Disraeli thereupon used the threat of military intervention to bring the Russians to the conference table. By the Treaty of Berlin (July 1878) Bulgaria was cut in two: northern Bulgaria remained independent but the southern half (Rumelia), though receiving a large measure of self-government, remained subject to Turkey; it was not reunited with Bulgaria until 1885. In addition Dobrudscha, in the north-eastern corner of the country, was ceded to Romania. Disraeli thus claimed that he had achieved Balkan independence without permitting Russia to use a 'big Bulgaria' to spread her influence in the Near East.

Disraeli's Eastern policy had the warm approval of most British Jews. In the first place Jews had considerable investments in Turkey, and were loath to see them thrown away because of Gladstone's conscience. Beyond that, British Jews, in common with their co-religionists in Austria-Hungary, Germany, France, and America, looked at the situation from the point of view of Balkan Jewry. Turkish rule had allowed these Jews 'a degree of tolerance far beyond anything conceded by Orthodox Christianity'.[24] A. L. Green, minister of the prestigious Central Synagogue in London's West End and 'a Liberal in politics all my life',[25] instructed the Liberal *Daily News* 'The Christian populations of the Turkish provinces have held, and continue with an iron hand to hold, my co-religionists under every form of political and social degradation.'[26]

With very few exceptions (John Simon was one of them) British Jews did not merely refuse to be associated with Gladstone's Bulgarian Agitation; they actively opposed it. The opening phase of the Agitation happened to coincide with the Buckinghamshire by-election, held on 21 September 1876. Buckinghamshire was Rothschild country, but it was also the seat which Disraeli had vacated, in August, on his elevation to the peerage, and the attempts of the Liberals to make the Agitation a major issue in the campaign there so enraged the Rothschild family that they were 'practically in open revolt', and by the beginning of October had 'gone Tory altogether'.[27] Steps had already been taken to convene a conference of European and American Jewish organizations to discuss ways in which advantage might be taken of the reopening of the Eastern Question to improve the lot of Balkan Jewry.[28] A memorandum on the position of Eastern Jews was drawn up, and on 27 December 1876 the Anglo-Jewish Association presented it to the Government.[29] When war broke out between Russia and Turkey the following year, Sir Moses

Montefiore made no secret about where his sympathies lay; he contributed £100 to the Turkish Relief Fund.[30]

But this was merely the beginning of a spirited campaign to obtain guarantees for Jews in those Balkan countries whose independence from Turkey was obviously imminent. The *Daily Telegraph,* owned by the Jewish Levy-Lawson family, swung its influence behind Disraeli's policy. Jewish pressure was brought to bear upon the most influential section of the Vienna press to support the side of Turkey.[31] In June 1878 the Board of Deputies and the Anglo-Jewish Association submitted a memorandum to Disraeli and Lord Salisbury, the Foreign Secretary, asking them to secure guarantees for the 'social, civil and political rights' of the Jews in the area of conflict.[32] But it was the aged Lionel de Rothschild who, in the year before his death, exerted the greatest influence. From Disraeli he could expect nothing but sympathy, and a letter he had written to the British premier, on the subject of ill-treatment of Jews in eastern Europe, was actually read to the peacemakers at Berlin. At the same time Lionel used his German Jewish banking associate, Gerson von Bleichröder, to bring pressure to bear upon Bismarck, President of the Berlin Congress, and he also sent appeals to the French and Italian delegates; the Vienna branch of the House of Rothschild made a similar appeal to the Austrian government.[33] The result was that the western delegates refused to sign the Treaty of Berlin unless the countries whose independence, complete or partial, was being established agreed to grant civil and political rights to the Jewish populations in them. The Treaty, when signed, thus contained definite guarantees of these rights for the Jews of Romania, Bulgaria, and the Danubian principalities.[34] Little wonder that, when Disraeli and Salisbury returned in triumph from the Congress, Montefiore, despite his ninety-four years, was the first to greet them at Charing Cross station.[35]

British Jews had not prevented Balkan independence, but had supported the Conservative Government in delaying the process of self-rule for about a year until Jewish rights were safeguarded and Russian influence minimized. This alone was sufficient to damn them in the eyes of many Liberals. The Bulgarian Agitation, in fact, had unpleasant anti-Jewish overtones, in which Disraeli's own ethnic origins were exploited to the full. A section of the intelligentsia, led by the historians Goldwin Smith, Edward Freeman, J. A. Froude, and John Morley, and the future socialist William Morris, jumped on the bandwagon.[36]

Most outraged of all was Gladstone himself. During the general election of 1874, which brought Disraeli to power, Gladstone, probably acting upon information supplied to him by Liberals with more feeling than sense, had taken it for granted that the Jewish Liberal vote was copper-bottomed.[37] But the appearance of Jewish Conservatives at that election, and the coming to power of a Jewish (albeit baptized) Prime Minister, seems to have unnerved him. When it became clear that British Jews were not going to support the Bulgarian Agitation, the full fury of his oratorical powers was unleashed upon them. 'I deeply deplore', he told Leopold Gluckstein, author of a pamphlet on *The Eastern Question and the Jews,* 'the manner in which, what I may call Judaic sympathies, beyond as well as within the circle of professed Judaism, are now acting on the question of the East.'[38]

Not even personal appeals from sympathizers such as Abraham Benisch could make the Liberal leader withdraw his condemnation of Jewish influence over British foreign policy.[39] By the time the Treaty of Berlin had been signed, little was left of the close relationship of the previous generation between Liberalism and Anglo-Jewry. Francis Goldsmid refused to support his party on the Eastern question.[40] Gladstone, for his part, refused categorically to take any initiative in healing the breach.[41] The virtual secession of the Rothschilds turned a great many City Jews into Conservatives, and seems to have acted as a green light to provincial Jewish communities also to demonstrate their support for Disraeli's government.[42] This happened at Liverpool in 1876 and in 1879 at Sheffield, where the Conservative candidate, C. B. Stuart-Wortley, won the support of Jews specifically because of issues of foreign policy.[43]

Thus far John Simon had kept his peace. In 1876 he had indeed gone out of his way to support Gladstone, publicly, over the Bulgarian question. But when at the end of 1879, Gladstone refused to accede to a request from Manchester to use his influence to obtain better treatment for the Jews living under Christian rule in Romania, Simon's patience ran out:

> Is all sympathy [he asked in a letter to *The Times*] reserved for the
> [Christian] 'subject races' and none to spare for the unhappy Jewish
> people? ...
>   I should deeply deplore anything like a considerable secession of
> Jews from the Liberal party, to which three-fourths of them belong ...
> But the repeated attacks upon Jews during the last two or three years
> by Liberals, some in high places, ... have a tendency to bring about
> these results, or at least to estrange the Jews from those whose lead
> they have been accustomed hitherto to follow.[44]

During the subsequent three years Simon did his best to
repair the damage. He was particularly anxious that the Conservatives should not be allowed to reap any further political
advantage from Jewish questions.[45] Thus in January 1882 he
acted quickly to prevent a Conservative motion from being
brought forward in the Commons concerning persecution of
Jews in Russia. Simon wrote to Gladstone, who had been
returned to Downing Street in the general election of 1880,
suggesting that he should put down a question to the Prime
Minister, in reply to which Gladstone could say a kind word for
the Jews, and thus steal the Conservative thunder.[46] A few
days later he returned, more insistently, to the same theme: 'I
have ventured to trouble you ... from a deep conviction that the
interests of the Liberal party as well as of the Government re-
quire that something should be said and that it had better be
elicited by a supporter of the Government than by a member
on the opposite side of the House.'[47]

Simon put his question, and the Conservative motion was
withdrawn. But this was, as Simon must have realized, a short-
term procedural victory; Gladstone was, and remained, unmoved by the plight of Russian Jews, and he certainly did not
intend to get up an 'agitation' on their behalf.[48]

A wedge has thus been driven between the mass of Anglo-
Jewry and the Liberal party. It remains, therefore, to consider
the precise impact of the Bulgarian Horrors upon the affilia-
tions of Anglo-Jewry between the accession of Disraeli to power
(1874) and the fall of Gladstone's third ministry (1886). That
there was a shift in Jewish opinion is certain. It was worrying

enough to Jewish Liberals to cause Arthur Cohen, the brilliant barrister and MP for Southwark, 1880-7, to advise Gladstone to make some public gesture of support for oppressed Jews during the 1880 election campaign.[49] Clearly the Jewish vote, which had never been wholly Liberal, never became wholly Conservative. But, equally clearly, now that the Liberal leader had blotted his copybook so thoroughly, it was eminently respectable to be a Jewish Conservative. 'Are we, [one writer asked the readers of the *Jewish Chronicle* in 1888] because there was once a Liberal party, to bow down and worship Gladstone —the great Minister who was too Christian in his charity, too Russian in his proclivities, to raise voice or finger to protect them?'[50]

In 1880 Saul Isaac lost his seat at Nottingham, but Henry de Worms was elected Conservative MP at Greenwich. Any doubt which might have remained concerning the propriety of Jews becoming Conservative supporters was removed in 1885, when Lionel Louis Cohen announced his intention of fighting the North Paddington seat in the Conservative interest. Cohen was a communal leader of the first rank, and a Vice-President of the National Union of Conservative Associations. His work in the Commons—he died in 1887 after less than two years as an MP—was of less significance than the fact of his having been elected to Westminster, for he had spent the best years of his life fighting, as he put it, 'the domination so long exercised by the so-called Liberal party over the Jews, and the monopoly of the Jewish vote which they have exercised and even yet claim to enjoy'.[51]

Cohen's successful candidature at Paddington was a shot in the arm for the Conservatives. His adhesion to the party had nothing to do with the Bulgarian Agitation; he was a lifelong Conservative and had done yeoman service on behalf of the party in the City of London in 1874. But the alienation of Jews from the Liberal party in the late 1870s and early 1880s made his work much easier. Thus, in 1885, he found he could take time off from campaigning in his own constituency to speak on behalf of Charles Thomson Ritchie, who was fighting the Tower Hamlets seat of St. George's-in-the-East. Ritchie had a formidable opponent in the person of Sir David Lionel

Salomons, nephew and heir of the pioneer of Jewish emancipation, but he won the constituency none the less.[52]

One other obvious factor facilitated the propaganda work of Jewish Conservatives. This had nothing to do with Jewish affairs, but was provided by the division within the Liberal party which was made manifest by the Home Rule split in 1886. Those who led the Jewish community in the late Victorian period were financiers, merchants, and industrialists. They shared the fear of their much more numerous Gentile counterparts that the Liberal party was moving too far towards the radical camp. The Liberal Unionist secession was the ultimate result. In 1850 the Conservative party had been the party of the Land and the Church; by 1900 it had become the party of Big Business as well. This fundamental shift in opinion naturally affected the Anglo-Jewish establishment. In 1886 Sir Julian Goldsmid and Ferdinand de Rothschild became Liberal Unionists. Ferdinand had already warned the radical Liberal MP Sir Charles Dilke that he was opposed to his and Joseph Chamberlain's attempts 'to court popularity with the masses by ... stimulating an unhealthy desire for social & pecuniary equality'.[53] After 1886 no Rothschild was elected to the House of Commons under the auspices of the Liberal party. In 1880, 8 of the 13 Jewish parliamentary candidates were Liberals, and 4 Jewish Liberal MPs were elected, as against 1 Conservative. In 1900, 11 of the 23 Jewish candidates were Unionists, of whom 7 were elected as against 3 Liberals.

The Jewish middle classes therefore finally cut the umbilical cord which had tied them to Liberalism. It was a conscious and deliberate act, and was seen by them as a necessary demonstration of political maturity and, no less important, of social integration and acceptance.[54] The Jews, the *Jewish Chronicle* proclaimed in 1885 'are too powerfully dominated by the desire to see that party controlling affairs which each considers the more calculated to perform the task successfully, to allow mere considerations of racial pride or interest to influence them.' And the newspaper added, somewhat optimistically, 'the Jewish electors ... vote, not as Jews, but as Englishmen'.[55]

The switch to Conservatism even affected the Jewish clergy. Professor D. W. Marks, minister of the West London Reform Synagogue, publicly supported the Conservative candidate at Holborn in 1888.[56] In 1895 two Jewish clergymen canvassed on behalf of Claude Hay, the Unionist candidate for Hoxton.[57] Nathan Marcus Adler, the Chief Rabbi, was very careful never to enter into the political arena, but his son, Hermann, who deputized for him as 'Delegate' Chief Rabbi from 1879, and who became Chief Rabbi in his own right following his father's death in 1891, was a pillar of the establishment and a staunch Conservative.[58] So was Hermann's elder brother, Marcus, Actuary of the Alliance Assurance Company. Hermann's major political outbursts were directed against the socialists, but in 1898 there was a remarkable intervention by the Adler family in Plymouth.

Plymouth was a double-member constituency which had been Conservative since 1885. But in the 1895 general election one of the seats had been lost to the Liberals, and when a by-election occurred for the other, in January 1898, the Liberals put up a Jewish candidate, S. F. Mendl. Marcus Adler at once wrote to Myer Fredman, a prominent member of the Plymouth Jewish community, 'stating that he had been requested by leading members of the [Jewish] community in London to ask Jews residing in Plymouth to give their support to Mr Guest', the Conservative candidate.[59] This appeal, rightly interpreted as 'a *quasi*-pastoral letter to the Plymouth Jews on the subject of the election', caused a local sensation.[60] Hermann wrote to *The Times* protesting that he had always kept 'aloof from party politics'—which was not true—and telegraphed the Plymouth Liberals that 'My brother wrote without my authority.'[61] This was a red herring, as Marcus did not need his brother's authority, certainly not in secular matters. In any case, Hermann was exceedingly careful not to repudiate the letter, and Marcus never issued a disclaimer or a withdrawal. Mendl won the seat by 164 votes.

The Plymouth affair did not in the least dampen Hermann's enthusiasm for publicizing Conservative causes. When the Boer War broke out, he did not confine himself to suitable prayers for the safety of British troops, but went out of his way to justify the policy of Lord Salisbury's Government, in spite of the fact that this policy was very much a party political issue. 'The government of our Queen', he told the congregation of the North London Synagogue, 'had no alternative but to resort

to the fierce arbitrament of war, with the view of restoring just
and righteous government to the Transvaal, and to vindicate
the honour of England.' Specially bound copies of the sermon
were presented to the Queen, the Prince of Wales, Lord
Salisbury, Arthur Balfour, and Joseph Chamberlain (now
Unionist Colonial Secretary), but not, it would appear, to any
Liberal leaders, and 600 copies were distributed to the British
press.[62]

To what extent did the mass of Anglo-Jewry follow the
political example of the leadership? It is tempting to think that
the majority of Jewish voters remained Liberal.[63] The career of
Sir Samuel Montagu, banker, philanthropist, and Liberal MP
for Whitechapel, 1885-1900, seems to reflect the endurance of
Liberal loyalties among, at least, working-class London Jews.
Montagu was a very strict orthodox Jew and, though a brother-
in-law of Lionel Louis Cohen, was never tempted out of the
Liberal camp. He won Whitechapel in 1885 after a vigorous
and blatantly 'Jewish' campaign, during the course of which he
attacked Cohen mercilessly and counted him one of 'a few
shallow-pated, ignorant people who thought it more respectable to call themselves Conservatives'.[64] In 1886 he declared
publicly that he hoped not a single Jew would vote Conservative.[65] In 1892 he retained the seat even though the Conservative candidate claimed to have a letter of support and
recommendation from Lord Rothschild, and in 1895 he retained it again, by thirty-two votes, even though his opponent actually did possess such a letter.[66] 'It is only natural', one local
paper observed, 'that a constituency which contains 50 per cent
if not more, of Jewish people should return a Hebrew representative.'[67] Whitechapel was one of only two Tower Hamlets
constituencies that never went Conservative between 1885 and
1900 (the other was Poplar). Montagu seemed somehow to
have kept its large Jewish element loyal to the Liberal party.

However, certain features of the Montagu-Whitechapel connection need to be taken into account when assessing the
strength of Jewish Liberal support there. Firstly, although the
constituency became very heavily populated with Jewish immigrants during the 1880s and 1890s, so that in 1901 aliens accounted for 31.8 per cent of its population, most of them, not
being naturalized, did not have the vote.[68] In 1900 the

registered electorate of Whitechapel (5,004) formed only 6.4 per cent of its total inhabitants.[69] The actual number of Jewish voters in the constituency in 1895 was put at 1,500, of which the Conservatives claimed half.[70] Secondly, Montagu was a particularly charismatic figure for East End Jews. His rigid orthodoxy was beyond doubt. He was connected with every important Jewish communal organization, and was himself a disburser of charity on a grand scale. He was the founder of the Federation of Synagogues, which catered exclusively for the chronically poor immigrant community, and he could address his fellow-Jews in Whitechapel in the one language they all spoke and understood, Yiddish.[71] This wealthy banker was therefore able to enjoy a rapport with them which the anglicized Rothschilds could not have established. The Jewish vote which Montagu created was, in the deepest sense, a personal vote built upon a very personal relationship between MP and constituents.

Whitechapel under Montagu was, in short, *sui generis*. An examination of the surrounding constituencies between 1885 and 1900 supports this view. St. George's (whose alien proportion in 1901 amounted to 28.8 per cent) only went Liberal once during this period—in 1892; the same was true of Limehouse. Mile End was never lost to the Conservatives. The Conservatives captured Stepney in 1886, and though they lost it at a by-election in 1898 they won it back in 1900. And lest it be thought that the Jews did not contribute towards these Conservative victories, the testimony of contemporary observers is worth recalling. At Stepney, in 1892, the defeated Liberal 'declared that he had been beaten by the Jewish vote alone'.[72] In 1895 the Jewish vote in Stepney was also thought to have been responsible for the Conservative victory, while at Limehouse, in the same election, the Conservative candidate, Harry Samuel (who, though a Jew, had declared himself in favour of 'the absolute prevention of Alien Pauper Immigration') had the support of 'nearly all the local Jews'.[73] When H. H. Marks, another Jewish Conservative and editor of the *Financial News*, won St. George's, the Jewish vote 'was cast almost wholly' for him; this was crucial, for the number of Jewish voters was put at about 200, and Marks won the seat by only 4 votes.[74] The President of the St. George's Conservative

Association, Joseph Abrahams, was himself Jewish.[75] In 1900 a Jewish resident of Stepney declared its west ward, 'packed with Jews', to be 'a hot-bed of Toryism'.[76] Bertram Straus, the affable and much respected Jewish Liberal who lost at St. George's, in 1900, by 296 votes, explained that the 'Jews of London are generally Conservative in politics, they having got all they want, namely their freedom and the franchise, from the Liberals: they now belong to the party who opposed them tooth and nail'.[77]

Of course this was a bitter over-simplification, but it contained a kernel of truth. Liberalism was no longer the dominant political force moving among British Jews. The Conservative victories in East London, and particularly the victories of Jewish Conservatives, were obtained because of, and not in spite of, hostility to Jewish immigration. Jewish candidates fell over themselves in the rush to support restrictions on the entry of Jewish immigrants from eastern Europe. In 1900 Lord Rothschild gave his stamp of approval to Major William Evans-Gordon, the (Gentile) Unionist candidate at Stepney and a leading spokesman of the restrictionist lobby.[78] Even Samuel Montagu jumped on the bandwagon. He had assured his electors in 1892 that he had spared no effort 'to divert the stream of emigrants [*sic*] from this crowded city and land' and he boasted, at a meeting at Brick Lane, the heart of the Jewish East End, that he had been 'the means of preventing the immigration to this country of thousands of foreigners'.[79]

If Liberalism and radicalism did have a Jewish future in Great Britain, it was most assuredly not to be found within the Jewish communities already established in the country, but rather among the as yet largely unenfranchised pauper immigrants whom Lord Rothschild and Sir Samuel Montagu were doing their best to keep out of the country.

4. The Socialists Arrive

Socialism was practically unknown among British Jews before the 1880s.[1] The early British socialist movements, such as the Owenites and the Chartists, contained no Jewish elements.[2] Popular anti-Semitism was partly to blame for this state of affairs, but so also was the social structure of the Anglo-Jewish community. In 1883, just as the mass immigration from eastern Europe was gathering momentum, Joseph Jacobs completed a study of the social and economic structure of Anglo-Jewry. Of the 46,000 or so Jews in London, he estimated that 36,000 were professional people, merchants, shopkeepers, and petty traders. The rest were made up of servants, assistants, and paupers (most of whom were maintained by the Board of Guardians and other Jewish charities).[3] There was really nothing corresponding to a manual working class, a Marxist proletariat upon whom socialist teachings might have had some positive effect. There were plenty of poor Jews, but they were too dependent upon the wealthy ones to undertake a class struggle against them—even if they had wanted to. The only substantially Jewish industrial employment to be found in London before 1880 was the cigar- and cigarette-making activities of a small community of Dutch Jews. Significantly, the first strike of Jewish workers in Britain involved this community, in 1858.[4]

If socialism were ever to take root within Anglo-Jewry it obviously needed a much broader base. Prior to the 1880s this base simply did not exist. Thus the early efforts of immigrant Jewish socialists to organize Jewish workers in London were completely unsuccessful. In 1874 one Lewis Smith, a Polish Jew who had come to England by way of the Polish uprising of 1863 and the Paris Commune of 1871, attempted to form a union of Lithuanian tailors in Whitechapel; 72 members were enrolled, the organization lasted a few weeks and disappeared without trace, and its founder left England for New York.[5]

Two years later a more ambitious socialist organization was established. A small group of intellectuals and semi-intellectuals discovered a leader in the person of Aaron Lieberman, a twenty-seven-year-old drop-out from both orthodox Judaism and the Technological School in St. Petersburg, who had fled to Germany from the Tsarist police in 1875, and who came to London the same year to work on *Vperyod*, the Russian underground newspaper founded by Peter Lavrov. Lieberman hoped to be able to spread socialism and trade unionism among the working-class Jews of the East End. On 20 May 1876 he and nine other politicized Russian-Jewish immigrants met at No. 40 Gun Street, Spitalfields, and, with Lavrov looking on, founded the Hebrew Socialist Union.

Lieberman's ideas were big indeed. A revolutionary himself, he wished to convert the poor Jews of Whitechapel to his anti-bourgeois and anticlerical views, and involve them in a full-blooded uncompromising, and atheistic, class struggle. But his idealism prevented him from being realistic about the likely impact of his propaganda. The membership of the Hebrew Socialist Union never exceeded forty. It never managed to reconcile its proletarian aims with the fact that those whom it hoped to recruit (especially tailors) were in fact self-employed. It hoped to unite Jewish and Irish immigrants in the East End, but forgot that the Irish were vehemently anti-Jewish. Most damaging of all was the Union's anticlericalism, which enabled its enemies among the Anglo-Jewish establishment to accuse it of aiding and abetting the work of Christian missionaries. The nearest the Union ever got to becoming a mass movement was on 26 August 1876, when a meeting held under its auspices attracted several hundred workers. The demand for a ten-hour day was well received, but when Lieberman attacked local Jewish leaders, mentioning the Chief Rabbi by name, there was uproar and the meeting broke up in confusion.[6]

Jewish communal leaders had already taken steps to eradicate the socialists from their midst. At one level there was blatant economic pressure upon Hebrew Socialist Union members by their employers. At another, Zvi Hirsch Dainow, a popular Russian *maggid* (preacher) recently arrived in England, was persuaded to use his oratorical powers against the socialists. A tailors' union was formed, but it was certainly not socialist, and collapsed after three months when its treasurer fled to America, taking the funds with him. But Lieberman was, in truth, killing off his own movement by his refusal to compromise his own lofty principles. He quarrelled with his associates, who accused him of being more Jewish than socialist, and left the Union, and England, suddenly in December 1876. Imprisoned for his revolutionary activities first in Vienna and then in Berlin, Lieberman returned briefly to London in 1879. He and some former comrades established a Jewish Working-men's Benefit and Educational Society, which had no impact whatsoever. Lieberman left for America and there, in Syracuse, New York, he shot himself in November 1880, not, it must be added, as an act of revolutionary martyrdom, but through unrequited love.[7]

It is difficult to arrive at an objective assessment of Lieberman's work in London. The *Jewish Chronicle* was hopelessly biased, and dismissed the Hebrew Socialist Union as a 'Conversionist Trick'.[8] Morris Winchevsky, Lieberman's disciple, who came to London in 1879, stated that he could find no trace of his mentor's work.[9] The organization was always minute, 'an élite of thinking people, who were acquainted with Socialist thought, and wanted to improve the lot of the Jewish workers in London'.[10] But the Union should not be belittled simply because, as an organization, it did not survive. Most of its members found their way into the Third Section of the Communist Workers' Educational Union.[11] The short-lived tailors' union which it promoted did attract 300 members. And the hostility which Lieberman's activities provoked from the Jewish press, the master tailors, and the clergy was probably the best compliment that anyone could have paid him. What blighted its growth from the very beginning was the fact that the Hebrew Socialist Union's political creed was repudiated (if, indeed, it was ever properly understood) by those whom it wanted to win to its side. It sought to propagate its political faith at the very moment—1876—when, through the Bulgarian crisis, the Conservative Government was becoming ever more popular with Anglo-Jewry. 'We socialists', one of its leaders candidly admitted, 'are widely hated in the city.'[12] Had Lieberman arrived in London a decade later, his impact would have been very different. As it was, he was fortunate in achieving the following in the East End that he did, even if it survived for only a few months.

Shortly after Lieberman's suicide, Tsar Alexander II was

assassinated. A wave of officially inspired pogroms spread across the Pale of Settlement, in which lived over four million Russian and Polish Jews. The attacks were renewed and intensified between 1882 and 1889, when the economically oppressed Russian peasantry found an outlet for their discontent in anti-Jewish violence. There was a further wave of pogroms between 1902 and 1906. The trickle of Jewish refugees from Russia before 1880 became a flood thereafter. The pogroms were destined to change the face of Anglo-Jewry; in so doing, they deeply affected its political complexion.

The Jews searched desperately for places not merely of refuge but of economic opportunity. For the Pale of Settlement was a land of social deprivation as well as of religious persecution. Poverty forced the Jews to think of emigration; pogroms intensified their search for new opportunities. For most, the goal was the United States of America, the *Goldene Medina* (Golden Country), where so many of Europe's refugees and dispossessed had built new lives. Few Jews thought of permanent settlement in England. England was merely a stopping place on the way to America, a point of arrival at Grimsby or Tilbury, a cross-country train journey, and then a point of departure at Liverpool.

Sometimes, however, the immigrant's cash ran out; he could reach England but go no further, at least until more money had been earned and saved. More often, a sojourn in England that was intended to be temporary became permanent settlement. The artisans and craftsmen, the tailors, dressmakers, glaziers, and furniture-makers who came from the Pale of Settlement found they could exist—just—by working exceedingly long hours and living, as immigrants newly arrived in England have always lived, in the poorest and most squalid parts of the great cities. No one supposed that the life was pleasant; it wasn't. But it was free from persecution and terror and, however meagre the financial rewards, there was economic opportunity of a sort, some hope of advancement, whereas in the Pale of Settlement there had been none at all. There was also an established, well-to-do Jewish community, which had clearly made its way in the Gentile society that surrounded it. This fact itself gave grounds for optimism.

Whatever their motives, between 1881 and 1914 150,000

Jews from eastern Europe settled in the British Isles.[13] Demo-graphically this amounted to a revolution. The existing Anglo-Jewish community, estimated in 1880 at about 60,000 (of whom over three-quarters lived in London) was swamped by the newcomers.[14] The London community alone increased threefold by the turn of the century. More importantly, the immigrants built up and revitalized provincial congregations; in 1881 the entire provincial Jewish population amounted to barely 20,000, but on the eve of the Great War it had grown to about 100,000.[15] Towns such as Leeds, Manchester, Liver-pool, Birmingham, and Glasgow became Jewish centres in their own right, and were no longer mere adjuncts of London. The largest of them, and pre-eminently Manchester and Leeds, developed their own independent communal institu-tions. On a wide variety of religious and social matters these provincial communities became less and less willing to look to London or to take their cue from the Anglo-Jewish leadership which they found in control there. This tendency was ac-celerated and reinforced by the fact that the immigrants were, at the same time, repudiating the Jewish establishment and all its works in the metropolis itself.

A clash of cultures and of priorities took place at every level. This was inevitable. On a purely religious plane Anglo-Jewry in 1881 was not particularly orthodox in practice, and was becoming less so. In this respect the establishment of Reform congregations in London, and later, through the agency of cen-tral European immigrants, in Manchester and Bradford, was less important than the reformist tendencies within the recently created United Synagogue; the liturgical modifications to which Nathan Adler was persuaded to agree in 1880 were said to have been partly responsible for his virtual retirement from the Chief Rabbinate that year.[16] In 1888 Adler addressed an impassioned circular to his rabbinical colleagues in eastern Europe begging them to prevail upon their congregants 'not to come to the land of Britain for such ascent is a descent'.[17]

Most of the immigrants were devoutly orthodox and when they reached Britain they instinctively rejected the religious institutions they found here. They had come from self-govern-ing communities, each with its own rabbi, and the very idea of a Chief Rabbinate was foreign to them. In any case they had

little regard for Hermann Adler, whose orthodoxy they
doubted and whose authority some were prepared openly to
repudiate.[18] They shunned the cold formalism and the ca-
thedral-like structures of the United Synagogue in London,
and set up instead their own small, noisy, informal synagogues
—*chevras*—by the dozen in the East End and in the provinces.
In this way they hoped to preserve the religious and cultural life
of the east European ghettos whence they had fled, and preserve the Yiddish language they all spoke. If integration with
British Jews meant adopting the ways of Anglo-Judaism, they
wanted no part of it.[19]

The Anglo-Jewish leadership, for its part, was dismayed and
terrified by the mass immigration. The prime cause for concern
was the effects which the influx of thousands of Jewish pauper
refugees was having upon the standing and safety of the community already here, for it was not long before the presence of
the refugees gave rise to an anti-Jewish agitation which affected
all political parties. The so-called problem of aliens from
eastern Europe became a political football, and in this way the
spotlight was turned upon the Jews in a manner which was
novel in its intensity, and the like of which had not been seen
since the 'Jew Bill' agitation a century and a half earlier. For
that reason alone Anglo-Jewry did not welcome the refugees.
The Board of Guardians advertised in the Jewish press in
Russia and Romania that Jews who sought to escape persecution by coming to Britain would face many hardships, and
would not obtain relief from the Board during the first six
months of residence—when they needed it most. Those refugees who did reach Britain were encouraged to continue their
journeys to America or South Africa, and some were persuaded
to return whence they had come. Jews in both the Liberal and
Conservative parties supported legislation to restrict the flow of
immigrants into Great Britain; in so doing they were merely
giving practical expression to the feelings of a great many
British Jews.

Beyond this consideration, however, there were other reasons
why the immigrants were most unwelcome to the Jewish leadership. For they were the means by which entirely new political
philosophies made their way into Anglo-Jewish thinking. This
threatened to mark out Anglo-Jewry as the carrier of 'foreign'

and, in the view of many, extremist doctrines into the United Kingdom, and was itself a powerful element in the anti-alien agitation of the period. Specifically, the immigrants brought into Anglo-Jewish life three political elements which had been but barely discernible within the community before: socialism, trade unionism, and Zionism. Powerful pressures were brought to bear by the established Jewish community to eradicate these novel tendencies. But the most that could be achieved was a tightening of controls to prevent the immigrants, and hence, it was hoped, their doctrines, from reaching the British Isles.

The immigrants came to Britain from a Jewish society in Russia and Poland which, though enclosed, was none the less rich in political and industrial organization. In the Pale of Settlement 'the Jewish strike movement ... struck terror in the hearts of the employers'; Jewish factory-owners actually preferred hiring non-Jews because, in the words of one factory-owner, 'the Jews are good workers, but they are capable of organizing revolts ... against the employer, the regime, and the Tsar himself'.[20] In towns such as Vilna, Vitebsk, and Gomel, Jewish trade unions flourished, at least for a time, at the end of the nineteenth century, and achieved considerable short-term successes.[21]

Many of these unions owed their inception and organization to socialists. The spread of socialism among the Jews of the Pale reached its apogee in the famous October 1897 meeting, in Vilna, of social-democratic delegates from Minsk, Warsaw, Vitebsk, Bialystock, and Vilna itself, at which the decision was taken to form 'The General Jewish Labour Alliance in Russia, Poland and Lithuania'.[22] The Bund, as it was popularly known, was anti-Zionist; initially, at any rate, it sought a solution to the Jewish problem in Russia not through nationalism but within the framework of the Russian Social-Democratic Labour Party, in the formation of which it played a prominent part, and its ideology was thoroughly Marxist. Zionism was, in the eyes of the Bund, a reactionary bourgeois movement.[23]

The organization of a socialist-Zionist movement took somewhat longer to work out. But when, at the turn of the century, conditions in Russia seemed to rule out co-operation between working- and middle-class Zionists, the proletarian Zionist groups seceded from the Russian Zionist Organization and

formed the Zionist Socialist Labour Party (February 1905). A
year later the Jewish Social Democratic Labour Party, Poale
Zion, was formally instituted at Poltava. Both parties held to
the view that the lack of a national homeland rendered impossible the normal development of a Jewish proletariat; Poale
Zion favoured Palestine, whereas the Zionist Socialist Labour
Party thought a suitable territory might be found elsewhere.[24]

Even for those Jewish socialists who were not particularly
moved by Zionism, the advantage of adopting a Zionist platform was obvious. The concept of a return to the Promised
Land was deeply rooted within religious orthodoxy, and was
bound, therefore, to attract the observant masses. It also
helped counteract the view that socialism was nothing less than
atheism. It is true that the majority of Russian rabbis were
hostile to socialism. But this was partly because they feared it
would foment anti-Semitism and invite Tsarist interference
with Jewish religious institutions, particularly the theological
seminaries which were often hotbeds of socialist propaganda;
there are several well-attested cases of collusion between rabbis
and the Russian police in the arrest of Jewish agitators.[25]

None of this meant that socialism and religious orthodoxy
were incompatible. On the contrary, there were elements within orthodox teaching which, it could be argued, were heavily
socialist: the pietistic Chassidic movement, for example, which
arose at the end of the eighteenth century as a reaction by the
poorest Jews to the conditions in which they lived, demoted
rabbinical scholarship, elevated the concept of charity, and
taught that the poor had a right to demand a share in the
wealth of the rich, for were not all earthly possessions enjoyed
only as a loan from the Almighty?[26] Many of the Jewish trade
unions in the Pale combined industrial militancy with fervent
religious devotion.[27] Far more significant than the handful of
publicity-seeking Jewish socialists, both in Russia and
England, who organized ham-sandwich picnics on the fast of
Yom Kippur, the Day of Atonement, were the mass of working-
class Jews who experienced no inner conflict when they repaired to the synagogue for religious services three times each
day, and then used the same premises to discuss socialist principles and organize industrial stoppages.

The mass immigration to Britain thus created a Jewish proletariat in the East End of London and other areas of immigrant settlement, such as Manchester and Leeds. Here, living in conditions of extreme poverty and working incredibly long hours, was a ready-made audience for socialist propaganda. And there happened to be, settled in London, a Yiddish writer and socialist philosopher of great eloquence who was able, for a time, to hold its attention: L. Benzion Novochovitch, better known by his pseudonym, Morris Winchevsky. Winchevsky had all the qualifications needed to make himself a superb socialist propagandist in the East End. Born in Lithuania in 1856, he had attended the famous Vilna Rabbinical Seminary and was able, in his writings, to summon up a rich variety of religious images. He had got himself a secure job (under another pseudonym) with a Jewish banking firm in the City of London, and had already acquired, during a sojourn at Königsberg, some journalistic experience as editor of the vaguely socialist Hebrew periodical *Asefat Hachamim* ('Assembly of the Wise'). On 25 July 1884 he and a friend, Elijah Wolf Rabbinowitz, founded in London, the first socialist newspaper in Yiddish, *Der Polisher Yidl* ('The Little Polish Jew'). Between July and October 1884 sixteen issues of the paper appeared. Much of its content was concerned with the plight of East End Jews, and it was not above taking the Jewish workers themselves to task for indulging in vices such as gambling.[28] On the subject of anti-Semitism it was refreshingly frank, and warned its readers that in the East End dislike of Jews was rampant.

But the socialism of *Der Polisher Yidl* was implicit rather than explicit. Rabbinowitz was moving closer to Zionism, and accepted religious advertisements for the paper; Winchevsky, however, had already published a brilliant parody on Maimonides' Thirteen Articles of Faith, entitled *Yeho Or* ('Let There Be Light').[29] The inevitable split came when Rabbinowitz accepted an election advertisement from Samuel Montagu. This was more than Winchevsky could stomach. He left the paper and, with a group of like-minded friends, some of them social democrats and some anarchists, founded the *Arbeter Fraint* ('Worker's Friend').[30] The first issue, which appeared on 15 July 1885, declared that the aim of the new paper was 'to spread true socialism among Jewish workers', but made it clear that it was open to all modes of radical thought. It remained the major Yiddish socialist newspaper in the country for the next decade.[31]

As with any small circulation journal, the precise impact of the *Arbeter Fraint* is not susceptible of calculation. It began as a monthly publication, and only appeared weekly from December 1886. In trying to occupy the middle ground (it assumed such ground existed) between radicals, social-democrats, collectivists, communists, and anarchists, it could please no one. Of course the small band of Jewish socialist revolutionaries in London (pre-eminently Winchevsky; Philip Krantz, the paper's first editor; and Isaac Stone) could agree with their anarchist friends that the existing social order had to be swept away, and with it all forms of religion, and hence any separately organized Jewish community. But how, and with what, were these pillars of established society to be replaced? The third issue of the *Arbeter Fraint* urged socialists to participate in the 1885 general election 'in order to prove to the public how little it has to expect from Parliament, trade unions, co-operation, and the like, with which the capitalists deceive the workers'.[32] The protests which this appeal evoked from the anarchists foreshadowed the split between them and the socialists which resulted, in 1892, in the paper becoming a vehicle of the anarchist movement.

More importantly, the socialists slavishly followed Lassalle's 'iron law of wages', which taught that wage rises won by trade unions would always be followed by commensurate increases in the cost of living. Trade unionism, as it was then developing in Britain, was, by this model, ruled out as a waste of time and— worse still—a harmful diversion of the energy of the workers from the struggle to attain revolutionary socialism; if there were to be trade unions, they must devote themselves exclusively to socialist ends, and if there were to be strikes their sole aim must be to foment revolution. When one remembers that such lofty exhortations were spiced with relentless anti-religious propaganda, it is not difficult to conclude that, as a vehicle for converting the Jewish proletariat to socialism, the *Arbeter Fraint*'s impact was muted to say the least. There was no Jewish socialist uprising in London, or anything remotely resembling one.

But, as so often happens with radical journals, the currents generated by the *Arbeter Fraint* proved to be longer-lasting and more significant than the paper itself. In 1884 a Society of Jewish Socialists was established, and it in turn founded an International Workers' Educational Club, with premises at No. 40 Berner Street, off the Commercial Road. In June 1886 the Berner Street Club, as it was popularly known, took over publication of the *Arbeter Fraint*, and became the meeting-place for every sort of radically orientated Jewish immigrant in London. Similar clubs were established in Manchester, Leeds, Liverpool, Hull, and Glasgow. The clubs, by attracting non-socialists, forced the socialist elements to recognize the necessity of coming to terms with trade unions, and they therefore provided a stimulus to the organization of trade unions among Jewish workers. Secondly, the clubs stimulated the first contacts between Jewish workers and British socialists. The Berner Street Club was visited by William Morris, Herbert Burrows, Harry Quelch, and H. M. Hyndman, the last three of whom spoke at public meetings of an East End (Jewish) branch of the Social-Democratic Federation, organized in the mid-1880s.[33] Jewish social-democratic groups sprang up in the provinces, and in September 1905 a League of Jewish Social-Democratic groups in England was formed, affiliated to the Social-Democratic Federation.[34] These links paid dividends, because although some British socialists adopted an increasingly anti-Semitic stance (particularly as the Boer War approached), enough sympathy with the plight of the Jews was generated to evoke protests from both Hyndman and James Keir Hardie against the Kishinev pogrom (1903), while the following year Hyndman actually denounced the Aliens Immigration bill, designed to curb Jewish immigration to Britain.[35]

But as propagandists for their own causes the 'Berner-Streeters' were failures, just as, during the 1880s and 1890s, the combined efforts of the Social-Democratic Federation, the Independent Labour Party, and the Fabian Society did precious little to convert the British trade-union movement to socialism. The Jewish immigrants were too busy keeping body and soul together to worry about social revolution; that could be left to their children. Winchevsky himself came to doubt the value of socialist propaganda among the immigrants, few of whom, he observed, had acquired citizenship and therefore the right to vote.[36] The situation was different in the United States of America and, one by one, the leading Jewish socialists left London for New York. Those who remained were largely won over to Zionism, much to Winchevsky's disgust; in his collected works he called them 'heretics and traitors'.[37] Winchevsky also lost the battle with the anarchists. In April 1891, by a vote of 25 to 22, the Berner Street Club, and therefore the *Arbeter Fraint*, adopted an anarchist position. By June the paper's sales in London had dropped to 200. The Club left its Berner Street premises and began 'a period of wandering through the meeting rooms of London'.[38]

Winchevsky and his remaining associates naturally quit the paper, and founded another, *Freie Welt* ('Free World'), nine issues of which appeared between May 1891 and November 1892. This managed to achieve an average paid circulation of 509 per issue, but most of the sales were to America, and although its revolutionary tone was as strident as ever its appeal for 'violent social revolution' fell on deafer ears than had that of the *Arbeter Fraint*.[39] Inevitably, in 1894, Winchevsky too left for the relatively lusher pastures on the other side of the Atlantic. In England, Jewish non-Zionist utopian socialism was dead. The way forward for Jewish socialism lay through trade unionism or nationalism. Winchevsky took a long time to learn the lesson. But he repented in the end, became a Zionist, and wrote *My Nationalist Confession*, in 1911, to prove it.[40]

To the Jewish masses in London and other urban centres socialism meant little as an ideology, but much as a framework for industrial organization. The small band of Jewish social-democrats and anarchists in England found that they were in demand not as political publicists but as trade-union managers; it was, consequently, through trade unionism that the socialist message made its greatest impact.

The premature beginnings of Jewish trade unionism in England were outlined at the beginning of this chapter. The flood of immigrants provided a wholly new impetus for union activities, and not only, or even primarily, from the workers themselves. The overcrowding and the sweat-shops in London and Leeds became topics of national concern. In March 1884 the *Lancet* began publishing reports by its 'Special Sanitary Commission' on the condition of Jewish immigrant workers.

Four years later both Houses of Parliament began investigating all aspects of the immigrant problem, and the Board of Trade conducted its own inquiry into the sweating system in Leeds and the East End of London. These investigations prompted the leaders of Anglo-Jewry to try to put their own house in order without government interference. One way of doing this was to promote the formation of 'respectable' (i.e. non-socialist) trade unions, whose major task it would be to see that existing factory legislation was enforced in the sweat-shops. In 1884 the *Jewish Chronicle* urged the Board of Guardians to undertake such a promotion, but the Guardians were, in truth, too closely identified with the Anglo-Jewish ruling élites to be taken seriously in this regard.[41] Samuel Montagu had a much better chance of success. He knew from his own constituency how quick socialists (Jewish and Gentile) were to exploit industrial and social grievances for political ends, and he had already put himself forward as a labour arbitrator and patron of the Jewish Working Men's Club. In 1886 he founded and supported the Jewish Tailors' Machinists Society, whose (unsuccessful) aim was to achieve a twelve-hour day without recourse to the strike weapon.[42]

Montagu feared socialism not in a religious sense but because of the bad name which he felt would accrue to Anglo-Jewry through the work of socialists within the immigrant community. Just at this time the socialists began to adopt an Irish tactic, that of using funerals for propaganda purposes. In February 1887 they issued an invitation, in Hebrew, to the Jewish workers of the East End, calling upon them to attend 'the funeral [at West Ham] of our comrade Simon Sweed, boot-finisher, 26 years of age, who fell a victim to the present system of production'.[43] Montagu felt the time for strong measures had come. In the early summer he and F. D. Mocatta made a heavy-handed attempt to suppress the *Arbeter Fraint* by bribing the compositor and printer to sabotage its production; the stratagem misfired, for within three months the paper had acquired its own printing press and was back on the streets.[44]

Subtler tactics were obviously called for. Montague needed a platform from which he could talk to the immigrants and super-intend their affairs. At Berner Street he was *persona non grata*. But in the *chevras* it was a different matter. Montagu therefore hit upon the idea of sponsoring a federation of them, under his own patronage, in order to show the world that Jewish immigrants were by no means socialists and republicans. 'Although there might be one or two Socialists', he told the preliminary meeting of his federation on 16 October 1887, 'these were quite the exception to the rule.'[45] A week later The Federation of Minor Synagogues came into being. As befitted such an instrument of social control in Anglo-Jewry, Lord Rothschild became Honorary President of the new body, but Montagu, the 'Acting President', supervised its day-to-day affairs, provided it with funds, and presented it with its own burial ground at Edmonton, at which, presumably, socialist propaganda was not to be permitted. In January 1890, again at Montagu's insistence, the Federation appointed its own Yiddish-speaking minister, Dr M. Lerner, in order to help combat a 'most serious evil', namely 'the influence of a few Atheists [i.e. socialists] over Jewish Working Men'.[46]

Built on the firm foundations of Montagu's money, the Federation survived, and did much to bring order into the chaos of the *chevras* without making their members feel that anglicization was being forced upon them. To this extent it undoubtedly made more difficult the work of socialist propagandists. But it did nothing to impede the sprouting of trade unions from the grass roots of the community, and it was based exclusively upon the Jews of London's East End, upon whom the public gaze was largely focused. Montagu ignored the provinces. But it was in the provinces, or, more exactly, in Leeds, that authentic Jewish trade unionism took a firm hold.

If class conflict existed anywhere within Anglo-Jewry in the age of immigration, it was to be found in the Leeds ghetto, known as the Leylands. In 1877 Leeds had only 500 Jewish families; by 1900 the community there numbered about 12,000, engaged primarily in the ready-made clothing industry.[47] A Leeds Jewish Working Tailors' Trade Society had been formed as long ago as February 1876.[48] The great majority of these Jewish workers were employed by Jewish masters, who were engaged in cut-throat competition for orders from the big factories. Consequently little regard was paid to Factory Acts or the limits of a working day. With the influx of the immigrants the Trade Society revolted against these conditions. The machiners and pressers were organized and the Society was able, with little difficulty, to persuade both orthodox and socialist Jewish workers to support its campaign.[49] In April 1885 it conducted a successful two-weeks' strike, at the end of which the masters agreed to a one-hour reduction in the working day, without loss of pay.[50] Three years later, however, another strike, revolving largely around a demand for the closed shop, was defeated by the masters and the Society, then numbering some 3,000 members, collapsed.[51]

Although the 1885 strike had been conducted without the aid of English trade unions, some Gentile socialists were already taking an interest in the Leeds Jewish proletariat. Prominent members of William Morris's Socialist League, such as James Sweeney, Tom Maguire, Tom Paylor, and J. L. Mahon, involved themselves in Jewish labour problems in the city.[52] In the 1880s the organization of the Leeds Jewish tailors came to be dominated by Jewish socialists, such as Lewis Frank and Morris Kemmelhor.[53] The disappointments of 1888 seem, moreover, to have brought English and Jewish socialists closer together; by January of the following year the *Arbeter Fraint*'s reporter found the Socialist Club in Leeds to be of mixed English and Jewish membership.[54] This was the prelude to a totally unprecedented pooling of resources, which took place in February 1890, when the Jewish tailors amalgamated with the gasworkers to fight for shorter hours. In August the tailors struck, and by the end of that month had won a uniform twelve-hour day.[55]

The union of Jewish tailors and gasworkers in Leeds came to an end in 1891. But in 1893 the entire Jewish branch of the Leeds tailoring trade was reorganized as the Leeds Jewish Tailors' Machinists' and Pressers' Union, with (from 1895) a full-time paid General Secretary, Sam Freedman. The union was regularly represented at the Trades Union Congress and became an early affiliate of the Labour Representation Committee, the forerunner of the Labour party.[56] Membership rose from 1,180 in 1902 to 4,465 in 1913. The union, with its social clubs and sickness and unemployment benefits, became 'in the public mind, more than any religious or charitable institution, the representative communal body' in Leeds, encompassing 'proletarians of immeasurably different types; ranging from those obeying the onerous and multifarious injunctions of the Mosaic Code and the Talmud, to those practising Free Love and Free Marriage'.[57]

In a Jewish no less than an English milieu, therefore, socialism was most widely welcomed when it addressed itself to practical industrial problems, and was prepared to suppress, if not abandon altogether, its anti-religious elements. What was true of Leeds was also true of London. In the metropolis the major socialist impact came, not through theorists such as Lieberman and Winchevsky, but via the doers, who were prepared to help the immigrants in practical ways. Pre-eminent among these was Lewis Lyons, who, in 1889, took over the leadership of the East End garment workers. Lyons, an English-born machinist, had once been a contributor to the *Arbeter Fraint*, and had briefly published his own paper, the *Anti-Sweater*. He was a social democrat of independent views, not trusted by the mainstream of Jewish socialists at that time because he believed, rightly, that the only way to improve the lot of the garment workers was to organize a combination of the workers and the small master tailors (whose situation was often no better than that of their employees) against the wholesalers.[58] For daring to suggest such a combination the *Arbeter Fraint*, already under anarchist influence, never forgave him.

In January 1889 Lyons and Philip Krantz formed a Committee for Jewish Unemployed and tried, unsuccessfully, to enlist the aid of Chief Rabbi Hermann Adler in their campaign against sweating.[59] But Adler, though acknowledging the evil complained of, would of course do nothing which might have linked his name with those of Jewish socialists.[60] In the early summer Lyons was again at work, organizing a strike for a twelve-hour day, including one hour for lunch and a half-hour for tea. The secretary of the strike committee was Wolf Wess, a Jewish immigrant from Libau who was also a prominent member of the Socialist League. The strike was widespread and bitter, and lasted for five weeks. Help came from some unexpected quarters. The strike committee of the London dockers gave £100, and the Amalgamated Society of Tailors and the London Society of Compositors £10 each; Lord Rothschild contributed £73 and Samuel Montagu £30. 10*s*.[61] The grievances of the workers were real, and even the *Jewish Chron-*

icle expressed its sympathy; what was worrying, it declared, was 'the leadership of men conspicuously associated with Socialist movements'.[62] Montagu offered himself as a peacemaker and persuaded the masters to agree to the demands of the men, on condition that the latter did not bring up the question of wages for one year.[63] At the same time a Jewish tailors' strike in Manchester was similarly successful.[64]

Though ardently celebrated at the time, these victories were short-lived. It was difficult to maintain the enthusiasm of the workers over a long period, when unemployment was rife, wages depressed, and when new immigrants were arriving daily looking for work. The evil of sweating needed parliamentary action to combat it, and this did not happen until the passage of the Liberal government's Trade Boards Act in 1909. In any case, by themselves the Jewish trade unions never had a broad enough base to affect the great mass of the new Jewish proletariat; in 1892 the *Arbeter Fraint* itself estimated that, of some 30,000 immigrant Jewish workers in London, only about 1,200 were members of Jewish trade unions.[65]

But the roots of Anglo-Jewish socialism had been planted, the memories remained, and a generation grew up in the knowledge that socialists had something to offer it. What precisely was on offer was never spelt out. Perhaps that was all to the good. The doctrinal arguments between socialists and anarchists did not concern the bulk of the immigrant generation. The ascendancy in London of the Yiddish-speaking, German, Gentile anarchist, Rudolf Rocker, is the story of the triumph of a man's personality over his principles. In October 1898 Rocker took over the editorship of the *Arbeter Fraint*, which became the outlet for his considerable literary and philosophical talents.[66] A sincere friend of the poor and the oppressed, Rocker became something of a legend in his own lifetime in the East End of London, but, as befitted an anarchist, he turned his back on parliamentary politics, refused to use the masses as a vehicle for the advancement of his own ideas, and consequently was singularly unsuccessful in raising Jewish anarchism in London from a clique into a movement.

Between 1898 and 1914 Rocker achieved a tremendous following in the East End, but it was personal to him alone. The Workers' Friend Club, which the anarchists opened in

February 1906, was the meeting place for a wide range of radical views, and though the anarchists did not support trade union development *per se*, they inevitably came to act, individually, as union sponsors, and they figured prominently in the great East End tailors' and garment workers' strikes of 1906 and 1912.[67] 'The Anarchists', Mr Fishman writes, 'had achieved such popularity that they became almost respectable. A sympathiser could lay on his *tefillin* (phylacteries) on the morning of an Anarchist-sponsored strike, bless Rocker, and still go off to evening service as an orthodox Jew.'[68]

Mr Fishman also asserts, less convincingly, that 'in 1914 the Anarchists were the most dynamic element in East End political life'.[69] But it was precisely in the *political* sphere that the anarchist impact was most muted. When the Great War broke out Rocker was arrested and interned, the *Arbeter Fraint* suppressed, and the anarchist club closed by the police. The movement disappeared because its following was emotional, not political. In 1918 Rocker was repatriated to Germany. Of East End Jewish anarchism nothing remained, though many friends of the movement had already committed themselves to established Labour and Zionist causes. And as the immigrant generation became anglicized even the need for separate Jewish unions was called into question; the Jewish tailors' unions in London amalgamated with the Tailors' and Garment Workers' Trade Union, and the Leeds Jewish Tailors' Union followed suit in 1915.[70]

Jewish socialism, established more solidly now because it had developed upon an industrial base, fared somewhat better but, before 1914, it was still a delicate creature. Since most of the immigrants were without a vote, its electoral strength is impossible to determine. Membership of Jewish socialist organizations was very small. In 1907 the Marxist Jacob Lestschinsky observed, somewhat pessimistically, that the total number of Jewish socialists in London amounted to no more than about 200, in a community of some 130,000 persons. He attributed this to the 'reserve army' of Jewish workers, whose presence prevented the emergence of effective unions and the development of a specifically Jewish working-class consciousness.[71] The truth was that in England, unlike Russia, a vibrant Liberal party existed as a counterweight to revolutionary socialism and that, hanging on the coat-tails of this Liberal party was a reformist, but not socialist, Labour party which was soon to achieve the backing of the British trade-union movement.

The truth—which Jewish Marxists often dared not admit even to themselves—also was that Zionism had taken a strong hold of the Jewish immigrants in England. More important than the Jewish section of the Social-Democratic Federation was the establishment of the Poale Zion movement in Britain. By November 1903 two branches had been formed in London, one under the auspices of the garment workers, the other in connection with the Independent Cabinet Makers' Union.[72] In February 1904 the movement in London opened permanent headquarters in Whitechapel Road.[73] Poale Zion groups were already in existence in the major provincial centres, and the British Poale Zion was formally constituted at a meeting in Liverpool on 25 December 1906.[74]

So the work of Lieberman and Winchevsky, Kemmelhor and Lyons, Wess and Rocker was not without results, though the results were clearly not what these pioneers had intended. Socialism came to the Jewish immigrants slowly, without the revolutionary passion it had assumed in the Old Country, and through an industrial rather than an ideological medium. Liberalism and Zionism proved very powerful counter-attractions. The children of the revolutionaries eventually found their way into the Labour party.[75] Some of them even found their way into Parliament, there, in due course, to fight not for international socialism but for Jewish national self-determination.

5. The Alien Makes His Mark

Between the general elections of 1900 and 1910 one issue dominated the politics of the Anglo-Jewish community: immigration. The Jewish refugees from Tsarist Russia became an issue in British domestic politics; at the same time they were becoming part of that political system. Jewish voting strength was exploited to the full, and without embarrassment or diffidence. The generation of the emancipation was giving way to its successor, the emancipated generation, the members of which exercised their rights without any special regard for the feelings of the Gentile majority. The Jewish vote thus came of age. But it was a very different political animal from that which had held sway during the nineteenth century.

With the appointment in 1888 of the Select Committee of the House of Commons on Alien Immigration, and of the House of Lords on the Sweating System, Jewish refugees became a political issue. They were soon to become a political football. The Select Committees themselves gave the immigrants a reasonably clean bill of health. The Lords' inquiry concluded that 'undue stress has been laid on the injurious effect on wages caused by foreign immigration, inasmuch as we find that the evils complained of obtain in trades which do not appear to be affected by foreign immigration'. The Select Committee of the lower House felt that the immigrants were 'generally very dirty and uncleanly in their habits' but none the less showed themselves to be 'quick at learning, moral, frugal and thrifty and inoffensive as citizens'.[1]

The only practical result of these inquiries was that the Board of Trade instituted annual returns of immigrants. At this stage the opposition to the Jews was multi-party in character. The Association for Preventing the Immigration of Destitute Aliens, for instance, could claim support from both Conservative and Liberal MPs, and from labour leaders such as J. Havelock Wilson and Ben Tillett.[2] But the agitation was led by a group of Conservative politicians, foremost amongst whom were Howard Vincent, MP for Sheffield Central, and James Lowther, MP for Thanet, and it soon became clear that the Conservative leadership was prepared to use anti-alienism as a vote-catcher.[3] In May 1892, two months before it faced a general election, Lord Salisbury's Government anounced that an Aliens' bill was being prepared. Whether true or not (the Liberal minister A. J. Mundella later claimed that it was not[4]), it is a fact that the issue was widely exploited by East End Conservative candidates in the election the following July.

The Liberals, in office between 1892 and 1895, refused to legislate on the aliens question, in spite of the fact that in 1892 the Trades Union Congress passed a resolution against the entry of 'pauper aliens' and that similar resolutions were passed in 1894 and 1895. Many Liberals were no doubt motivated by nostalgia and altruism in their refusal to placate popular misinformed opinion about Jewish refugees. But there was also an element of self-interest at work: to have agreed to restrict the entry of the Jews would have been tantamount to stabbing Free Trade in the back, for many Liberals could rightly see very little difference between tariff barriers to keep out foreign, cheaply produced goods and legal barriers to keep out foreigners who (allegedly) produced goods more cheaply than the native English.[5]

The Conservative party suffered from no such dogmatism. In July 1894 Lord Salisbury himself, acting as a private member of the House of Lords, introduced an Aliens' Bill which passed all its stages in the upper House but was then dropped. And in the general election the following year the issue was again exploited, both in London and in provincial constituencies. That more was not made of it between 1895 and 1900 was due in part to declining unemployment, and hence lack of trade-union concern about the matter, but partly also to the fact that the Conservatives simply did not need to exploit it; the Liberal party had been reduced to 177 MPs and was bitterly divided by both personal and doctrinal issues.

The aliens' card was therefore put on one side. But it was not given up. And by the time of the next general election, in October 1900 the card was pulled out of the pack once more. The

omens were favourable. During 1899 and 1900 there was an
exodus of several thousand Jews from Romania; nearly 3,000
reached England, whence the Jewish Board of Guardians did
its best to repatriate them.[6] Further pogroms, and the outbreak
of the Russo-Japanese war in 1904, added to the Guardians'
difficulties. Moreover, just at this time (1902-4) the Atlantic
Shipping Ring broke up, and the resultant price war made it
cheaper to travel from Hamburg to New York via England
than to go direct. The consternation within the Anglo-Jewish
leadership was great. By this time, as was shown in Chapter 3,
many of the leading families, and many of the Jewish voters, at
least in London, had become Conservatives. It was therefore
open to the Conservative party to peddle anti-alienism more
seriously without the fear of being accused of anti-Jewish prejudice.[7] The opportunity was too great to miss.

Politically, the Conservative parliamentary party which was
returned to Westminster in 1900 was more receptive to restrictionist propaganda. A number of East End Conservative MPs
had made much of the need for such legislation in their campaigns: Thomas Dewar (St. George's); H. Forde-Ridley
(Bethnal Green South-West); Cluade Hay (Hoxton); and the
Jew Harry S. Samuel (Limehouse).[8] At Stepney a new and
imposing figure emerged, Major William Evans-Gordon, who
won the seat back from the Liberals in a campaign in which
anti-alienism was the major issue. Moreover several of these
MPs could claim that Jewish voters had helped them to victory.
This was particularly true of Dewar and Evans-Gordon.[9] Most
remarkable of all in this connection was the campaign of David
Hope Kyd at Whitechapel. Samuel Montagu had retired from
the Whitechapel seat in favour of his nephew, Stuart Samuel.
In a strong bid to wrest the constituency from him, Hope Kyd
cleverly coupled his desire for an aliens' immigration bill with
heart-rending support for the infant Zionist movement. This
earned him the accolade of Lord Rothschild, and he came
within seventy-one votes of victory.[10]

Rothschild also supported Evans-Gordon, who celebrated
his own success by helping to organize a highly vocal pressure
group, the East-End-based British Brothers' League, to press
for restrictive legislation.[11] The League was formally inaugurated in May 1901.[12] The following August a 'Parliamen-

tary Alien Immigration Committee' came into existence, consisting of fifty-two MPs, who at once wrote to Lord Salisbury,
the Prime Minister, demanding legislation.[13] All this agitation
was taking place against a background of mounting, country-
wide anti-Semitism, fostered by the right-wing jingoism and
left-wing anti-capitalism which accompanied the Boer War,
and from which even the Liberal party was not immune.[14] In
January 1900 J. A. Hobson, then on the staff of the *Manchester
Guardian,* had told the National Liberal Club that 'the war was
due to Jewish capitalists'.[15] At the general election some Jewish
Conservative candidates were viciously abused by the local
Liberal press; Nathaniel L. Cohen, for instance, lost Penryn
and Falmouth by twenty votes after a campaign which consisted largely of crude attacks on him as 'a stock exchange
operator and a Jew'.[16]

   The British Brothers' League was a Conservative-led and
Conservative-dominated body, but it could boast all-party support.[17] What is more, Jews participated in its activities. At a
public meeting (variously estimated to have consisted of from
4,000 to 6,000 people) which it held at the People's Palace,
Mile End, in January 1902, speeches were made not only by
Evans-Gordon and Forde-Ridley, but also by Harry Samuel
and Henry Norman, the Jewish Liberal MP for Wolverhamp-
ton South.[18] The Government was only too happy to appease
such a combination of interests and announced, the following
month, the setting up of a Royal Commission on Alien Immigration.

   The Royal Commission reported in August 1903. The substance of its report was less important than the time at which
its findings appeared. The report itself was not unanimous.
The majority report rejected the total exclusion of alien immigrants in the future and refuted most of the charges made
against those already here; it was, however, in favour of limit-
ing the entry of certain classes of aliens, repatriating those
found to be 'undesirable', and controlling the settlement of
those allowed to stay by prohibiting settlement in certain areas
In two dissenting memoranda Sir Kenelm Digby, Permanent
Under-Secretary at the Home Office, and Lord Rothschild,
the only Jew on the Commission, argued that the recom-
mendations as to prohibited areas were unworkable, and they

objected to the repatriation of 'undesirable aliens' because, in Lord Rothschild's words, even if such measures 'were directly aimed at the so-called undesirables, they would certainly affect deserving and hard-working men, whose impecunious position on their arrival would be no criterion of their incapacity to attain independence'.[19]

At any other time such a report, dissented from by the highest permanent civil servant in the Home Office, would have been subject to detailed scrutiny by any government, however determined on legislation. But within two months of the report's appearance the position of the Unionist coalition altered dramatically. In September 1903 Joseph Chamberlain, the Colonial Secretary, resigned from the Government in order to be free to pursue his policy of tariff reform; four 'free trade' members of the Cabinet also resigned. Arthur Balfour, who had succeeded his uncle as Prime Minister the previous year, found his Government falling apart and his party, both in the country and in Parliament, in disarray. More importantly, the Liberal opposition was presented with an issue—the defence of free trade—on which it could unite at last. A party which defended free trade could hardly support restrictions on immigration. Balfour, on the other hand, desperately needed to restore his popularity. The majority report of the Royal Commission was thus not shelved, but was turned into a set of legislative proposals as quickly as possible. On 2 February 1904 the King's Speech announced the Government's intention to legislate that session; a bill, based on the majority report, was unveiled in April.

The Aliens' Bill of 1904 never reached the statute book. Consisting of a hastily prepared and probably unworkable set of proposals, the Bill suffered the ignominy of being condemned, in the correspondence columns of *The Times,* by Kenelm Digby, who had retired from the Home Office the previous year.[20] The Board of Deputies was more restrained. A deputation which went to the Home Office in May objected to certain parts of the Bill, but did not oppose it root and branch.[21] What sealed the Bill's fate, however, was the parliamentary assault on it by the Liberal opposition, who were as determined to make electoral capital out of its defeat as were the Conservatives to try and win popularity by pushing it thought Parliament. The Liberals won this particular battle on two counts. Firstly they exploited every parliamentary tactic to delay the Bill. Secondly, sensing that the Anglo-Jewish leadership did not speak for the Jewish masses, and particularly not for those recently arrived in this country, the Liberals appealed to the latter over the heads of the former.

The most brilliant stroke in this game was played by Nathan Laski, president of the Manchester Old Hebrew Congregation. In May 1904 Laski, a leading Manchester Liberal, obtained from Winston Churchill (who had just left the Conservative for the Liberal benches) a strong condemnation of the bill; the following month Churchill was adopted as Liberal candidate for North-West Manchester, in which there was a large Jewish electorate.[22] Later Churchill freely admitted that, in the Grand Committee of the House of Commons, he had 'wrecked the Bill'.[23] Led by Churchill the Liberals, Evans-Gordon asserted, 'choked it [the Bill] with words until the time-limit was reached'.[24] In July Balfour announced that the bill would be withdrawn. A jubilant Laski wrote to Churchill: 'I have had over 20 years' experience in elections in Manchester—& without flattery I tell you candidly—there has not been a single man able to arouse the interest that you have already done—thus I am sure of your future success.'[25]

The Conservative Government, however, had no intention of abandoning legislation altogether. Between July 1904 and April 1905 the party had to defend ten seats at by-elections; half were lost to the Liberals. One contest which was not lost, though, was that a Mile End in mid-January 1905; the turn of events there seemed to indicate that legislation on the aliens' question might still prove to be a life-support for Balfour's tottering administration.

Both candidates at Mile End were of Jewish origin. The Unionist, Harry Lawson, though born a Christian was in fact the grandson of Joseph Levy, founder of the *Daily Telegraph*, and later admitted to being 'half a Jew'.[26] The Liberal candidate, Betram Straus, was a professing Jew and a representative of the East London Synagogue on the Board of Deputies.[27] Normally the seat would have been considered a safe Conservative one; the party had held it since 1885, and in 1900 had obtained almost two-thirds of the votes. Straus hoped

to pull off a coup by running a campaign in which a robust
attack on tariff reform would be bolstered by a specific appeal
to Jewish voters for support against aliens' legislation. The
electorate, 5,380, was minute in proportion to the total population of 78,000, but about 10 per cent of the voters lived in 'the
alien quarter', in the West ward, and there is some evidence,
based on the testimony of the Conservative agent, J. Forest,
that many Jews there who had not been naturalized had none
the less been put on the electoral register.[28]

Straus boasted that 85 to 90 per cent of the Jewish voters
would support him.[29] This is probably what happened.[30] But,
in a close-run contest, Lawson held the seat (by a mere 78
votes) and had the additional satisfaction of seeing Straus panic
near the end of the campaign and declare that 'on the question
of excluding the undesirable, diseased and criminal I am in
agreement with my opponent, and would support any measure
that would provide for this'.[31] The lesson of Mile End was thus
twofold. Opposition to aliens' legislation was a vote-winner
with voters who were themselves immigrants, or not far removed from the immigrant generation; elsewhere it was a vote-
loser. For while the Liberal vote at Mile End had increased by
nearly 800, the Unionist total had fallen by only 302. This
seemed to indicate that the immigrant Jewish vote, where it
existed, could be sacrificed to the prospect of holding seats
elsewhere, the more so in the knowledge that the anglicized
Jewish vote would probably not desert the Unionists either.
The Liberals themselves seem to have reached this conclusion.
When the Government introduced a modified Aliens' Bill in
mid-April 1905, a meeting of east London Liberal MPs and
candidates, Betram Straus among them, sent a resolution to
Liberal leader, Campbell-Bannerman, expressing the hope
that the Liberal party would *not* oppose the Bill's second
reading.[32]

The Bill of 1905 was in any case very different from that of
1904, and this fact alone made Liberal opposition more difficult. The classes of aliens proposed to be excluded from Britain were more closely defined, and there was a right of appeal
to an immigration board; the provisions of the 1904 Bill as to
areas prohibited to immigrants were dropped altogether. Given
these changes, the Liberal party put up no more than a token

resistance. On the second reading the Liberals largely abstained from voting, so the Bill was easily carried by 211 votes to 59.[33]

The Jewish community was in a difficult position. That the Bill was going to become law was certain. The Board of Deputies itself might have brought greater pressure to bear, but was dissuaded from so doing by Jewish Unionist MPs, particularly Benjamin Cohen, a vice-president of the Conservative National Union and president of the Board of Guardians.[34] The Deputies therefore busied themselves with the advocacy— through Jewish Liberal MPs such as Stuart Samuel, Maurice Levy, and Rufus Isaacs—of amendments designed to provide safeguards for refugees from religious persecution, and a right of appeal (to the King's Bench Division) against expulsion. The *Jewish Chronicle* printed a model form of letter for Jewish constituents to send to their own MPs to support these amendments, and Jewish communities throughout the land bestirred themselves by forming committees to press these amendments locally.[35]

This was certainly pressure-group activity on a grand scale, but it lacked conviction because the Board of Deputies was unwilling to invoke even the threat of organized electoral reprisals against the Government. It seems that some wealthy Jews threatened to withdraw their support and their money from the Conservative party, and it is possible that a few actually did so.[36] The fact remains that David Lindo Alexander, president of the Board of Deputies, had to report in mid-July that none of the amendments framed by the Board of Deputies, had been successful.[37] Another weakness of the Jewish campaign was the reluctance of the Chief Rabbi to condemn the Bill, and the evident desire of Jewish Conservative MPs that it should go through with as little Jewish interference as possible.[38] On this point even Alexander—himself a Conservative—was moved to condemnation:

I have for some time past felt [he admitted in December] ... that this Board on many occasions does not receive that co-operation and assistance from some of the Jewish members of Parliament, which it has a right to expect ... and, further, that its efforts to procure the adoption of provisions and amendments, safeguarding Jewish interests are not infrequently hampered—if not rendered altogether abortive—by the want of unanimity amongst the Jewish members of Parliament.[39]

So it was that the Bill, as it finally emerged from the Commons, gave a right of entry to immigrants seeking to avoid 'prosecution' on religious or political grounds, but not 'persecution'; another group of amendments, excluding transmigrants from the provisions of the legislation, owed their incorporation to pressure from the shipping companies, not from the Jews or the Liberal parliamentary party.[40]

Outright opposition to the measure, which became law on 10 August, was left to a group of radical Liberals, led by Charles Dilke and C. P. Trevelyan, and to the immigrants themselves. It was not at the Board of Deputies that the principle of the bill was condemned, but at the Jewish Working Men's Club, Great Alie Street, Aldgate, and by Poale Zion at Whitechapel.[41] The immigrant generation at last found its political feet. Many immigrants had adopted English names and (albeit illegally) found their way on to the electoral register; others had saved up the five pound fee and become naturalized.[42] The children of immigrants had come, or were shortly to come, of age. The net result was that in a substantial number of constituencies— perhaps as many as twenty in London alone—small 'immigrant' Jewish electorates had come into existence since the aliens' agitation had begun in the 1880s.[43] And at the general election of January 1906 these electorates wreaked a terrible vengeance upon those politicians who had supported the passage of the Aliens' Immigration Act.

Although the Jewish vote played an important part in the 1906 election there is only limited evidence that it was organized and none that it was centrally directed, in spite of pleas for such organization which had been made but a few months previously.[44] Some Liberal candidates, Jewish and Gentile, deliberately brought the aliens' question into their campaigns. At St. George's, William Wedgwood Benn made 'a great effort to obtain the Jewish vote' on this issue, even though he was one of those Liberals who had signed the April 1905 petition to Campbell-Bannerman not to oppose the legislation. Benn told his Jewish voters that Herbert Samuel, Under-Secretary at the Home Office in the new Liberal Government formed in December 1905, had been appointed to administer the Act, but he warned that if the Conservatives were returned the administration of it would be consigned to the tender mercies of

Evans-Gordon.[45] At Mile End Betram Straus made an unequivocal appeal to Jews to vote for him, not only because of
the aliens' issue, but also because he pledged himself to speak
out against atrocities in Russia, and he even argued that the
return of a Liberal Government at the polls would help prevent
the pogroms. For good measure Straus obtained a letter of
approval from Samuel Montagu.[46]

At Whitechapel Stuart Samuel, one of the few Jewish MPs
who had spoken out against the 1905 Act, was assured of Jewish
support. But the fate of his opponent, Hope Kyd, seems to
have been sealed when a leading Jewish Conservative in the
constituency, Alderman John Harris, appeared at an election
meeting and proposed a motion that Hope Kyd was not a fit
Conservative candidate, as he had referred to aliens as 'the
very scum of the unhealthiest of the Continental nations'; the
motion was approved 'amid a scene of great enthusiasm, during
which Alderman Harris was carried shoulder high'.[47] The
Conservative share of the vote at Whitechapel fell by 4 per
cent; at Mile End it slumped by 17 per cent, thus bringing
Straus into Parliament; and at St. George's it fell by just over
17 per cent.[48] The Jewish anti-alienist Harry Samuel lost
Limehouse with a drop of over 15 per cent in his share of the
poll; and the Conservatives also lost both Bethnal Green seats
with falls in their vote of over 16 and 19 per cent. To put these
defeats in perspective it must be remembered that, in England
as a whole, the Conservative share of the vote fell by only 8.1
per cent. So at Whitechapel they really did not do too badly,
perhaps because of strong anti-Jewish feeling among Gentile
electors. Elsewhere in the East End the size of the Liberal victories were substantially above average.

In none of these reverses was the Jewish vote decisive,
though in all of them it played a part.[49] But there were two
Conservative defeats, both in the provinces, in which the behaviour of the Jewish electors was of major importance: Leeds
Central and Manchester North-West. The Manchester seat
contained about 1,000 Jewish voters in an electorate of 11,411.
As there had been no contest in 1900 it is difficult to estimate
the size of the Jewish defection in 1906, but Winston Churchill's
canvassers claimed that five-sixths of the Jewish voters there
were pledged to him, and it was certainly the experience of

Jewish observers that Churchill's victory (his majority was
1,241) 'was in considerable measure due to the support of the
Jews'.[50]

A more spectacular demonstration of Jewish voting strength,
however, was at Leeds Central, which had a Jewish vote estimated in 1906 at about 300, and which was being defended
for the Conservatives by Arthur Balfour's younger brother,
Gerald.[51] Here, although the Jewish vote (predominantly
working-class) had always been largely Liberal, nothing was
left to chance. A Leeds Jewish Electoral League was inaugurated by Edward E. Burgess, who described himself as 'the
"official" Jewish political organiser' in the constituency.
Members of the Jewish clergy were prevailed upon to speak
against the Aliens' Act and in favour of the Liberal candidate,
Robert Armitage; this clerical assault was led by Dr Moses
Gaster, *Haham* (spiritual head) of the Sephardic community in
London, who hastened to Yorkshire to proclaim the Liberal
cause when it became known that the Chief Rabbi had sent his
nephew, Herbert Adler, to Leeds to preach the virtues of Conservatism.[52] Conservative meetings were deliberately packed
with Jews and, as a result, resolutions proposed at them in
favour of Balfour were resoundingly defeated. By all accounts
the overwhelming majority of Jewish voters supported Armitage.[53] The Conservative share of the vote fell by 15 per cent,
and the unfortunate Balfour was deprived of his seat by 1,069
votes.

The immigrant generation, and the agitation over aliens
which its presence had provoked, thus gave Liberalism a new
lease of life among Jewish voters. The Reverend Goldstein, of
the Federation of Synagogues, told a meeting of Jewish electors
at the King's Hall that the return of the Conservatives would
be the 'death blow to Jewish freedom in England' and urged
his audience to vote against Conservative candidates.[54] Even
the *Jewish Chronicle*, in the heat of the moment, came down
from its non-partisan pedestal and celebrated the return to
power of the Liberal party, with a parliamentary majority in
the Commons of 130 seats, as 'this wonderful election ...
[which] instals in power a Ministry which is thoroughly friendly
to our people'.[55]

The Liberal leadership, it was true, had never promised to

repeal the 1905 Act. Nor did it do so, for it was, after all, a popular measure. What the Liberal Government did do was to work the Act with considerably less ferocity than might otherwise have been the case. In a circular letter to the Immigration Boards in February 1906 Herbert Gladstone, the new Home Secretary, expressed the hope that 'the benefit of the doubt, where any doubt exists, may be given in favour of any immigrants who allege that they are fleeing from religious or political persecution'.[56] The Government's own Immigration Officers were instructed to approach their work in a similar fashion.

To that extent, Jewish loyalty to the Liberal party in the 1906 election had not been misplaced. But that loyalty had been based on something more than assurances of administrative leniency; in some cases pledges had been given that the Act would actually be modified to accommodate Jewish criticisms of it; in particular, the alteration of the procedure adopted by the Immigration Board to the benefit of the immigrants and the granting of a right of appeal from the Boards to the High Court had been promised. During the course of 1907 it became clear that Gladstone was not prepared to move in any of these directions, and certainly did not intend to introduce an amending bill.[57] The Board of Deputies, under increasing pressure from the numerous and growing immigrant communities, became openly more hostile to the Liberal Administration. Furthermore, the immigrants found a new ally in Leopold Greenberg, himself a Liberal, and a Zionist, who in January 1907 became editor of the *Jewish Chronicle* (a position he held till his death in 1931) and who early declared himself in favour of the use of the Jewish vote to protect Jewish interests.[58]

In terms of its practical effect, it is a matter of dispute whether, in the long term, the Act of 1905 made much difference to the rate of Jewish immigration to Britain. The number of immigrants dropped sharply, from over 11,000 in 1906 to under 4,000 in 1911. But by 1906 immigration from Russia and Poland had probably passed its peak; the Act applied only to 'undesirables'; and the bulk of the new arrivals were admitted without inspection. Evans-Gordon and his associates were soon complaining bitterly about the negative impact of the measure. On the other hand, the psychological effect of the Act was undeniable. News of it spread through the Pale of Settlement and prospective immigrants were encouraged to avoid Great Britain, into which entry might now be refused, and to make directly for the United States, where entry was, for the time being, still assured. The Act undoubtedly acted as a deterrent; and as long as there were Russian and Polish Jews wishing to enter the United Kingdom, and an Act deterring them from applying, that Act was bound to be regarded with hostility by the Jewish immigrants already in the United Kingdom, and by those who sympathized with their plight.

Greenberg demonstrated at once where his sympathies lay. Under him, the *Chronicle* rapidly moved away from an establishment position on communal affairs; specifically, on the aliens' question, it attacked the elder statesmen of the Board of Deputies for wanting modification rather than repeal of the 1905 Act. 'The political emancipation of Jews in England is reduced to a sham', Greenberg argued, 'when its representative body feels that because an Act specially affects Jews, Jews must put up with it.'[59] Eventually, at the end of January 1908, the Board sent a Memorial to the Prime Minister, asking for the establishment of receiving-houses at all immigration ports, better provision of interpreters, a revision of the lists of members of the Immigration Boards, and a right of appeal. On 31 March Herbert Gladstone gave the Government's reply: the Board's requests were rejected out of hand and, for good measure, abolition of the naturalization fee was also refused.[60] 'The Board asked for the driest of dry bread', Greenberg thundered; 'it was given the hardest of hard stone.'[61]

In other ways, too, relations between Anglo-Jewry and the Liberals deteriorated after the euphoria of the 1906 election. The Government's attempts to legislate on the education question worried the community, for the Jews had benefited from the Conservative's 1902 Education Act, which had provided for rate aid to voluntary schools. Since 1870 the Jewish voluntary schools had been maintained by the community, but with grants from the Board of Education. Under the 1902 legislation the schools were handed over to the local education authorities for secular purposes, and the committees which had formerly run the schools were henceforth responsible only for religious instruction; at the same time the Jewish community was relieved of much of the cost of maintaining the schools. In 1906 the Liberal Government proposed to overturn this settlement, by insisting that extended facilities for religious education in aided schools could only be provided if four-fifths of the parents in a school demanded it; and this provision was to be permissive only, not mandatory.[62] The 1906 Education Bill was one of those emasculated by the House of Lords, but few Jewish tears were shed over its demise.

1907, apart from being a year of frustration over the Aliens' Act, was also the year of the Anglo-Russian Entente. The signing of a diplomatic agreement with Tsarist Russia shook Jewish faith in the Liberal Administration more than any of its domestic acts of commission or ommission.[63] Coupled with the evident unwillingness of the Government to amend the immigration legislation, the Entente was received in some Jewish quarters as proof positive that the Liberals were really little better than the Conservatives in their dealings with Jewish people. At the Board of Deputies discussion of the arrangement with Russia was deliberately stifled, but locally communal feelings ran high, and it is noteworthy that, for the first time, Jewish socialists received favourable publicity—and praise—in the columns of the *Jewish Chronicle* for their unequivocal condemnation of the *rapprochement* with Nicholas II.[64]

Anger at Liberal policies was compounded by frustration at the inability of the community to do much about them. In 1906 a record number of Jewish MPs had been returned, twelve Liberals and four Conservatives; but few of them seemed inclined to put Jewish interests above party considerations. Betram Straus, Stuart Samuel, and Sir Philip Magnus (Unionist MP for the University of London) could always be relied upon to liaise closely with the Board of Deputies, but most of the others could not usually be induced to do more than append their signatures to memorials and petitions.[65] Even Straus, who during his four years as an MP might be regarded as the leading Jewish spokesman in the Commons, was against any more formal organization of the Jewish MPs, 'as the Jewish members must remember that they represented their constituents and not their co-religionists'.[66]

By the end of March 1908, therefore, when Herbert Gladstone's letter rejecting Jewish demands over the Aliens Act arrived at the Board of Deputies, Jewish-Liberal relations had

reached a fresh nadir; nor, with another general election not
due until 1913, did there seem any prospect of successful
pressure by the Jewish community. But by the end of the first
week in April 1908, the situation had changed dramatically.
Campbell-Bannerman, fatally ill, resigned as premier on 5
April, and was succeeded by Herbert Asquith. In the Government reshuffle that followed, David Lloyd George left the
Board of Trade for the Exchequer and was succeeded by
Winston Churchill. The law at that time required Churchill,
because of his elevation to the Cabinet, to resign his seat and
fight a by-election. In 1906 Churchill had gone out of his way
to woo the Jewish voters of North-West Manchester and his
success had largely depended upon their loyalty.[67] In 1908 his
dependence upon them was even greater. Since the general
election the Liberals had lost five by-elections to the Conservatives. Churchill's majority, in a marginal constituency, was
thus vulnerable in any case. The particular circumstances of
the by-election only served to increase this vulnerability.

Jewish activists in the constituency were determined that the
maximum amount of leverage would be derived from the contest taking place so soon after the Government's *non possumus*
on the aliens' question. David Garson, a leading Jewish Conservative in North-West Manchester, and President of Manchester's Spanish and Portuguese congregation, had already
given notice that he would exploit the Government's failure to
fulfil its—or rather Churchill's—pledges to repeal or amend
the 1905 Act.[68] But Jewish opposition to Churchill's re-election
also came from the grass-roots level. An all-party committee of
Jews, consisting of 21 Liberals, 20 Conservatives, and 2 socialists, went to see Churchill on 14 April to discuss with him
various points in relation to the Aliens' Act, the Education Bill,
and also the Sunday Opening of Shops Bill. Churchill's replies,
on his own behalf, were eminently satisfactory: for instance, he
pledged his support in the Cabinet for the lowering of naturalization fees, he declared that 'in his opinion' immigrants ought
to have the right to be legally represented before the Immigration Boards, and he stated that he 'was personally in favour' of
a right of appeal to the High Court. But speaking as a member
of the Government, the only promise Churchill was prepared
to make was that receiving-houses would be set up 'where it

could be shown' that such houses were necessary; he also specifically ruled out any repeal of the 1905 Act.[69]

Nathan Laski at once took advantage of Churchill's undoubted personal goodwill towards the Jews, and at a meeting of Jewish electors held at the Jewish Working Men's Club asked for their support for the Liberal minister. The meeting gave its approval, but by no means unanimously.[70] Jewish Liberals sensed that all was not well. A letter, in favour of Churchill, was procured from Moses Gaster; circulars were also distributed in the name of Sir Alfred Turner (like Gaster a prominent Zionist) saying that 'any vote given by a Jew to Mr Joynson-Hicks is a vote given for anti-Semitism'.[71] William Joynson-Hicks, Churchill's Conservative opponent, as in 1906, was a totally unrepentant supporter of the Aliens' Act, and had made it clear that he was not going to 'pander for the Jewish vote' on this issue.[72] But it only needed the defection of 621 Jewish voters to him to deprive Churchill of his seat, and Joynson-Hicks knew (or, if he did not know, his Jewish friends soon told him) that there were other ways in which such defections might be procured. At a late stage in the campaign, therefore, Jewish Conservatives introduced the education controversy into the campaign.[73] Sir Philip Magnus told the Jews of North-West Manchester that the repeal of the 1902 Education Act would place intolerable financial burdens on the Jewish voluntary schools.[74] A correspondent of the *Jewish Chronicle* estimated that in Manchester the burden would amount to £2,000 per annum.[75]

Joynson-Hicks's campaign also benefited from the activities of Jewish socialists. The Social-Democratic Federation in Manchester decided (without Labour party approval) to put up a candidate of its own, Dan Irving. The Manchester section of the Social-Democratic Federation was particularly strong in the largely Jewish Cheetham district, within Churchill's constituency, and had played a prominent part in socialist propaganda against the excesses of Tsarist Russia and against the Entente.[76] Appeals were issued in English and Yiddish calling for support for Irving who, for good measure, pledged himself to support free naturalization.[77] In 1906 there had been no socialist candidate in North-West Manchester. So Irving's intervention, and in particular his play for Jewish support, which might otherwise have gone to Churchill, was doubly dangerous.

Polling took place on 24 April, the day after the termination of the Passover festival. The gallant Irving obtained 276 votes, Churchill's vote fell by 651 compared with 1906, and Joynson-Hicks's increased by 1,019, thus giving him a majority of 429. The *Jewish Chronicle* was stunned, and Greenberg went to great lengths to convince his readers that the Jews had stayed loyal to Churchill and had had nothing to do with his defeat.[78] The *Chronicle*'s special correspondent tried to argue, for example, that the fact that Irving obtained only 276 votes in all was 'a sufficient refutation of the story that there are 200 Jewish socialists in the division'.[79] In fact it was probably a confirmation of it.

Mr John Garrard, in his examination of this by-election, contrives to quote the victorious Joynson-Hicks in support of his view that Churchill lost in spite of, and not because of, the Jewish voters in the constituency. Mr Garrard states that, in a speech to the Maccabeans (a Jewish fraternal society and dining club of select membership), the Conservative MP 'placed the Liberal Jewish vote at 900'.[80] What Joynson-Hicks actually said was that 'there were in North-West Manchester 11,500 voters, of whom 900 were Jews', not that 900 of the Jewish voters were Liberals.[81] Churchill's official biographer, his son Randolph, relied for a similar argument upon the assurance which Dr Joseph Dulberg, President of the Jewish Working Men's Club in Manchester, had given Winston, that '95 per cent of the Jewish votes were for him'.[82] Yet, after the result had been declared, Dulberg confessed that 'it had made my blood boil ... to see Jewish electioneers busy' helping in Churchill's defeat.[83]

It cannot be said for certain that the Jews, by themselves, kicked Winston Churchill out of the North-West Manchester constituency.[84] But it can be asserted that they gave a big helping hand, some by voting socialist, others by abstaining, a few by switching to the Conservative party.[85] When the shock had subsided a quiet glow of satisfaction came over at least some sections of the Jewish community. Preaching at the Birmingham synagogue, the Reverend G. J. Emanuel expressed his

approval of what the Manchester Jews had done.[86] An un-
named correspondent to the *Jewish Chronicle* argued that:

> Jews are expected to act as no other section of the population ever
> dreams of acting ... The Jew always votes as an Englishman, but, if
> he is true to his Judaism, he will vote as *an Englishman who is a Jew.*
>   We Jews do not know our own power; the sooner we realise it and
> exert it in the interests of our political freedom the better it will be.[87]

The general consensus of opinion within the community was
that Churchill had been an innocent victim of a righteous campaign to force concessions from the Government. Develop-
ments over the following two years to some extent justified this
view. Churchill was found a safe seat at Dundee, and at the
end of May 1908 announced that he would insert amendments
in the Port of London Bill making the provision of receiving-
houses for immigrants obligatory; outside London, receiving-
houses began to be established towards the end of 1909. There
was better provision of interpreters. And, as Home Secretary
in 1910, Churchill announced that he would allow legal assistance at Immigration Board proceedings, provided the cost was
borne by the immigrant himself.[88] But this last concession
represented the absolute limit to which the Liberal Government was willing to go in appeasing the Jews and it came, significantly, after a deputation had travelled to Scotland, during
the general election of January 1910, to remind Churchill of his
pledges at North-West Manchester.[89]

On the strength of these concessions the Liberals recaptured
North-West Manchester in January 1910 and retained it in
December.[90] Central Leeds was also retained.[91] But in January
Betram Straus had lost Mile End by 57 votes, and at the same
election North Hackney (into which there had been a Jewish
middle-class migration since the turn of the century) also re-
verted to the Conservative party.[92] One feature of the January
1910 election which caused particular concern was a vitriolic
attack by Lloyd George upon Lord Rothschild. Rothschild,
though nominally still a Liberal, had opposed death duties and
old-age pensions, and had proudly led the opposition of the
City and the peers to Lloyd George's 'People's Budget'—he
called it the 'Robber's Budget'—which the House of Lords had

refused to pass. So 'Natty' was certainly fair game for the Welsh politician's verbal assaults. But Lloyd George chose to attack him, in a speech at Walworth on 17 December 1909, in a particularly crude way, linking his earlier demand for eight Dreadnought battleships with his refusal to support taxation to pay for them, and thus likening the premier Jewish peer (and in many ways still the premier British Jew) to Pharaoh, who had oppressed the Jews by forcing them to make bricks without straw.[93]

This astonishing attack, followed almost at once by the launching of a viciously anti-Semitic campaign at Salford South by the Liberal candidate there, Hilaire Belloc, struck deep into the hearts of many Jewish Liberals.[94] Lucien Wolf, who a quarter of a century previously had berated Lionel Louis Cohen for daring to stand as a Conservative, now announced in the correspondence columns of *The Times* that he would vote Conservative himself and that, in so doing, he would 'not be conscious of any betrayal of Liberal principles, and still less of any ingratitude to Liberalism'.[95] Another prominent Jewish Liberal who announced he would vote Conservative was Sir John Simon's son, Oswald.[96] Rothschild himself lost no time in pointing out that if the House of Lords were swept away the Liberals would pass the Education Bill, which would mean that Jewish parents would have to pay for religious education after school hours.[97] And, he added, the Liberals had no intention of repealing or amending the Aliens' Act.[98] This last point was now abundantly clear. In February 1909 Herbert Gladstone had told the Commons that 'under my administration of the Act the ingress of the most undesirable aliens had been prevented'.[99] In July 1910 Churchill, no longer dependent on Jewish votes, spoke in glowing terms of the 1905 legislation which, he declared with an ominous air of finality, had 'taken its place in the legislative and administrative machinery of the country'.[100]

The Liberal Government claimed that the Act could not be modified because any modification would be rejected by the peers.[101] Yet the fact remains that no modification was ever attempted by the Governments of Campbell-Bannerman or Asquith. Even Leopold Greenberg had to admit that the Liberal

party's historic claims upon Jewish loyalty were no longer
relevant:

To argue [he told his readers in January 1910] that the fact that the
particular party which enfranchised the Jew is entitled to eternal
Jewish allegiance is to ask the Jew to abdicate his powers of reason ...
The Jew cannot be tied to the chariot wheels of Liberal or Conservative ... both parties are almost equally badly tarred by their attitude
towards the Aliens Act.[102]

In the two general elections of 1910 the Conservative vote
fell in Whitechapel (from 44.9 per cent in 1906 to 40.8 per cent
in December 1910) and in Stepney (from 57.3 per cent to 48.5
per cent over the same period). But in other constituencies with
large Jewish populations it rose: in St. George's from 38.7 per
cent to 42.2 per cent; at Mile End (where Straus was defeated
in both 1910 contests) from 48.6 per cent to 50.0 per cent; and
by an average of over 5.0 per cent in the two Bethnal Green
seats. It rose by over 4 per cent in North-West Manchester, by
nearly 5 per cent at Leeds Central, and by over 5 per cent in
North Salford. While these improvements were by no means
spectacular they were well above average, for nationally the
Conservative share of the poll in December 1910, as compared
with 1906, had increased by only 2.7 per cent. The second
honeymoon between Anglo-Jewry and the Liberal party was
well and truly over.

6. The Zionist Dimension

The alacrity with which newer generations of British Jews hastened to use such political influence as the State gave them in order to combat aliens' legislation was paralleled by an unprecedented amount of overtly Jewish political activity in other spheres. In September 1908, for instance, a meeting of Jews at the Mansion House, Dublin, announced the formation of a Judaeo-Irish Home Rule Association, which offered Jewish support for Home Rule.[1] Exactly a year later a Jewish section of the National Liberal Federation was established at Leeds with, significantly, a member of the Jewish clergy, the Reverend Manson, as Vice-President.[2] Jewish ministers of religion had, indeed, become far less inhibited about entering the political arena. The Chief Rabbi could always be counted on to use his influence in the Conservative interest, and *Haham* Dr Gaster was an enthusiastic Liberal. But it was not only at parliamentary elections that clerical influence was used. On 26 May 1906 the Reverend Simeon Singer delivered a powerful sermon at the New West End synagogue against sweated industries.[3] In October 1909 a circular letter, in favour of Bertram Jacobs, was sent to Jewish electors of Islington Borough Council by Dr Moses Hyamson, a *Dayan* (Judge) of the London *Beth Din*, the ecclesiastical court of the Chief Rabbi.[4] And in November 1912 a number of Jewish ministers, among them the Reverend A. A. Green of Hampstead and Rabbi Dr S. Daiches of Sunderland, became Vice-President of the Jewish League for Woman Suffrage.[5]

The League, a pacific drawing-room affair, had substantial support, at least in London; Israel Zangwill, the foremost Jewish writer of the period, was numbered among its patrons.[6] But the Jewish suffragette movement also had its violent wing, and the fact that the Jewish MPs Herbert Samuel and Rufus Isaacs were then, as members of the Government, responsible for the incarceration and forceful feeding of suffragettes provoked Jewish direct action of an altogether novel kind. In March 1913 Hugh Arthur Franklin, a member of the Men's Political Union for Women's Enfranchisement, was sentenced to nine months' imprisonment for setting fire to a railway carriage at Harrow.[7] In October the solemnity of the *Yom Kippur* service at the New West End synagogue was shattered by three Jewesses who shouted an invocation to the Almighty to 'forgive Herbert Samuel and Sir Rufus Isaacs for denying freedom to women ... [and] for consenting to the torture of women'.[8] In June 1914 a similar demonstration at the Brighton synagogue likened British treatment of suffragettes to Russian treatment of Jews.[9]

Though violence and the disturbance of religious services were not to be condoned, and though there were some misgivings at Jewish involvement in the Irish question, in general the elder statesmen of Anglo-Jewry welcomed evidence of deepening Jewish participation in British politics. It was, after all, but the logical outcome of the campaign for political emancipation a half-century before, and if it was sometimes taken to excess (the Board of Deputies did not like separate Jewish sections of political parties, and actively discouraged them[10]) it was, for all that, the best evidence of Jewish acceptance into the host society. The Board itself was obliged to take a much closer interest in political affairs. In 1911, for example, D. L. Alexander chaired a protest meeting, estimated at over 6,000, at Mile End in connection with the Sunday Closing of Shops Bill; letters of support were obtained from national figures as far apart in their views as the Chief Rabbi, Claude Goldsmid Montefiore (the founder of the Jewish Religious Union and of Liberal Judaism in Britain), and the Labour MP George Lansbury.[11] Alexander brought together every Jewish MP to help in the campaign. In October of the same year the Board had to frame amendments to the Slaughter of Animals bill to safeguard *shechita*, the Jewish method of slaughtering food animals.[12] And at the same time Stuart Samuel was heavily involved in obtaining concessions for Jewish friendly societies in the National Insurance bill.[13]

In short, as the Welfare State began to be shaped in the years immediately preceding the Great War, a 'Jewish dimension' in British government and politics was bound to arise, and the free passage of Jews within the corridors of power—symbolized by the entry into the British Cabinet in 1909 of the first professing Jew, Herbert Samuel—was an integral part of this process.

Partly in consequence the Anglo-Jewish leadership became, by way of gratitude, ultra-patriotic. The *Jewish Chronicle* was full of enthusiasm for the Boer War, as was the Chief Rabbi.[14] The relief of Mafeking was celebrated as warmly in synagogues throughout the land as in churches.[15] When Hermann Adler died, in 1911, and the difficult search began for a successor who would be as acceptable to East End as to West End Jews, the choice eventually fell upon Dr Joseph Herman Hertz, formerly Rabbi of the Witwatersrand Old Hebrew Congregation, Johannesburg. In 1913 Lord Rothschild insisted upon Hertz's election after learning from Lord Milner of his outspoken opposition to, and eventual expulsion by, the Boers.[16]

And it goes without saying that when the Great War began, involving as it did the pitting of Jew against Jew, the *Jewish Chronicle* forgot its former condemnations of Russia and of the Aliens' Act, and declared (in print and in a banner outside its office) that 'England has been all she could be to the Jews; Jews will be all they can be to England.'[17] 'Now is our time', declared the Reverend Michael Adler, Chaplain to His Majesty's Forces, 'to prove the genuine loyalty and patriotism of the English Jew, and may the community rise worthily to the height of the occasion.'[18] It did so. It has been calculated that the number of British Jews who served in the armed forces during the First World War totalled 41,500, thus representing about 13.8 per cent of Anglo-Jewry (about 300,000 strong in 1914); among the general population of Great Britain at that time those who served in the armed forces amounted to only 11.5 per cent.[19] Those few Jews who had the temerity to take an anti-war stance were quickly disowned by the leadership. In Liverpool the Reverend John Harris, minister of the Old Hebrew Congregation, was dismissed after refusing to give an undertaking that he would cease supporting Jewish conscientious objectors before recruiting tribunals.[20] Religious services themselves were turned into manifestations of patriotism. The 1915 *Yom Kippur* service for the poor at the Pavilion Theatre, Mile End, was interrupted in order to welcome and present a loyal address to the Lord Mayor, while the choir ceased their penitential melodies in order to give a rendition of Rule Britannia.[21]

There is little doubt that the Great War acted as a force for assimilation, like the Napoleonic Wars a century before.[22] Immigration ceased, and the immigrant generations already here were urged by their communal leaders to bind themselves as never before to their adopted country. Unnaturalized Russian Jews (estimated at between 25 and 30 thousand) who refused to volunteer for a war (as they saw it) to preserve Tsarist Russia were threatened with deportation under a law, passed in July 1917, which had the full backing of Jewish leaders. Herbert Samuel, when Home Secretary in 1916, had written: 'If the mass of Russian Jewry in this country refuse to lift a finger to help when this country is making immeasurable sacrifices in a war in which the cause of Liberty all over the world is bound up, the effect on the reputation of the Jewish name everywhere will be disastrous.'[23] At the end of September 1917 deportations actually began, but a month later the Bolshevik Revolution took Russia out of the war, and it is most unlikely that Jews so deported would ever have seen active service in the Tsarist armies.[24]

At all events the Jewish East End and the areas of Jewish immigrant settlement in the provinces ceased to grow. What is more, the pre-war movement of immigrant Jews out of the East End, to form new communities at Walthamstow, Bow, Leyton, Stoke Newington, Hackney, and Stamford Hill, was accelerated by increasing prosperity which the war brought to those engaged in the clothing industry and the boot and shoe trades.[25] As they moved northwards and eastwards out of the ghetto, the immigrants and their children took their socialist proclivities with them, for as the parliamentary representation of the Labour party increased, and particularly once Labour had entered the Coalition Government in 1915, the socialist strain within Anglo-Jewry was no longer seen as a stigma, something to be belittled and, if possible, hidden from view. The 1918 franchise reform gave the vote to many Jewish immigrants for the first time because the suffrage, hitherto linked to the payment of rates, was henceforth bestowed upon men on the basis of six months' residence, and upon women, over thirty years of age, if they were local-government electors; the local franchise was, at the same time, extended to all owners or tenants of property. So a new Jewish electorate was ushered into existence, and, though not overwhelmingly Labour, it was substantially so. The links between Jewish socialism and Labour became stronger and were cemented in 1920 when Poale Zion officially affiliated to the Labour party.[26]

From the foregoing brief overview it might be supposed that, with the post-emancipation generations playing a full part in Liberal and Conservative politics, with the absorption of the pre-war immigrant generations into the body politic, and especially into the Labour party (in the general election of 1918 three Jews stood, unsuccessfully, as Labour party candidates), and with the withering away of the aliens' question as the Great War approached, the political assimilation of Anglo-Jewry was an established fact. This was not so. For as some issues (such as the aliens' question) which had provoked a specific Jewish voting response were disappearing, a new one, not itself of any importance in British domestic politics, arose, out of which certain sections of Anglo-Jewry were determined to make electoral capital. This was Zionism. Jewish voters made an election issue out of Jewish nationalism; without these voters Zionism would not have existed in an electoral sense. Moreover, the responses of the politicians to Zionism modified, and have continued to modify, the political attitudes of the Jews themselves.

This is not the place to examine the history of Zionism, or even of British Zionism.[27] Nevertheless some examination of the Anglo-Jewish response to the Zionist movement is necessary in order to understand the precise impact which the movement had upon the politics of Anglo-Jewry. The first point to be made is that Theodor Herzl did not invent Zionism. The idea of a 'Return to the Promised Land' was deeply rooted within orthodox Judaism. During the nineteenth century wealthy English Jews gave generously towards the maintenance of the impoverished Jewish communities of the Holy Land and when, in the early 1880s, the *Hovovei Zion* ('Lovers of Zion') movement to promote Jewish immigration to Palestine grew up in eastern Europe, English Jews supported these settlements too.[28] But there was a world of difference between Jewish *settlements* and a Jewish *State*. When Herzl published his pamphlet *Der Judenstaat* ('The Jewish State') in 1895, and when he summoned the first Zionist Congress, at Basle, two years later, he gave to Zionism an entirely new meaning, and one against which the Anglo-Jewish gentry instinctively rebelled.[29]

Herzl hoped to find support for his movement from among the Anglo-Jewish leaders whom he visited in the 1890s, but he was sadly disappointed. Samuel Montagu gave him a warm reception. 'He confessed to me', Herzl recorded in his diary, '—in confidence—that he felt himself to be more an Israelite than an Englishman.'[30] Montagu, however, was very much the exception to the rule, and was, in any case, alienated in due course by Herzl's lack of orthodox scruples. Most of the Anglo-Jewish leadership were repelled by the very idea of Jewish nationality; they regarded being Jewish simply as having a religious connotation. The possibility of Jewish nationhood struck at the heart of the process of social, cultural, and political assimilation of which they were so proud. Without a Jewish state they were well-bred British Jews. With it, they automatically became exiles in the land of their birth, and their loyalty to Great Britain could be questioned.[31] The battle for Jewish emancipation had been fought and won on the grounds that an English Jew was different from an English Christian only by virtue of his religion; admit the Zionist claim (so the argument went) and you admitted too that the Gentiles had been deceived at the time emancipation was being fought for.[32]

It was little wonder, therefore, that at the turn of the century most English-born Jews set their faces against Herzl's movement.[33] Herzl himself was regarded with bitter hostility, of which there was no greater purveyor than Chief Rabbi Hermann Adler. Addressing the Anglo-Jewish Association, in July 1897, Adler condemned the forthcoming First Zionist Congress as 'an egregious blunder', and denounced the idea of a Jewish state as 'contrary to Jewish principles'.[34] Had there been no Jewish immigration into Britain in the 1880s and 1890s, there is little doubt that Anglo-Jewry would have followed its supreme religious head in rejecting the Zionist creed.

But the presence of the immigrants provided an entirely new audience for the Zionist message in Great Britain.[35] Driven from Russia and Poland they had little reason to feel that Britain would offer them a settled future any more secure; anti-Semitism was rife at all levels of British society, and the newly arrived immigrants were usually the first to feel its effects. Zionism held out the promise of a permanent solution to their problems of persecution and wandering, and they responded warmly to it. Aba Werner, the extremely orthodox and much-respected rabbi of the *Machzike Hadass* ('Upholders of the Religion') synagogue in Brick Lane was a fervent Zionist who actually attended the Second Zionist Congress in Basle in 1898 and the Eighth at the Hague in 1907. And if the immigrant Zionists lacked the patronage of the Chief Rabbi they gained that of Dr Moses Gaster (himself an immigrant), who was one of Herzl's earliest English supporters.[36] 'The East End', Herzl announced to a packed Zionist meeting at the Great Assembly Hall, Mile End, 'is ours.'[37] In January 1899 the English Zionist Federation was launched.[38] The following year it managed to acquire as its President Sir Francis Montefiore, a handsome but ineffective great-nephew of Sir Moses, and a staunch Conservative.[39]

The fact that at this time a Jewish Conservative should have consented to lend his name to the Zionist movement was surprising but, on closer examination, not astonishing. The Conservative policy of keeping Jews out of Britain was perfectly compatible with—indeed, it could be said, was complementary to—that of supporting the establishment of a Jewish state for the refugees elsewhere.[40] Ignored or attacked by the (largely Conservative) Anglo-Jewish establishment, therefore, the early English Zionists were none the less very careful not to identify themselves too closely with any political group, and particularly not to throw themselves into the arms of the Liberals. In 1900 a suggestion from Herzl that the English Zionist Federation should put up a candidate of its own in Whitechapel at the general election was rejected on the grounds that it would not be wise to obtain the backing of either of the main parties, and that an independent Zionist candidate would be bound to suffer ignominious defeat.[41] Instead the Federation addressed an inquiry to all parliamentary candidates and, on the basis of the replies received, issued a circular strongly urging electoral support for those candidates who favoured the Zionist cause; the circular naturally contained Conservative names, and made the point that the realization of Zionist aims would 'practically solve the ever-growing Jewish problem in Europe, and will tend to divert the tide of emigration which now takes place to Western countries'.[42] A similar exercise was undertaken in 1906.[43]

Both attempts to influence Jewish voters were doomed to failure. The immediate concern of the immigrant voters was the question of aliens' legislation and, with it, the possibility of compulsory repatriation. In 1900 the Zionists supported Gentile, Conservative anti-alienists such as David Hope Kyd, but opposed Jewish Liberals who were sympathetic on the aliens' question, such as Kyd's opponent at Whitechapel, Stuart Samuel.[44] The 1900 circular was a damp squib; many candidates, such as Kyd, lost even though they had the Zionist stamp of approval.[45] In 1906 the Zionist circular was simply buried in the swell of Jewish support for the Liberal party. In its early years, moreover, the Zionist message in Britain was itself muffled by differences within the movement.[46] To Herzl, a completely irreligious Jew, the plight of east European Jewry was a severely practical one, and he did not care particularly whether the Jewish State was set up in Palestine, El Arish, Cyprus, or east Africa. Only after Herzl's death, in 1904, did leadership of the movement pass to those for whom a Jewish State elsewhere than in Palestine was unthinkable. But the idea of supporting Jewish settlements world-wide, already entrenched in nineteenth-century Anglo-Jewish philanthropy, retained a certain popularity. Israel Zangwill abandoned official Zionism in 1905 to found the Jewish Territorial Organization, 'dedicated to the creation of a Jewish territory in some country that need not necessarily be Palestine'.[47] Lord Rothschild, Lucien Wolf, and other Anglo-Jewish leaders joined him in this venture. As far as Palestine itself was concerned, the British Government was not in a position to do very much about aiding Jewish settlement there, even had it wanted to; Palestine was under the control of the decaying Ottoman Empire and that Empire was, by the turn of the century, moving rapidly towards the German sphere of influence. In the world Zionist movement as a whole the British section at this time was a very small and unimportant part.

Before 1914, in short, the potential which Zionism had for influencing Jewish voters was bound not to be great, except where, as with Poale Zion, it carried a domestic ingredient as well. But this was not always appreciated by British politicians. The last chapter demonstrated how the Conservatives, hampered by their position on the aliens' question in and after 1905, were eager to exploit other issues in order to gain Jewish votes. Education was one such issue with immediate appeal. Zionism was another.

On 27 January 1905 Prime Minister Balfour addressed a Conservative meeting in his constituency of East Manchester. In the audience was a young chemistry lecturer at Manchester University, Chaim Weizmann. Weizmann, a native of Russia, had arrived in England, and Manchester, barely six months before. He knew very little about British politics. In September 1902, while in Pinsk, he had met William Evans-Gordon who, as a member of the Royal Commission on Alien Immigration, was on a fact-finding tour of the Pale of Settlement. Evans-Gordon was naturally anxious to deflect Jewish refugees from Britain and apparently affected an interest in Weizmann's Zionist plans. Weizmann, who cannot then have known about the anti-Semitism of the British Brothers' League, was evidently charmed by the MP for Stepney.[48] When Weizmann came to England, in the summer of 1904, he re-established contact with Evans-Gordon, who arranged an audience for him with Earl Percy, Under-Secretary at the Foreign Office.[49] Nothing came of this approach, but the whole episode evidently left Weizmann with a favourable impression of Conservative politicians and of the Conservative party.[50] Once in Manchester he made contact with the Manchester Zionist Society, whose president was Dr Charles Dreyfus. Dreyfus, a refugee from Alsace, was managing director of the Clayton Aniline Company and in November 1904 had taken Weizmann on to his staff as a part-time researcher.[51] Dreyfus was also a member of the Manchester City Council and a leading light in the East Manchester Conservative Association, of which he became President in 1906. As such he was a close friend of Arthur Balfour and, almost certainly, it was he who introduced Balfour to Weizmann at the January 1905 constituency meeting. 'We couldn't talk much', Weizmann recorded, 'but he invited me to see him in London.'[52]

The London meeting did not materialize. But when the hardpressed Conservative Government finally collapsed, on 4 December 1905, an idea germinated in Dr Dreyfus's mind and, simultaneously, in that of the leading Jewish Liberal in Manchester, Nathan Laski. The idea was to persuade Weizmann to use his influence with immigrant Jewish voters in the

North-West Manchester constituency. Winston Churchill's claim to the Jewish vote there, on the basis of his opposition to the aliens' legislation and his espousal of Zionism, was already strong; Weizmann's backing was bound to make it stronger. Nathan Laski had prepared the ground by inviting Weizmann to a dinner party to meet Churchill on 10 December 1905.[53] On 27 December Churchill's election agent wrote officially to Weizmann asking for his support.[54] In Weizmann's eyes, but not in those of Jews generally in the constituency, Churchill had one drawback: many of his principal Jewish supporters, such as Dr Dulberg and Samuel Finburgh, were members of the Manchester branch of Zangwill's Jewish Territorial Organization. Weizmann was definitely not a Territorialist; the Liberal request was refused.[55]

Dr Dreyfus's approach was altogether more subtle. Balfour's standing with the immigrants was low, and Churchill's Jewish support threatened to bring it lower still. There was not much that Jews could do in Balfour's constituency, for Jewish voters were thin on the ground in the heavy industrial areas of East Manchester. But the defeat of Churchill, the most brilliant of the ex-Conservative free traders, would do Balfour a power of good, by removing Churchill from Parliament and by demonstrating that the Jewish vote was not in the Liberals' pocket. Dreyfus evidently realized, especially if he knew that Weizmann had been approached by the Liberals (which was quite probable given the friendship between the two men), that a direct approach to him to act on Balfour's behalf was doomed not to succeed. He therefore arranged, with Balfour's prior approval, that Weizmann should meet Balfour in the Queen's Hotel, Manchester.

The meeting took place on 9 January 1906. Ostensibly the object was to discuss the east African offer, which Balfour's Government had made and which the Zionists had rejected. Weizmann thought that the object of the meeting was to have Balfour convince him that he had been wrong to reject out of hand the east African option.[56] And, to Balfour, Dreyfus 'had suggested that Weizmann might be able to throw some light' on the Zionist rejection of east Africa.[57] Neither of these explanations is plausible as a reason for Balfour, who a month before had been Prime Minister, agreeing to meet a Russo-Jewish *émigré*, to discuss east Africa, just when a crucial general-election campaign was about to start.

What the two men talked about, for over an hour, was certainly Zionism, and what Balfour told Weizmann was that he saw 'no political difficulties in the attainment of Palestine— only economic difficulties'.[58] There was never the slightest possibility of Balfour convincing Weizmann that he should accept east Africa, nor is there any evidence that he seriously tried to do so, and it is highly improbable that so astute a man as Dreyfus could have supposed for one moment that this might have happened. Balfour told Weizmann what Dreyfus knew he wanted to hear; that the Conservative leader, who had so recently legislated to keep Jews out of England, was none the less willing to support politically Jewish settlement in the Holy Land. Did Dreyfus hope that this meeting would pay political dividends at home too? The meeting was in no sense secret, and there is no hint that Weizmann was supposed to have kept details of it, or even the fact of its having taken place, to himself. Weizmann wrote at once to his fiancée, Vera Chatzman, to tell her of the meeting, and it is most unlikely that, in the following weeks, he would not have spoken widely, and with some pride, of his satisfactory interview with the Conservative leader, and that word of this encounter, and its outcome, would not have filtered back to the Jewish voters who were being urged to give their all for Churchill. And if Weizmann did not spread the word Dreyfus and his Conservative friends certainly would have. The suspicion must remain, therefore, that in January 1906 Weizmann allowed himself to be used for the propaganda purposes of the Conservative party.

Churchill won his seat but Balfour, like his brother Gerald at Leeds Central, lost his; a telling verdict upon Zionist political influence at the time. Weizmann did not meet Balfour again until 12 December 1914, when he found him 'much more than sympathetic'.[59] By then Weizmann had widened his political contacts, especially with the Liberal party.[60] In September 1914 he had met C. P. Scott, editor of the *Manchester Guardian*, and it was through Scott that he made contact with Lloyd George and also with Herbert Samuel, who, unknown to any of the English Zionists, with the exception of Samuel's confidant, Moses Gaster, was already sympathetic to the Zionist cause.[61] As it turned out these contacts were to be crucial in the chain of events which led to the issue of the Balfour Declaration on 2 November 1917. Throughout them the English Zionists were generally careful not to involve themselves in domestic party politics.

In this regard Poale Zion was exceptional. Though its formal adhesion to the British Labour party was still some years away, it had already decided that it could work only within the framework of the Labour movement, partly by popularizing Zionism within trade unions and among Labour politicians, and partly by attempting to deliver the Anglo-Jewish working-class vote into the hands of the Labour party. It claimed some credit for the insertion, in the War Aims Memorandum approved in December 1917 by a special conference of the Labour party and the Trades Union Congress, of a paragraph referring with approval to the hope that Palestine might become a 'Free State', under international guarantee, to which such of the Jewish people as desired to do so might return 'and work out their salvation free from interference by those of alien race or religion'.[62] In gratitude for this mark of favour Poale Zion issued a manifesto on the eve of the December 1918 general election, urging Jewish voters to vote Labour:

The Labour Party [the manifesto declared] stands strongly for progress and challenges reaction. We, the Jewish people, have always suffered under reaction ... it is only from the forces of Labour and Progress that we can expect justice, tolerance, equality, and redemption of our own National Home, Palestine ... the Labour Party stands for labour under good conditions, and as the great majority of the Jews in this country are working men, it is of the utmost importance that we support the demand for better labour conditions.[63]

It is difficult to assess the impact of such an appeal, and the fact that the 1918 election took place on a Saturday might have blunted its edge in those areas of the East End where social conformity to the outward appearance of religious observance was still strong. But it is certainly true that by December 1918 the world of Anglo-Jewry had undergone a transformation which made Labour all the more attractive to Jewish voters, among whom working-class Jews in the inner cities were now in the majority. Some of the elements in this transformation, such as the rise of the Labour party and the 1918 franchise reform, have already been referred to, and they, like others, such as the breakup of the Liberal party and the political pre-eminence of Lloyd George, were quite external to Anglo-Jewry itself. But the promulgation of the Balfour Declaration had set in train a series of events within the community which sharply altered the face of its leadership and which also reacted upon its political stance. These events must now be briefly sketched in.

By 1914 the English Zionist Federation had some fifty branches, and during the war its support grew both in London and the provinces.[64] In 1915 a petition in favour of the establishment of a 'publicly recognized, legally secured home for the Jewish people in Palestine' was signed by 50,000 members of the Anglo-Jewish community.[65] This evidence that Zionism had taken firm root in the community alarmed the ruling families of Anglo-Jewry. The Jewish establishment had hoped that the English education system would have transformed the sons of the immigrants into English nationalists, and turn their thoughts away from Zion. They were wrong. 'Zionist propaganda has gained ground with adult English Jewry', L. G. Montefiore observed in 1914, 'but this is little in comparison with that which it has gained with the Jewish youth.'[66] Zionist societies flourished as well in the major universities as in the slums of Whitechapel, the Leylands (Leeds), or Cheetham Hill (Manchester).[67]

While Hermann Adler was alive the anti-Zionists could count on the support of the Chief Rabbinate.[68] But his death and replacement by Joseph Hertz brought to this position a man of strong Zionist convictions.[69] Hertz's election, moreover, coincided with a movement for more democracy within the two leading organizations of Anglo-Jewry, the Board of Deputies and the Anglo-Jewish Association. The latter was a self-elected body, upon which the immigrants were not represented at all; the constitution of the former—'conceived on whig principles'—did not allow for the representation of the many friendly societies and small synagogues to which the immigrants belonged and which they had created.[70] Zionists were particularly anxious for the democratization of these two bodies because each of them elected half the members of the

'Conjoint Foreign Committee', whose claim to represent the views of Anglo-Jewry on foreign affairs had hitherto been unquestioned.[71] In January 1915 Dr Gaster made an unsuccessful attempt to persuade the members of the Anglo-Jewish Association to allow Zionist representation on the Conjoint. The proposal was voted down and, as if to add insult to injury, almost at once Lucien Wolf, the arch-anti-Zionist, became the Conjoint's secretary.[72]

Wolf, 'a gifted but embittered man', 'looked upon the Foreign Office as his patrimony'.[73] Like Claude Montefiore, president of the Anglo-Jewish Association, he regarded Zionism as 'dangerous and provoking anti-Semitism', and rejected out of hand attempts by Zionists to formulate a common approach to the British government on the Palestine question.[74] The Conjoint, meanwhile continued to deal with the Foreign Office under a veil of secrecy which David Lindo Alexander, at the Board of Deputies, made clear he was not prepared to lift.[75] From the Zionist point of view, therefore, the dissolution of the Conjoint became an imperative. Since this could obviously not be done through the Anglo-Jewish Association it would have to be achieved through the Deputies; and the way to do it was to exploit and reinforce moves already afoot to have the Board of Deputies enlarged, and to allow the immigrant communities and their leaders a much greater say in the Deputies' activities.[76] In January 1916 a National Union of Jewish Rights, consisting of representatives from twenty-three Zionist and friendly societies, was launched to achieve this end.[77]

During 1916 the split between the Zionists and the anti-Zionists grew ever wider. Weizmann, Gaster, and their friends busied themselves in bypassing the Conjoint to make direct contact with senior civil servants and ministers. Wolf was adamant that the Conjoint was not to be enlarged so as to 'submerge the English-born elements in the community'. To a meeting of the Council of the Anglo-Jewish Association in April 1916 he 'proceeded to make some observations concerning our brethren in the East End', the *Jewish Chronicle* announced, 'which we think it not in the general interest to reproduce'.[78] In late 1916, as the British expeditionary force occupied the Sinai peninsula, the Anglo-Jewish gentry took

fright. Lord Rothschild (who was not a Zionist) would not lead
them, but Montefiore and Alexander filled the gap. Alexander
told the Deputies in October that co-operation between the
Conjoint and the Zionists could not take place 'on an overt or
official assumption of the existence of a Jewish nationality for
the Jews all over the world'.[79] In March 1917 the British invasion of Palestine began. Wolf, who had seen Balfour in
January, had gained some impression of how the mind of the
Government was working, but he had no idea when, or in what
manner, a definitive statement of the Government's view
would emerge.[80] A manifesto against the Zionist movement
was prepared and it appeared, in the form of a letter over the
signatures of Alexander and Montefiore, in *The Times* of 24
May.[81]

The contents of the letter—'a venomous stab at the Zionist
movement', as Greenberg called it—were less important than
the manner in which it had appeared.[82] Alexander and Montefiore, in pleading that 'emancipated Jews in this country ...
have no separate aspirations in a political sense', were saying
nothing new, and the attack upon the Zionist movement was
much less biting than one which Wolf had launched in person
at the Liberal Jewish synagogue a week before.[83] But the letter
of 24 May purported to represent the views of Anglo-Jewry; yet
its contents, indeed its very existence, had never been disclosed
at the Board of Deputies, let alone discussed.[84] The letter
evoked widespread communal protests.[85] Even non-Zionist
deputies were outraged. Repudiations of the letter quickly appeared from Lord Rothschild, Weizmann (by now president of
the English Zionist Federation), and the Chief Rabbi.[86] At the
Anglo-Jewish Association Montefiore was sure of support and
was unrepentant. Alexander appeared unmoved. On 17 June,
by 56 votes to 51, the Deputies condemned the letter and passed
a vote of censure on the Conjoint. Alexander resigned, and
the Conjoint was wound up.[87]

These revolutionary events were as important for the future
of Anglo-Jewry as the Balfour Declaration the following
November. The revolution, it must be stressed, was not
primarily about Zionism; Stuart Samuel, who was elected
president of the Board of Deputies in Alexander's stead, was
not a Zionist.[88] The revolution certainly made the Zionist task

easier. But it was, in truth, 'a revolt against a system of oligar-
chical repression'.[89] It was a rebellion against the old ruling
cliques within the community. It was an attack by the provincial communities, which the immigrants had largely created,
against the leadership in London.[90] And it was followed, not by
a resolution placing the Board of Deputies at the disposal of
the English Zionist Federation, but by an inevitable revision of
the Board's constitution which was completed in 1919 and
broadened considerably its representative base.[91] Thus did the
reins of power within the Anglo-Jewish community pass from
the 'old regime'—the coterie of interrelated anglicized families
that had held sway over the community since the early nineteenth century—to the pogrom refugees and their children.

For the old élites it was all too much. Edwin Montagu,
Samuel Montagu's second son, who had become Secretary of
State for India in July 1917, fought a rearguard action to try to
sabotage the proposed Balfour Declaration, and he did, indeed, succeed in having it altered in several important
respects.[92] 'All my life', he told Lloyd George, 'I have been trying to get out of the Ghetto. You want to force me back
there!'[93] A week after the Balfour Declaration had been
issued, the new outcasts of Anglo-Jewry decided to form a
League of British Jews 'to uphold the status of British subjects
professing the Jewish religion', 'to facilitate the settlement in
Palestine of such Jews as may desire to make Palestine their
home' (a sop to the old philanthropic ideals), and most importantly, 'to resist the allegation that Jews constitute a separate
Political Entity'.[94]

The irony was that the League itself constituted a separate
political entity. It embraced all the leading Jewish anti-Zionists
in the country at that time and it soon launched its own
newspaper, the *Jewish Guardian* (1919-31) as a platform for its
views. The League's utter hostility to Zionism was basic to its
existence.[95] But it went further and from the start adopted an
ultra-patriotic tone by deliberately and openly refusing
membership to Jews living in Britain who were not British subjects.[96] Did it hope none the less to recruit 'second-generation'
immigrants? In theory, certainly. But, by its own admission,
membership never exceeded about 1,300, and after an initial
burst of enthusiasm attendance at its meetings fell drastically.[97]

By 1926 the League was an empty shell, a movement led by the aristocracy of Anglo-Jewry but followed by few others.[98]

One other feature of the League, and that which, as much as its anti-Zionism, prevented it from becoming a mass movement, was its close identification with the extreme right wing of the Conservative party. The League's leadership was largely Conservative in composition anyway, including as it did Lionel de Rothschild, MP (President of the League), Sir Philip Magnus, MP (one of the Vice-Presidents), and David Lindo Alexander (a founder member). The only prominent non-Conservative was its treasurer Sir Charles Henry, Coalition Liberal MP for the Wrekin, who died in 1919. Henry, a wealthy metal-broker, had once cheekily described himself as a 'Lib-Lab'. As President of the Jewish Soup Kitchen during the Great War he had announced that the Kitchen would not extend its benefits to any Russian Jews or their families who refused to volunteer for service in the British army.[99] A year or so after its foundation the League's members appear to have convinced themselves that 'the Jewish Relief Act of 1858 might be repealed in 1919 if Zionists convinced anti-Semites that the Jews were a nation in Palestine and if anti-Semites prevailed upon Parliament to legislate them into foreigners in England'.[100] At that time the High Tory *Morning Post* was engaged in an attack upon Russian Jews in Britain as emissaries of Bolshevism, a line of argument which had featured significantly during the general election the previous December.[101] While the Board of Deputies and the English Zionist Federation did their best to dispel groundless fears, ten leading members of the League of British Jews wrote to the *Post* accusing the *Jewish Chronicle* and its sister paper, the *Jewish World* (also edited by Greenberg), of promoting the Bolshevik cause.[102]

During the remaining years of the Lloyd George Coalition, and especially once Britain had assumed the Mandate for Palestine, in 1920, the Conservative Press became ever more vocal against the implementation of the Balfour Declaration. Lord Northcliffe was a declared opponent of Zionism.[103] His newspaper, the *Daily Mail*, launched a campaign against the Mandate during the 1922 general election, and it was joined by Lord Beaverbrook's *Daily Express*.[104] The burden of their argu-

ment was that the British taxpayer was being mulcted in order
to build up a Jewish National Home, and that this would
influence Muslim opinion against the British Empire.[105]
Beaverbrook at once disclaimed any intention of launching an
anti-Semitic campaign, but his propaganda gave plenty of am-
munition to genuine anti-Semites, and the election of 1922 was
in fact marked by more anti-Jewish feeling than any since
1906.[106] The visible decay of the Liberal party made a Labour
government a realistic possibility for the first time. To the extreme right the unthinkable seemed to lie just around the corner.
The Labour party was thus branded as 'pro-Jewish' in an effort
to harness popular anti-Semitism against it.[107] At the same time
the revolt of Conservative back-benchers, which had brought
the Lloyd George Coalition to an end, was justified on the
grounds that the Coalition was under Jewish control; Lloyd
George's sympathy with Zionism, and his many Jewish
friends, gave this argument a veneer of plausibility.[108] Both the
Morning Post and the *Spectator* went further, by alleging that
British politics was dominated by Jews and Jewish considerations; only a government of loyal Conservatives would be
strong enough to resist these tendencies.[109]

   The positions taken up by important sections of the Conservative press could not but affect Anglo-Jewish opinion. Firstly,
Beaverbrook's revelation, while on a visit to Palestine in
March 1923, that the League of British Jews had asked him to
use his newspaper to oppose Zionism damned the League, in
the eyes even of non-Zionist Jews, as a treacherous organization.[110] Secondly, although there were Conservatives who
were staunch friends of the Zionist cause, the Conservative
party as a whole came under increasing suspicion—as it had
been between 1900 and 1905—as a willing refuge for enemies
of the Jewish people. The *Jewish Chronicle* noted, with dismay,
that the post of Secretary of the Overseas Trade Department in
Andrew Bonar Law's government of 1922-3 had been given to
none other than William Joynson-Hicks, 'the most avowed and
determined anti-Semite in the House', and that Joynson-Hicks
had become also a leading pro-Arabist.[111] In May 1922 he had
chaired a meeting at the Commons in support of the Arab community in Palestine; the following month the Conservative-
dominated House of Lords had passed a resolution denouncing

the Palestine Mandate.[112] Furthermore, it was noticeable that, although Jewish representation in Parliament remained at an embarrassingly high level (eleven MPs in 1918 and 1922, thirteen in 1923), over half the Jewish MPs returned at those three elections were Conservatives, some were intimately connected with the League of British Jews and were out-and-out anti-Zionists (none more so than Edwin Montagu), few could be relied upon to speak sympathetically on Jewish matters of any description, and only one, Alfred Mond, was a Zionist.[113] It was on their Gentile friends at the Palace of Westminster that Zionists had to rely for parliamentary support.[114]

Between 1918 and 1922 the mass of Anglo-Jewry observed all these tendencies but was not sure whether a pattern could be detected. For this reason alone, and in spite of its support for the notoriously anti-Semitic White Russians during the Russian Civil War, the Lloyd George Coalition had seemed a safe bet; under it the Mandate, incorporating the Balfour Declaration, had been secured and Herbert Samuel had been dispatched to Palestine, as first High Commissioner, to supervise the rebuilding of Zion. Anglo-Jewry forgave Lloyd George his pre-war indiscretions. He had become a hero in their eyes, and his downfall was 'very much deplored by the Jews in the East End'.[115] Had the Liberal party elected him as their leader there is no doubt that many pre-war Jewish Liberals would have been only too glad to have continued giving the party their support, and that a great many new Jewish voters would have followed them. But Lloyd George's assumption of the Liberal leadership did not take place until 1926. Until then Asquith remained at the head of the party. And Asquith lost whatever goodwill there remained for him within Anglo-Jewry by a speech he made at Paisley, on 1 November 1922, when he asserted that 'what was wanted was that we should cut down to the bone our external commitments in Mesopotamia, Palestine, or anywhere else in the world ... We had fulfilled every obligation we ever entered into, and it was now time to withdraw.'[116]

There were, of course, a great many Liberals who were ardent and committed Zionists. But a government with Asquith at its head obviously could not be trusted on this issue. It could not be said that the Conservative party was saturated with anti-

Semites. But there were too many powerful critics of Jewish aspirations within that party for it to be attractive to any but the Jewish establishment of old. Besides, the Conservative party was not a poor man's party, and the Liberal party (reduced, by 1924, to forty MPs) was clearly no longer a credible party of government. By a process of elimination, therefore, if for no other reason, new Jewish voters, including the many working-class Jews enfranchised for the first time in 1918, gravitated towards Labour.

Without doubt the deportation of Jews back to Russia during the Great War had aided this process. Those who had articulated Jewish immigrant opposition to conscription and deportation were, for the most part, socialists. They obtained support from other socialists, who were at that time campaigning against British involvement in a 'capitalist' war, and who were naturally sympathetic to the Bolshevik revolution when it came.[117] In Leeds and east London, where the conscription issue had triggered off anti-Jewish riots, revulsion at the policy of deportation initiated by Lloyd George's government had undoubtedly added warmth to the developing relationship between immigrant Jews and the Labour movement. A Jewish Labour supporter was not merely making propaganda when he told the *Jewish Chronicle* in 1922:

The Labour Party is a party of quiet men ... They are the true successors of the great Liberal tradition of tolerance, seeking peace at home and abroad ... On the Palestine policy, moreover, by no means the least of Jewish interests, the Labour Party is more completely sound than any other political group ... Alone of all the parties contesting the election [1922] the Labour Party has taken an outspoken and definite stand on the Palestine question.[118]

The truth of this last point could not be denied. Not only was the party on record as favouring the implementation of the Balfour Declaration, but Ramsay MacDonald had, as recently as February 1922, visited Palestine and reiterated this policy.[119] The following November Labour's commitment to the Mandate was reaffirmed by Arthur Henderson, Secretary of the party's National Executive Committee, when, alone of the major parties, Labour agreed to distribute to each of its candidates material relating to Palestine which had been prepared by the Zionist Federation; at the same time George Lansbury promised the support of the *Daily Herald,* of which he was the editor.[120] Thus, on the grounds both of its working-class appeal and of its Zionist sympathies the Labour party attracted large numbers of Jewish voters at the 1922 election.

That election saw the return to Parliament of the first Jewish Labour MP, Emanuel Shinwell. Shinwell's election, however, was symbolic only; his constituency, Linlithgow, was hardly awash with Jewish voters. The contest that mattered took place in Whitechapel, the seat which Stuart Samuel had vacated in 1916. In 1918, as part of the general redrawing of constituency boundaries, the old Whitechapel constituency (which had been held for sixteen years by Samuel and for fifteen years before that by his uncle, Samuel Montagu) had been amalgamated with that of St. George's; the new Whitechapel seat was therefore probably more thickly populated with Jewish voters than any other in the country at that time.[121] In 1922 a three-cornered contest was fought there. The Conservative candidate, Captain A. Instone, was both Jewish and a supporter of the Balfour Declaration; the Liberal candidate, J. D. Kiley, a former MP, was also a keen supporter of the idea of a Jewish National Home. But in 1922 Whitechapel was won by the Labour candidate for the first time; C. J. Matthew had a 528-vote victory over the Liberal, with the Conservative 2,337 votes behind at the bottom of the poll. Such was the extent to which the premier Jewish constituency in the country had swung Labour's way.[112]

As early as 1919 Greenberg, writing under the pseudonym 'Mentor', had told *Jewish Chronicle* readers that 'Jews have no better friends in this country than the Labour party and like political groups in other lands.'[123] At the general election of 1923 Poale Zion put out its strongest statement yet in support of Labour candidates, stressing most of all Labour's commitment to the Mandate; Conservative and Liberal messages to the Jews studiously avoided this subject.[124] By 1924 support for Labour had become respectable among British Jews. The minority Labour government that year received the *Jewish Chronicle*'s warm approval.[125] J. H. Thomas, Secretary of State for the Colonies in the Labour Administration, told the Commons that the Government would give effect to the Balfour Declaration.[126] And the new relationship between Anglo-Jewry and Labour was cemented at the Labour party conference in October 1924 when, immediately prior to the 1924 general-election campaign, Arthur Henderson announced that his close friend, the Jewish philanthropist and Russian refugee Bernhard Baron who was managing director of the Carreras tobacco firm, had sent the party a cheque for £5,000.[127]

7. Love Affair With the Left

The three-party nature of British politics in the inter-war years gave the Anglo-Jewish community a heightened awareness of its own importance in the election process. In certain constituencies Jewish voters held the balance, and this was a circumstance none of the parties could afford to ignore. At the same time the total number of Jewish MPs continued to remain high; in 1929 they reached the record number of 17, or 2.8 per cent of the Commons, although Anglo-Jewry could only then have accounted for about 0.7 per cent of the total population of the United Kingdom (45 millions). Inasmuch as several important issues concerning the Jewish community—and not just Jewish Zionists—came before Parliament at this time, this situation had obvious advantages. Yet it also had drawbacks, though these only became apparent during the fascist upsurge of the 1930s.

That the community possessed real political power was an open secret. With the coming of near-universal suffrage at the end of the 1920s, the urban constitution of Anglo-Jewry marked it out for special treatment by the political parties; Palestine was an added dimension of growing importance. Jewish leaders could hardly claim now, as they had been so fond of doing in the past, that Jews should vote as British citizens but not as Jewish citizens; Jewish issues demanded a Jewish response. In a leader on the eve of the 1923 general election Greenberg urged that 'where any candidate ... expresses himself as opposed to Jewish interests, then it seems to us the duty of Jewish voters to withhold from him their support ... the constitutional idea of the suffrage is that each voter shall employ it in what he conceives to be his own true interests'.[1] A year later, with Palestine in mind, the editor of the *Jewish Chronicle* returned more insistently to the same theme, and expressed the hope that no Jew would 'so mistake his duty as for Party reasons to support a candidate who has expressed himself in opposition to the development of the Jewish National effort'.[2] More explicit still was the plan of the young Ian Mikardo, the future left-wing Labour MP, for a 'Union of Anglo-Jewish Parliamentary

Electors' 'to unite every Jew and Jewess in Great Britain who
has the franchise, into a body, every one of whose members
would be pledged to vote as directed by the Council of the
Union, who would naturally be free of party influences and
would wield the Jewish vote purely as a weapon with which to
secure fair play for British Jews'.[3]

The Conservative party was well aware of the new mood
within Anglo-Jewry. On certain questions, notably aliens'
legislation, it was not prepared to compromise to win Jewish
votes. Joynson-Hicks, as Home Secretary between 1924 and
1929, proved absolutely unbending in the face of Jewish demands to relax the regulations governing the treatment of
aliens in Britain.[4] 'To become naturalised', he told a <i>Jewish
Chronicle</i> reporter somewhat menacingly in 1926, 'an alien
must cut himself off entirely from his old country and its sur-
roundings, its mode of life, language and ideas.'[5]

But the Conservatives knew that the Jewish community was
not monolithic and that many Jews were happy to see the
immigrant flood of pre-war days almost entirely shut off. On
occasion the aliens' legislation could prove a blessing in dis-
guise to Jewish leaders, and Joynson-Hicks knew it. Thus in
February 1926, at the behest of Chief Rabbi Hertz, he refused
to admit, from Poland, Rabbi Abraham Sacharov, whom certain orthodox Jews in Gateshead wished to have at the head of
a projected <i>Yeshiva</i> (Talmudical college) there. Hertz did not
want Gateshead to become an independent congregation, and
he did not want a <i>Yeshiva</i> to be formed there in opposition to
Jews' College, London; Joynson-Hicks was happy to be of
assistance.[6]

And even if Joynson-Hicks was hostile from the Jewish point
of view there were more attractive personalities in the Conservative party. Churchill, who had rejoined the party and who
was now Chancellor of the Exchequer, was a confirmed Zionist.
Baldwin's government did not, after all, abandon the Mandate.
Moreover throughout the 1920s the Conservative parliamentary party contained more Jewish MPs than were to be found
on the Labour or Liberal benches, and the Conservatives
happened to have in their ranks the foremost Jewish MP of
the period, Samuel Finburgh. Finburgh, a Manchester cotton
manufacturer and past President of both the Manchester

Shechita Board and the Higher Broughton synagogue, a member of the Board of Deputies, and a Zionist, was also President of the North Salford Conservative Association. In 1924, at the age of fifty-seven, he won the North Salford seat from the Labour demagogue Ben Tillett, after a campaign which was largely aimed at convincing the 1,500 or so Jewish voters in the constituency that Finburgh (who, as befitted the son of a Jewish minister, did not campaign on the sabbath) was the best person to represent them at Westminster. These tactics paid off and he emerged with a majority of 1,136: it was the first time in the history of Manchester Jewry that a Jew was an MP there.[7]

It must be said that if Finburgh manipulated Jewish voters for the greater glory of the Conservative party, Anglo-Jewry was exceedingly well served by having such a man in the House of Commons. On entering Parliament he observed 'that most of the Jewish Members ... were indifferent to matters affecting their own people'.[8] In the service of the community he rose head and shoulders above his parliamentary co-religionists. On the aliens' issue he was an outspoken critic of Joynson-Hicks, both in and out of Parliament.[9] In October 1926 he stole the Zionist limelight in the Commons, hitherto focused largely upon the Labour party, by organizing a 'Parliamentary Palestine Committee', an unashamed pressure group, consisting originally of 37 Conservative MPs, 19 Labour members, and 7 Liberals, whose aim it was to support 'the Balfour Declaration and ... the policy of Great Britain as the Mandatory Power'.[10] In 1927 Finburgh and another Jewish Conservative MP, Isidore Salmon, also a member of the Board of Deputies, blocked a private members' bill to prohibit *shechita*.[11] The same year the Member for North Salford launched an all-out attack on the Goverment's Aliens Amendment Bill. He told Conservative MPs who sat for Jewish constituencies 'that if this Aliens Bill goes through there will be an outcry in those constituencies which they represent'.[12] The Bill was dropped.

Had Finburgh been a younger man he might have been able to increase Jewish support for his party. But ill health forced him to retire in 1929 and he died six years later.[13] Today Anglo-Jewry hardly remembers him. He did not live long enough to prevent the rapid deterioration in relations between the community and the Conservative party in the 1930s. More importantly, while he lived, his efforts on behalf of Anglo-Jewry, though courageous and valiant, did little to persuade the Jewish masses that the Conservative party might be worth backing after all. There were a number of reasons why this should have been so. To begin with most of Finburgh's battles were undertaken against the Conservative party and against the policy of Baldwin's government. Secondly, with the solitary exceptions of Churchill and his Under-Secretary, G. Locker-Lampson, the Government contained no personalities whom Anglo-Jewry felt it could trust. Thirdly, as has already been observed, the Conservative party in the 1920s was just not a poor man's party. *The New Survey of London Life & Labour*, published in 1934, showed that whereas 12.1 per cent of the whole working population of east London lived in what was then considered poverty, for working-class Jews the proportion was 13.7 per cent.[14] To the extent that a large proportion of Anglo-Jewry was still relatively poor, living in crowded city centres with grave, and worsening, social problems, it was bound not to be attracted by the party which Bonar Law and Baldwin had built up. Even supposing Baldwin had declared himself an out-and-out champion of Jewish rights in Palestine, the economic and social facts of life at home would still have acted as a powerful countervailing force.

Non-socialist Jews, nurtured on pre-1914 politics, still hoped that Liberalism could be revived. When Lloyd George eventually succeeded to the leadership of the Liberal party in October 1926, their hopes rose and centred upon Herbert Samuel, who had completed his tour of duty as High Commissioner in Palestine the previous year. Samuel had tried to steer a middle course which had not always pleased the Zionists; yet under his administration the *Yishuv* (the Jewish community in the Holy Land) had taken firm root, and he returned to a hero's welcome from British Jews, who regarded him, rightly, as one of the few top-ranking Jewish politicians of the period. When Baldwin's Government lost the 1929 general election, and the succeeding minority Labour Government reacted to the increasing violence in Palestine by issuing a White Paper (11 October 1930) in which it declared publicly that Jewish immigration to the Holy Land would be suspended, there seemed a chance that the close relationship between Jewish Zionists and the Labour party was at last about to come to an end, perhaps to the advantage of the Liberals. And it so happened that almost at once the strength of that close relationship was put to the test.

In November 1930 a by-election occurred in the Whitechapel constituency, following the death of its Labour MP Harry Gosling, who was both a Gentile and pro-Zionist. Zionists, furious because of the White Paper, hoped that the Government could be taught a lesson. J. Rosenbloom, Chairman of the East London Young Zionist League, announced that local Zionists would officially campaign against the Government.[15] Accordingly, a 'Palestine Protest Committee' was formed to undertake this work; judging from reports of its meetings, and from correspondence printed in the *Jewish Chronicle*, it had plenty of local support from both lay and ecclesiastical leaders.[16]

The Liberal party thought it sensed victory. In 1929 Gosling had had a majority of 9,180 over his Liberal opponent; if 4,500 or so of Gosling's Jewish supporters could be persuaded to change sides, success was assured. To make this change of sides even more palatable the local Liberal party chose as its candidate an up-and-coming Jewish solicitor from South Wales, and a Zionist of rising fame, Barnet Janner. Leopold Greenberg was delighted. 'Now there is a Jewish candidate no Jewish vote need be lost', he told his readers.[17] Local Liberals put the number of Jewish voters in the constituency at roughly 12,000, in an electorate of 37,000. The omens, therefore, seemed propitious, particularly since Labour party workers themselves seemed to be admitting that all was not well. During the final week of the campaign local Jewish Labour supporters hurried to do some fence-mending. A special meeting of the executive committee of Poale Zion condemned the White Paper and the Labour candidate, James Hall, was prevailed upon to give an assurance that, if elected, he would vote against the Government should it attempt to put the White Paper into force.[18]

When polling took place, on 3 December, Janner did very well. With turn-out, at 59 per cent, practically identical with that at the general election the previous year, there was a swing of over 18 per cent against Labour, whose majority was cut to 1,099.[19] The Government had been shaken, certainly. Two months later, in a letter read by him in the House of Commons and printed in Hansard, Ramsay MacDonald told Chaim Weizmann that, in effect, the White Paper was dead.[20]

Locally, Labour activists believed strongly that there was political mileage to be made out of the issue of Zionism, and that the Whitechapel by-election had proved this to be the case. Before Hall had been adopted as Labour candidate, there seems to have been an attempt to persuade Selig Brodetsky, Professor of Applied Mathematics at Leeds University, and a member of the Jewish Agency for Palestine, to stand in the Labour interest.[21] Labour's worst fears seemed to be confirmed in the general election of October 1931, when Janner did win the seat with a majority of over 1,000; this was the famous occasion on which the Jewish boxer Ted 'Kid' Lewis stood for Oswald Mosley's 'New Party' and obtained 154 votes.[22] But Janner's 1931 victory did not last. In 1935, in a straight fight with him, Hall won the seat back for the Labour party.

From the Whitechapel contests of 1930, 1931, and 1935 several important conclusions emerge. Firstly, Zionism was not a guaranteed vote-winner. Gareth Jones, who visited Whitechapel during the 1930 contest, in order to make notes for a speech Lloyd George was to deliver, warned the Liberal leader that although 'the Jews would like to hear something brief and personal about Palestine ... they do not want the Government policy to be attacked at length ... Many of them are not keen Zionists.'[23] This was something Jewish Liberals easily forgot. Of course the Jews of Whitechapel were not *anti*-Zionist; Labour's sympathy with Zionism had been of immense importance in winning Jewish support in the East End during the previous decade. But it was not, and never had been, the sole basis for that support.

Secondly, in an atmosphere of increasing anti-Semitism in the East End in the 1930s Zionism—particularly when promoted by an assertive Jewish candidate—could have serious electoral drawbacks. Brodetsky realized this when he gave as one of the reasons for his refusal to stand the fact that 'my position in the Zionist movement would have made it a Zionist election'.[24] In a typescript note of a meeting between Neville Laski, President of the Board of Deputies, the Labour MP and former minister Herbert Morrison, and the Secretary of the Communist party, Harry Pollitt, held in October 1936 to discuss the situation in the East End, Laski recorded the following observation:

I do not like to put it in these notes, but M.[orrison] said and P.[ollitt] agreed, that the manner in which Janner fought his election on the suggestion that votes be given to him (Janner) because he (Janner) was a Jew, had done a great deal of harm. It was still remembered and talked about, and it was said that Jews were Jews first and Englishmen a long way after.[25]

Thirdly, and following from this, Janner's near success in 1930 and his victory in 1931 owed something to the political situation then current, and much to the fact that Pollitt himself had entered these two contests. In 1929 there had been no Communist intervention. In 1930 the Conservatives still thought the seat worth fighting; their candidate, Noel Guiness, managed to collect 3,735 votes, while Pollitt obtained 2,106. In 1931 the Conservatives dropped out of the fight and Pollitt increased his vote by just over 500; most of the Conservative votes seem to have gone to Janner (if they went anywhere) and though, on a larger turn-out, James Hall increased Labour's percentage, Pollitt undoubtedly deprived him of support. The result was a Liberal victory. But in 1935, with no Communist intervention, Hall won comfortably with a majority of over 2,000.

The message from Whitechapel was, therefore, that the Jews of the East End were turning to Labour, and that some of them were turning to Communism. So far as Labour was concerned, this shift, though aided by the party's record on Zionism, was not fundamentally dependent on it. It was a socio-economic shift, triggered by the decline of the Liberal party. As a Liberal MP Janner had resuscitated the Parliamentary Palestine Committee, of which he and Lord Hartington became honorary secretaries, and he also worked hard defending *shechita* and, later, attacking the National Government's attitude to the treatment of Jews in Germany.[26] But after his 1935 defeat he seems to have seen the writing on the wall, and a year later joined the Labour party. So did Major H. L. Nathan who, having been elected Liberal MP for Bethnal Green North-East in 1929 and 1931, joined the Labour party in 1934 and later sat as Labour MP for Wandsworth Central.[27]

Labour thus attracted into its ranks committed and professing Jews of high calibre, and of a younger generation than those still to be found in the Conservative party. Typical of this new breed was Michael Marcus, elected as Labour MP for Dundee in 1929 at the age of thirty-three. Born in Russia, Marcus was a religious Zionist who saw no difficulty in reconciling orthodoxy and socialism and who was an outspoken critic of the 1930 White Paper.[28] During his short stay in Parliament (1929-31) he assumed the mantle left by Finburgh as defender of Jewish rights at Westminster; in July 1931 he was asked by the Board of Deputies 'to look after Jewish interests' in the Commons in relation to *shechita*—the first occasion on which a Jewish socialist MP undertook communal duties of such a nature.[29]

Between 1931 and 1934 there were no Jewish Labour MPs. But the general election of 1935 saw the return of four: D. Fraenkel at Mile End, H. Day at Central Southwark, E. Shinwell at Easington, and Sydney Silverman (a founder member of Liverpool Poale Zion) at Nelson and Colne. By the mid-1930s the Labour party had become the normal political home of the mass of poor working-class Jews in Great Britain and, one suspects, of a significant number of middle-class Jews as well. This was true of both parliamentary elections and local elections. In the big cities Labour emerged as the only credible party of social welfare and reform. In March 1937 twelve Jews were returned as London County councillors, including Dr Bernard Homa, a grandson of Rabbi Werner of the *Machzike Hadass* synagogue in Brick Lane.[30]

The attraction of Jews to the Communist party was of an altogether different order, and a fundamental distinction must be drawn between those few Jews who became Communist party members from idealistic and intellectual considerations, and those Jews who supported Communism because of what the party stood for in the East End and in confrontation with the British Union of Fascists. The former category comprised a motley collection of children of the rich and influential Jews of pre-1918 days: Ivor Montagu, for instance, a grandson of Samuel Mongatu, joined the Communist party in the early 1930s 'simply as a mere honest act of gratitude for life'; fourteen other members of the Montagu family also became party members.[31] Jack Gaster, a solicitor and son of Dr Moses Gaster, also joined the party.[32]

These members had famous names and were Jewish personalities in their own right. But a more important influence in attracting Jews towards support of the Communist party was the species of non-Zionist socialism which, as was shown in Chapter 4, had a long history in Anglo-Jewish working-class politics. In 1909 a group of Russian Bundists had founded the Workers' Circle Friendly Society in the East End. Favoured with Communist goodwill the Workers' Circle became one of the largest associations of Jewish workers in England; by the end of the Second World War it had some 2,500 members.[33] Many members of the Workers' Circle gained their livelihood in the clothing industry. In the late 1920s a number of East End Jews, dissatisfied with the policy and Irish leadership of the Leeds-based United Garment Workers' Union, formed the United Clothing Workers' Union, one of two Communist 'breakaway' unions (the other being the United Mineworkers of Scotland) which enjoyed the official blessing of the party. Under the leadership of its founder, the able Russian-born Jew Sam Elsbury, the United Clothing Workers enjoyed a few years popularity. But Elsbury objected to the use of the union for directly political purposes, was expelled, as a 'social fascist', from the party and from his post as union secretary, and at the end of 1935 the union was dissolved.[34] Elsbury was not, however, the only Jewish trade-union leader to achieve prominence in Communist politics; another was P. Marks, of Leeds, a member of the Cabinet Makers' Alliance and, later, of the Amalgamated Society of Woodworkers, who had actually been a founder-member of the Communist party.[35]

Most potent of all, however, was the eruption of fascism in the East End between 1932 and 1936. The Board of Deputies at first refused to believe that the fascist threat was worth bothering about. Later Neville Laski, President of the Board from 1933 to 1940, accepted the analysis given to him by Morrison and Pollitt, that by their professional conduct Jewish landlords, estate agents, and businessmen had contributed much to the anti-Jewish feeling in the East End, which reached its climax at the 'battle' of Cable Street on 4 October 1936.[36] In consequence the Board came very close to appealing to Jews to accept second-class status at least temporarily in order to dampen anti-Jewish prejudices.[37] At St. John's Wood synagogue, for example, in

May 1939, Laski condemned 'the price-cutting activities of
some Jewish traders in the tobacco, grocery, cosmetic, and
chemistry businesses ... It was no use replying to these charges
by saying that there were non-Jewish price-cutters. He knew
there were. But Jews must not trade in this way. Those who did
were doing the greatest harm to their people.'[38]

Once the fascist threat became real—even physical—the
philosophy of the Board's Defence Committee (formed 1936)
was to keep the community out of public view if at all possible
and, in particular, to avoid street confrontations with the
fascists.[39] This was not to the liking of many East End Jews.
In July 1936 the Jewish Labour Council, which represented
Jewish trade unions, socialist societies, and branches of the
Workers' Circle, formally repudiated the advice of the Board of
Deputies and urged Jews not to stay away from Mosley's
march through the Jewish area of Stepney which was planned
for 4 October but to stop it.[40] An elaborate plan was devised for
this purpose, and there was open and enthusiastic co-operation
with the Communist party.[41]

The Communist party alone had taken the British Union of
Fascists seriously from the start. Whilst the Deputies strained
every muscle to avoid confrontation with Mosley and his
followers, the Communists provided a framework for action on
the streets, and at the same time tackled the social ills upon
which fascism fed.[42] The result was what Barnet Litvinoff has
aptly termed the 'Jewish infatuation' with Communism in
Britain, whereby Jews supported the party in spite of, and not
because of, its anti-Zionist and anti-religious stance.[43] Even
East End Jewish businessmen gave money to the party to help
combat the fascist menace.[44] As the struggle with the fascists
intensified the infatuation deepened, and it received a new
lease of life when the Soviet Union and the United Kingdom
became allies against Hitler at the end of 1941. The Communist party, on its side, sought to incorporate a specifically
Jewish dimension within itself. In 1945 the party's 'National
Jewish Committee' launched a monthly periodical, the *Jewish
Clarion*.[45]

In the same year, at the general election, the Jewish candidate Phil Piratin was returned as Communist MP for Mile
End.[46] In a three-cornered contest he obtained 5,075 votes as

against the Labour candidate's 3,861. The infatuation seemed to have entered a new phase. What it meant, in terms of numbers, is impossible to state with precision. Shortly after his election Piratin stated that the percentage of Jewish members of the Commmunist party corresponded to the percentage of Jews in the general population—i.e. about 1 per cent in 1945.[45] Even if party membership had reached 50,000 at that time the number of Jews in the party could only have been about 500.[48] But it is fair to add that in Stepney in the 1930s the Jewish proportion of Communist party members was certainly much higher than this, and may have represented as much as a third of the total.[49]

If the Communist share of the vote in 1945 (0.4 per cent) is assumed to reflect also the Communist share of the Jewish electorate (about 337,000), then the total number of Jews who *voted* Communist works out at about 1,500.[50] Yet it is difficult to believe that the Communist Jewish vote was actually as low as this; in Mile End, alone, in 1945, it probably amounted to at least 2,500 voters, or about half Piratin's total vote.[51] Over the country as a whole the total number of Jews who supported the Communist party at the end of the Second World War may have been as high as 5,000, perhaps even higher.[52] Most of these voters, too, were undoubtedly to be found in the East End, where the memory of the alliance between Anglo-Jewry and Communism lingers still. The infatuation was great fun while it lasted. But Piratin's victory marked its peak, and during the Cold War it quickly evaporated.

What did all this left-wing activity imply so far as the Jewish attitude towards Conservatism was concerned? There were plenty of Jewish supporters of the Conservative party in the 1930s, and they were to be found particularly in the new communities already being established in the suburbs of London, Leeds, and Manchester.[53] Just over half the Jewish MPs elected in 1931 and 1935 were Conservatives and they included some who held high communal office, pre-eminently Louis Gluckstein (Nottingham East), Vice-President of the Liberal Jewish synagogue, and Sir Isidore Salmon (Harrow), Vice-President of the United Synagogue and of the Board of Deputies. But the presence of such men was not sufficient to make up for the tendency of the Conservative party to harbour anti-Semites and their fellow-travellers, and this seems to have severely damaged the reputation of the party with Jews who had formerly been Liberal supporters but who did not want to vote Labour.[54] The forced resignation of the Minister of War, Leslie Hore-Belisha, in January 1940, was widely and correctly interpreted as an instance of the Conservative party's unwillingness to resist anti-Semitism in the Foriegn Office and among the army generals.[55]

Anti-Semitism, like anti-Zionism, was not confined to the Conservative party. Some supporters of appeasement towards Nazi Germany saw 'the Jewish problem' as an obstacle to good Anglo-German relations, and many more were open admirers of the Nazi regime.[56] The entry of Jewish refugees from Germany and Austria into Britain triggered a new wave of anti-Semitism which, because of the nature of the immigration, affected middle-class Gentiles rather than working-class ones. The Jews who fled to Britain in the 1930s were educated professional people, the earliest victims of Nazi discriminatory laws. In 1933 and 1934 the *British Medical Journal* began reporting hostility from the medical profession to refugee doctors, and in 1934 *The Times* carried a similar correspondence regarding university appointments.[57] 'Worst of all', the *Sunday Express* revealed in 1938, 'many of them [the refugees] are holding themselves out to the public as psycho-analysts.'[58] The total number of Jewish refugees from Nazism who came to Great Britain between 1933 and 1945 was not more than 65,000.[59] This hardly mattered; it was the quality, not the quantity, that was important.

The same was true of the anti-Semitic reaction to it. Mosley's 'New Party', and its successor the British Union of Fascists, formed in 1932, never had a parliamentary success, and its electoral impact was far less than that of the Communist party. Yet the British Union of Fascists gathered around itself leading political figures, most of whom were connected with Conservative politics.[60] When Lord Rothermere swung the *Daily Mail* and the *Evening News* behind the fascists, Jewish advertisers threatened sanctions (June 1934) unless he relented. He did so, in magnificent style, by devoting two leading articles in praise of the Jewish contribution to British life.[61] The fascist campaign against Anglo-Jewry became formal policy in the autumn of 1934; gradually Conservatives who had flirted with the movement melted away. But propagandists of the extreme right, such as Lord Londonderry, Admiral Sir Barry Domvile, and Sir Arnold Wilson continued to peddle the idea that Jewish refugees were purveyors of Marxist ideology 'and other forms of decadence'.

Pro-German groups such as the Anglo-German Fellowship and The Link (sponsored by Domvile) easily lent themselves to agitation against Jewish refugees. In December 1937 the Fellowship had 700 members, including important financiers, industrialists, and MPs.[62] It is also worth noting that, in the view of the Board of Deputies Defence Committee, the most prominent anti-Semite in the country was not Sir Oswald Mosley but the Conservative MP for Peebles and Southern from 1931 to 1945, Captain Archibald Henry Maule Ramsay, a fanatical anti-Bolshevik and a leading member of the Nordic League.[63] Ramsay, who made a habit of asking anti-Semitic questions in the Commons, was interned in May 1940 under Defence Regulation 18b, and not released until September 1944. He celebrated the end of the war with Germany by tabling a motion, which no other MP supported, calling for the 1290 Statute of Jewry, under which the Jews had been expelled from England, and which had been repealed in 1846, to be reintroduced.[64]

But if Ramsay was clearly in a class of his own, and an embarrassment to the Conservative leadership, he was most certainly not the only member of his party to hold anti-Semitic views.[65] The trend was particularly evident at constituency level, and the most notable instance of it occurred at the Cheltenham by-election of June 1937; against all expectations the local Conservative Association refused to adopt as their candidate the then Mayor of Cheltenham, Daniel Lipson, because he was Jewish. Lipson, an anti-Zionist, ran as an Independent Conservative against the official candidate, and narrowly won the seat.[66] He retained the seat, again as an Independent Conservative, in 1945, when his majority was much increased; ironically he was then the only Jewish Conservative MP, official or independent, in the House of Commons.[67]

The reaction of the Anglo-Jewish leadership to the resurgence of anti-Semitism in the 1930s was confused but predictable. On the one hand the Board of Deputies did not want to enter into public controversy with the Conservative-dominated National Government over its attitude to Nazi Germany. In April 1933 Neville Laski (as President of the Board), Lionel Cohen (Chairman of the Board's Law and Parliamentary Committee), L. G. Montefiore (President of the Anglo-Jewish Association), and Otto Schiff (Chairman of the Jewish Refugee Committee), gave a formal written undertaking to the Home Secretary that the Anglo-Jewish community would bear all the expenses, 'without ultimate charge to the State', incurred in giving shelter in Britain to German-Jewish refugees.[68] The Board consistently rejected calls for an official Anglo-Jewish boycott of German goods.[69] This refusal was the subject of bitter personal animosity within the community and led to the formation of a 'Jewish Representative Council for the Boycott of German Goods and Services' in November 1933. The Council's inaugural meeting was attended by 530 delegates representing 104 London synagogues, 87 provincial synagogues, 84 friendly societies, 63 zionist societies, and 22 trade councils, trade unions, and trade associations. This amounted, of course, to a widespread repudiation of the Board's attitude by British Jews, which perhaps accounts for the fact that the Council's activities were consistently under-reported by the *Jewish Chronicle*.[70]

At the same time, as has been noted, the Board of Deputies publicly sought to counteract anti-Semitism at home by calling upon British Jews to adopt a deliberately low profile. At Cardiff, in October 1933, Neville Laski blamed Jews who 'by their own conduct fostered anti-Semitism'.[71] In September 1934 his father, Nathan, threatened that he would block the appointment of a Communal Rabbi in Manchester by telling the authorities in London (he did not specify which) to 'prevent any foreign gentleman' from going northwards to fill such a post.[72] A handbook, in English and German, issued jointly by the Board of Deputies and the German Jewish Aid Committee in January 1939, warned refugees not to make themselves conspicuous, not to talk 'in a loud voice', and not to take part in any political activities.[73] Inevitably, perhaps, any idea of a Jewish vote in the Britain of the 1930s was officially and actively discouraged.[74]

Yet if the Board was to make any impact at all against home-grown anti-Semitism it had to enter political waters. Intelligence-gathering activities, and co-operative efforts with the Special Branch, were all very well, but they could not make any electoral impact, at least in the short term. But the Board did not wish to be seen in an overtly political role. During the late 1930s, therefore, a technique was developed which has been used periodically ever since, that of supplying election literature to candidates in the major political parties, who then distribute it as their own. The technique was first used against British Union of Fascists' candidates contesting the 1937 municipal elections. Sidney Salomon, secretary of the Defence Committee, later explained how it worked: 'The democratic parties opposing Fascist candidates were given such assistance as was necessary and, in addition, leaflets exposing the Fascist tactics were printed and circulated in these constituencies. There was nothing to 'tie up' the publications [*sic*] of these leaflets with the Defence Committee.'[75] Such tactics were also employed against the fascist candidates at the Leeds North-East and Middleton and Prestwich by-elections in 1940; both candidates lost their deposits.[76] Publicly, therefore the Board denied the existence of a Jewish vote, but surreptitiously it did its best to foster an anti-fascist vote, particularly in constituencies, of which North-East Leeds and Middleton and Prestwich were good examples, where there were sizeable Jewish populations.

In other ways, too, the leaders of Anglo-Jewry sought to influence both Gentile and Jewish public opinion. Sometimes this was done quite openly. In 1938 Salomon published *The Jews of Britain,* in which he played down the Jewish contribution to the world of finance and commerce, and emphasized instead Jewish involvement in the arts and medicine.[77] But sometimes the influence was less obvious. An agreement was reached with the British Broadcasting Corporation, which undertook to submit to the Board the scripts of any programme 'of Jewish interest', and to abide by the Board's decision or to 'further discuss the matter' before the programme was broadcast.[78] In November 1938 M. Gordon Liverman, Chairman of the Defence Committee, reached an agreement with Morris Myer, managing director of The Jewish Times Ltd., publishers of the Yiddish newspaper *Die Zeit* ('The Times'), by which Myer gave 'an unqualified assurance that at any rate during the war he would not allow the paper to advocate a contradictory attitude to the official policy of the Board at any time, and that this assurance would also extend to the general policy of any issue held by the responsible leaders of the Community'.[79] The Defence Committee, on its side, advanced Myer a loan of £500.[80]

In these ways the Board tried to tighten its hold upon Anglo-Jewry, to minimize the influence of 'wayward' Jewish elements, and especially to present Anglo-Jewry as politically non-partisan. 'Far from being wedded to one political creed', Salomon assured his Gentile readers, 'individual Jews, like their fellow-citizens of other faiths, hold different political views.'[81] But the creeping antipathy of Anglo-Jewry towards the Conservative party as the 1930s wore on could not be disguised. It was notorious, for instance, that the Jewish Conservative Maurice Bloch had tried repeatedly to win the Gorbals, which had a large Jewish population, but could make little impact upon his co-religionists.[82] In London the Conservatives managed to hold on to seats in the newer areas of Jewish settlement only until the mid-1930s: Hackney Central until 1931, Hackney North and Stoke Newington until 1935. The same was true of comparable seats in the provinces, such as North-East Leeds and North Salford. By the time of the next general election, in 1945, all these constituencies had become Labour strongholds.

The well-to-do image of the Conservative party, and the anti-Semitic proclivities of a certain section of it, inevitably affected the picture it presented to Jewish eyes. But beyond this there loomed the seemingly intractable problem of the Palestine Mandate, of which the governments of Stanley Baldwin and Neville Chamberlain became increasingly weary. Unwilling to permit Jewish immigration to Palestine (now ever more pressing because of the Nazi menace) in the face of Arab and Muslim opposition, the National Government first suppressed the Arab Revolt (1936-9) in the Holy Land, then from a position of strength, rejected the idea of partition (November 1938), and finally, on 17 May 1939, issued a White Paper which signalled what Zionists had always feared, the total abandonment of the Balfour Declaration. Instead the White

Paper looked forward to the creation of an independent Palestine in which Jews would be in a permanent minority. The House of Commons approved this policy by 268 votes to 179. Coming so soon after the Munich agreement, the White Paper was widely interpreted within Anglo-Jewry as proof positive that the Conservative party—albeit with some notable exceptions, such as Churchill—was prepared to turn a blind eye to the plight of German Jewry whilst depriving it of an escape route.

Perhaps it was as well for Labour that it was out of office during this unhappy period, for this enabled it to come to the Jewish community with clean hands. In the luxury of opposition, Labour could afford to be generous to the Jews, and its generosity was not found wanting. At successive Labour party conferences (Edinburgh, 1936; Bournemouth, 1937[83]; Southport, 1939; Bournemouth, 1940; and London, 1942 and 1943), and at the Trades Union Congresses of 1936, 1937, and 1938, as well as in Parliament, the British Labour movement demonstrated its backing for the Balfour Declaration and its opposition to the policy of the National Government on this question.[84] On the eve of the 1935 general election Clement Attlee, the new leader of the Labour party, sent a special message to Zionists reminding them of the party's support for 'a national home in Palestine for the Jewish people'.[85] In 1938 Poale Zion published a booklet, *British Labour Policy and Palestine*, written by Dr S Levenberg, which boasted an introduction by the Labour party's General Secretary, J. S. Middleton; the same year the 'Palestine Labour Political Committee' was resurrected to maintain contacts with the Labour party, the trade unions, and the Co-operative movement, on Zionist matters.[86]

By the outbreak of the Second World War Zionists, and especially Poale Zion, had managed to build up a great deal of goodwill within the Labour movement. And although it is easy to point to instances of electoral opportunism, it would be wrong to ignore or even underestimate the genuine and deep-seated admiration for Zionism within Labour circles. 'The Socialist element in the Jewish settlement [in Palestine] and the social ideals of the Histadruth [the General Trade Union of Jewish Workers of Palestine], Dr Levenberg wrote in 1945, 'have a strong appeal for British Labour.'[87] Once Nazi persecution of Jews began in earnest (and 1938, the year of the Kristallnacht, was the turning-point here[88]), and once Chamberlain's Government had published its White Paper, Labour's support for Zionism became overwhelming. Opposition to the White Paper became official Labour party policy.[89] The 1944 party conference adopted a resolution which came as a pleasant shock to Zionist spokesmen: 'Let the Arabs be encouraged to move out', it read, 'as the Jews move in. Let them be compensated handsomely for their land and let their settlement elsewhere be carefully and generously financed.'[90]

But the most sensational expressions of Labour's support for Zionism came in May 1945, in the final weeks of Churchill's Coalition Government. On 6 May, at a Poale Zion meeting in Manchester, Professor Harold Laski, Neville's left-wing brother and soon to become Chairman of the National Executive of the Labour Party, announced a personal conversion; 'until the outbreak of war', he admitted, 'he had always been an advocate of assimilation', but now 'he was firmly and utterly convinced of the need for the rebirth of the Jewish nation in Palestine'. Laski then told his delighted audience that 'The British Labour Party ... had decided to urge H. M. Government to recognise the right of the Jews to recreate their national life.'[91] The party conference at Blackpool later that month gave Maurice Rosetté, the Poale Zion delegate, a rapturous welcome.[92] Hugh Dalton told the conference that 'it was morally wrong and politically indefensible to restrict the entry into Palestine of Jews desiring to go there'.[93]

No plan to capture the Jewish vote in 1945 could have had a better foundation. During the war, and because of the Holocaust, Zionism had gained many new adherents within Anglo-Jewry. By July 1943 the Zionists were strong enough to be able to 'pack' the Board of Deputies with their own nominees, thus ensuring that there could be no repetition of what had happened in 1917.[94] Relations between the Board and the Anglo-Jewish Association were practically severed. There was a last-ditch attempt by some anti-Zionists to reassert their authority. The social worker Basil Henriques and the former Conservative MP Sir Jack Brunel Cohen formed the Jewish Fellowship 'to uphold the principle that the Jews are a

religious community and not a national political group'.[95]
Henriques had 'found Zionism well entrenched in the East End
with flourishing Zionist youth groups and he feared that they
must somehow undermine the British loyalties of the Jewish
youngster'.[96] But even to say that the Fellowship's impact was
minimal is to exaggerate its importance. It was widely regarded
within Anglo-Jewry as a joke in bad taste.

Among British Jews Zionism, in the context of the
Holocaust, had now become not so much a narrow assertion of
Jewish national identity as a symbol of revolt against centuries
of Gentile oppression. This mood, as it happened, dovetailed
with the current of opinion and yearning for change which
swept Labour to power in 1945. In these circumstances Poale
Zion leaders were not the least bit afraid of criticism when they
asked Jews, as Jews, to vote Labour.[97] And Labour candidates
were not the least bit diffident in calling for the creation of a
Jewish Labour vote.[98] To what extent did the Labour party
capture the Jewish electorate in 1945? The parliamentary
evidence is misleading. Twenty-six Jewish Labour MPs were
returned, together with Piratin, the Communist, and Lipson,
the rebel Conservative. This was not only a record number of
Jewish MPs; it was the first occasion on which the Jewish lobby
in Parliament had been overwhelmingly socialist. Of 34 Jewish
Labour candidates only 8 had failed to secure election, whereas
all 5 Jewish official Conservatives had been defeated, and so
had all 16 Jewish Liberals[99]; in fact the 1945 election was the
first since emancipation at which no Jewish Liberals were
returned.

The evidence of the fate of parliamentary candidates,
therefore, points strongly to a massive turnabout in the
political preferences of British Jews. The Labour party had
clearly opened its arms wide to receive the sons of the immigrant generations of fifty years before, and many of the
Jewish MPs returned for Labour in 1945 were later to achieve
national reputations as political activists: Barnet Janner,
Harold Lever, Marcus Lipton, Ian Mikardo, Emanuel Shinwell, Lewis Silkin, Sydney Silverman, and Maurice Edel-
man being the most prominent among them. But in reality
the picture was not quite so straightforward as this parliamentary analysis might suggest. Only two of the Jewish Labour

MPs sat for constituencies with substantial Jewish electorates: Maurice Orbach at East Willesden and David Weitzman at Stoke Newington. By itself, therefore, the overwhelmingly socialist composition of the Jewish lobby could not be taken as evidence relating also to Anglo-Jewish voters. Moreover, as the *Jewish Chronicle* pointed out, the absence of Jewish Liberal and Conservative MPs was partly due to the fact that many Liberal and Conservative local associations had been 'averse' to the selection of Jewish candidates for fear of the electoral consequences.[100] The proportion of Jewish Labour MPs to all Jewish MPs (93 per cent) definitely did not reflect in any meaningful sense the proportion of Jewish support for Labour in the country as a whole.

On the other hand it is perfectly true that the vast majority of constituencies where Jews were to be found in large numbers (the two seats at Bethnal Green, the three in Hackney, two of the three in Stepney, the Stoke Newington seat, Hendon North, the two seats at Ilford, Central and North-East Leeds, North Salford, South Tottenham, the two Walthamstow seats, the two at Wembley, the two at Willesden, and Glasgow Gorbals) had all returned Labour MPs in 1945. This did not mean that all, or nearly all, Jews had voted Labour. There were a few constituencies, already heavily populated with Jews, which had been held by the Conservatives: Hendon South, Finchley, Leeds North, and Middleton and Prestwich. Significantly these were all marginal seats situated in the outer-suburban areas into which still more Jews were to move after the War.

What can be said is that in 1945 Labour had a chance to make itself the party to which Jews would naturally gravitate. But this, in turn, depended on two other factors: the policy of the party towards Palestine; and the nature of Anglo-Jewish society in the post-war era. Measured against these considerations the number of Jewish MPs in the Labour party really was irrelevant.

8. Return to the Right

The euphoria with which the Labour victory of 1945 was greeted in left-wing Jewish circles lasted barely four months. On 13 November 1945 Ernest Bevin, the new Foreign Secretary, shocked Anglo-Jewry by announcing that the Labour government would stand by the White Paper of 1939, and that future Jewish immigration into Palestine would therefore take place only with the consent of the Arabs.[1] So began the last and most unhappy phase of the British Mandate, which was to end two and a half years later with the rebirth of the Jewish state in blood and fire.[2] Given the choice between recognizing Jewish claims to statehood and placating the oil-rich rulers of the Islamic Middle East, the Labour government chose the latter course. In Britain, as in America, many Jews regarded (and still regard) Bevin as an anti-Semite; and the delay in the recognition of Israel (it was not recognized *de facto* by the United Kingdom until February 1949) seemed a quite gratuitous extra turn of the knife in the wound.[3]

To those at the very centre of the Zionist movement Bevin's policy came as a surprise but not a shock. During the war Weizmann himself had appreciated the need to use the weight of American Jewry against the implacable hostility of the British Foreign and Colonial Offices. In December 1944, at the time of the Labour party's conference resolution on Palestine, a leading British member of Poale Zion prophetically, but privately, warned the Zionist leadership in the Holy Land that the resolution was so much window-dressing, and that a future Labour government would never implement it.[4] But these misgivings were never communicated to the Anglo-Jewish electorate, certainly not in time for the June 1945 general election. The British Zionist Federation did a great deal of publicity work among the parliamentary candidates at that time; indeed a special conference was called for that purpose.[5] Yet the Federation seems to have been lulled by the satisfactory assurances given to it by Poale Zion, whose influence on successive Labour party conferences and Trade Union Congresses could not be denied.[6] Poale Zion membership now stood at about 1,300, and it boasted sixteen branches.[7] It had worked hard in support of Labour's election effort. Publicly its leaders gave not the slightest hint that Labour would not 'deliver the goods' on Palestine if and when elected to office; at East Willesden, for instance, Poale Zion members even campaigned against the outgoing Conservative MP, S. Hammersley, in spite of the fact that he was a well-known supporter of the Zionist cause.[8] And as late as October 1945 Ian Mikardo, speaking of the pledges the Labour party had given on Palestine, promised one Zionist meeting that the party leaders would not 'talk their way' out of them.[9]

But this is precisely what happened. For the mass of Anglo-Jewry anger and perplexity vied with each other as the dominant reaction. British Jews were asked to finance illegal activities in Palestine, to help purchase and smuggle arms, to smuggle refugees into the Holy Land, even to finance Jewish underground armies fighting against British troops. Many Jews gave generously to these causes without asking too many questions.[10] The Zionist Federation, and the Zionist-dominated Board of Deputies, quickly launched a constituency-by-constituency campaign against the Government's policy.[11] But the general election was now over. The Government had a comfortable majority. Few even of the Jewish Labour MPs were willing to step out of line. Maurice Orbach, newly elected at East Willesden, bluntly told a Zionist deputation that he would not vote against the Government.[12] In April 1946 only six Jewish Labour MPs, 'after desperate "lobbying" by the Poale Zion', could be persuaded to venture the slightest parliamentary opposition to Bevin's Palestine policy.[13] And at the Labour party conference, held in Bournemouth in June, Poale Zion itself was prevailed upon, at Bevin's own suggestion, to withdraw a resolution calling on the Government to fulfil its election pledges to the Jews.[14]

At grass-roots level, the helplessness of the Zionist movement in the face of Government intransigence led, inevitably, to a fundamental revision of Jewish attitudes towards the Labour party. Why had Labour turned against the idea of a Jewish State, and why had Labour Zionists been unable to do anything about it? Out of office it seemed Labour had been prepared to issue any number of blank cheques in order to gain Jewish votes; now the cheques had bounced, and the Jews, in the short run, were helpless. Although the threat of electoral reprisals against Labour could have been made, this weapon was not resorted to, at least officially.[15] One disincentive to militant action was undoubtedly the fact that the activities of Jewish underground fighters in Palestine led to widespread anti-Jewish riots throughout Britain. Mosley attempted a come-back.[16] The blowing-up of the King David Hotel in Jerusalem on 22 July 1946 lost Zionism many friends in the British Labour movement; a number of Labour MPs who had previously attempted to be 'even-handed' in their approach to the Palestine problem now openly supported Bevin's policy. Significantly, a proposal to outlaw anti-Semitism was rejected by the Labour party conference in 1946; a similar proposal in the House of Commons in 1948 failed to get past its first reading.[17] At the Board of Deputies in 1948 non-Zionist elements, led by Neville Laski, attempted to have Brodetsky removed as President; Brodetsky was also a member of the executive of the Jewish Agency for Palestine, and 'the continuation of this situation', Laski argued, 'is fraught with danger to the Anglo-Jewish Community'.[18] The motion was defeated easily, by 227 votes, but the re-emergence of anti-Semitism in Britain, so soon after the end of the war with Nazi Germany, clearly acted as a powerful argument against Zionists taking upon themselves a new political campaign against the Labour Government.

So, with a general election still some years away, Labour Zionists could do little beyond apologizing to Jewish audiences.[19] But it was widely admitted that a great rift had been created between Anglo-Jewry and the Labour party. Poale Zion made some attempts to repair the damage. In January 1950 a Labour delegation, led by Sam Watson, the Chairman of the Labour party, and Alice Bacon, MP, the Vice-Chairman, visited Israel under the auspices of Poale Zion and the Histadruth (the General Federation of Jewish Workers in Israel); at a reception given to the delegation on its return, Herbert Morrison was the guest of honour.[20] Two months later the Labour Government, at last, recognized Israel *de jure*.[21] But that, as observers were quick to point out, was only after a general election (23 February) in which Labour had seen its majority in the Commons slashed from 146 to just 5 seats.

Some Jewish Labour supporters hoped that, with Bevin's death (1951), and the State of Israel a fact of life, relations between the Labour party and British Jews could be restored to something like their former level; voters, after all, have notoriously short memories. But the Suez crisis of 1956 thwarted efforts at reconciliation, the more so because Labour was then out of office, and so could not plead the burdens of government in defence of its attitude in condemning the attacks (now known to have been co-ordinated) made upon Egypt by the British, French, and Israeli armed forces.

The Suez affair was a subject of great controversy within Britain at the time, and the passions it aroused have abated but little since then. The Conservative Government of Anthony Eden suffered defections because of it, and the Labour Opposition was roused to a frenzy of outrage made more intense still by the opportunity it provided for Hugh Gaitskell to unite the party in righteous indignation at (as he alleged) the flouting of world opinion by the Eden government.[22] But within Anglo-Jewry there was very little controversy, at least so far as Israel's part in the affair was concerned. To judge by the many Zionist and communal meetings held in October and November 1956 there was general unanimity that Israel was justified in attacking Egypt in order to bring to an end years of terrorist incursions across the Gaza Strip; the Israeli conquest of Sinai was a further source of pride and, if this had been facilitated to some extent by the Anglo-French intervention, so much the better.

The seventeen Jewish Labour MPs returned in the 1955 election were therefore expected to support Israel's position. This expectation was natural but most naïve. The MPs had never acted as a group, and they came from diverse social, cultural, and religious backgrounds; at least six had espoused the cause of Aneurin Bevan in the early 1950s and were, therefore, openly left wing.[23] In spite of discreet lobbying all seventeen obeyed the three-line whip and voted against the Government on 1 November 1956, and all but one behaved similarly a week later.[24] The exception was Emanuel Shinwell who, from the safety of Australia declared that 'Israel was right', and added 'I have the utmost contempt for those Jews, including

British M.P.s, who, though professed Zionists, claim to see in Israel's action an offence against international law. They ought to be ashamed.'[25]

Shinwell's strictures upon his fellow Jewish Labour MPs were widely reported in the British Press, and they had added force because Shinwell had also made it crystal clear that, in the first of the 'Suez' votes in the Commons, on 30 October, his abstention had been quite deliberate. That division, an un-expected one which took place a day before the Anglo-French attack, had not, however, carried a three-line whip. Seven Jewish Labour MPs had failed on that occasion to support their party in the division lobby. But, apart from Shinwell, only one made it clear at the time that his abstention was deliberate: Harold Lever, who sat for the Jewish constituency of Man-chester Cheetham.[26] Put another way, of the seventeen Jewish Labour MPs, only a handful showed the slightest inclination to support Israel rather than the party to which they belonged, and of the three who sat for constituencies where the Jewish vote was electorally important (Harold Lever, Maurice Orbach, and David Weitzman) only one, Harold Lever, could be con-sidered a 'rebel' against the party. The standard response of Jewish Labour MPs to criticism from the community was to state, quite properly no doubt, that in Parliament they repre-sented their constituents, not their co-religionists.[27]

Two of the MPs, however, had rough rides from the Jewish community, and one of these lived to regret his lack of sensi-tivity to Jewish aspirations. It so happened that at the time of the Suez affair Barnet Janner was President both of the Board of Deputies and of the Zionist Federation. He came under pre-dictable and heavy attack from Zionist groups for his failure to abstain in the two whipped divisions, and on 18 November 1956 the Deputies discussed his position. A large majority of those present expressed their full confidence in him as their president; in any case, any sanction against him would prob-ably have amounted to a breach of parliamentary privilege.[28] So Janner's leadership of Anglo-Jewry survived. But the affair did him little credit and his self-defence, in view of his past wooing of Jewish voters, seemed lame indeed.

Janner, now representing North-West Leicester, was not dependent upon Jewish voters. Maurice Orbach was. Orbach, a well-known figure in Anglo-Jewry, was General Secretary of the Trades Advisory Council, a body set up by the Board of Deputies in 1940 to remove causes of friction between Jews and non-Jews in commerce, trade, and industry; he was also a life-long Poale Zion member. But his East Willesden constituency, an area into which Jews had moved in large numbers during and after the Second World War, had become increasingly marginal.[29] Surprisingly, he had none the less thought fit to deliver a number of slaps in the face to his Jewish electors, perhaps in order to convince others in the party that he was not specially beholden to the Jewish vote. His support of the Attlee government in October 1945 has already been noted. At the end of 1954 he went on a mission to Cairo, ostensibly to try to save the lives of Jews who had been arrested for spying for Israel, but also to attempt a reconciliation between Israel and Egypt. On his return he was reported as saying 'Nasser was my brother', and although he subsequently denied this (Nasser later denounced him as a spy!) the recriminations against him in Jewish circles had the greater staying power.[30] His behaviour during the Suez crisis, when he had not even accidentally abstained, proved the last straw. Local Conservatives (including Jewish Conservatives) rightly guessed that Orbach had alienated sufficient Jewish voters to make the constituency vulnerable.[31] The issue of Orbach's 'disloyalty' was discreetly kept alive locally during the late 1950s, and at the general election of 1959 it was used to devastating effect against him. He lost the seat by over 2,000 votes and was out of Parliament until returned for the distinctly non-Jewish constituency of Stockport South, which he represented from 1964 until shortly before his death in 1979.[32]

At Suez, in fact, the special relationship between the Labour party and Anglo-Jewry, so carefully built up on both sides in the 1930s and early 1940s, was finally buried. Gaitskell, whose previous record had been that of a friend to Israel, and whose wife was Jewish, had likened Eden to a policeman whose policy had been 'to go in and help the burglar shoot the householder'.[33] The comparison of Israel with a burglar was not easily or quickly forgiven, and was naturally seized upon by the Conservative Press.[34] Poale Zion again moved quickly to try to paper over the cracks. It played a key role in the formation of the Labour Friends of Israel, an organization of Labour MPs and peers, whose inaugural meeting was held during the Labour party conference at Brighton in October 1957.[35] None the less it was obvious that Suez had given a unique opportunity to the Conservative party to rebuild its Jewish image.

Churchill's wartime leadership had done little by itself to endear the Conservative party to Jewish voters, certainly not at constituency level. A major stumbling block was the antipathy of many constituency Conservative Associations to Jews in general and Jewish candidates in particular. The presence of Daniel Lipson in the Commons from 1945 to 1950 was a constant reminder of this, but there were others. During the 1945 election campaign some Conservative candidates had made no secret of their desire to see Jewish refugees from Nazi persecution returned 'to their own countries'.[36] Sir Thomas Moore, Conservative MP for Ayr, 1925-64, was well remembered as an adherent of the pre-war Anglo-German Fellowship and as a public admirer, in 1934, of the British Union of Fascists.[37] In 1948 Commander F. Ashe Lincoln, KC, who had unsuccessfully fought Harrow East in 1945 as a Conservative, was passed over for readoption, and it was publicly stated by one local party member that the Commander had been prevailed upon to withdraw because of 'anti-Semitic feeling'.[38] In 1950 the Conservative party's Standing Advisory Committee on Candidates took the extreme step of vetoing the choice of the Chorley Conservative Association on the grounds that the candidate adopted, Andrew Fountaine, was an outspoken anti-Semite.[39] Throughout the 1950s, indeed, it was well known, and freely admitted by Conservative Central Office, that there was considerable anti-Jewish prejudice in some local Associations.[40]

Though some Jews were adopted as Conservative candidates they were not chosen for safe or winnable seats. An official Conservative MP who was Jewish did not reappear at Westminster till 1955, when Sir Henry d'Avigdor Goldsmid was elected for Walsall South. He was soon joined by Sir Keith Joseph, who had been unsuccessful at Barons Court at the general election but victorious at the Leeds North-East by-election in February 1956. Sir Henry was a highly successful banker and bullion-broker and (in keeping with family tradition) a member of the Reform synagogue; Sir Keith was a lawyer, a Fellow of All Souls College, Oxford, and (again in keeping with family tradition) a member of the Liberal synagogue in St. John's Wood.[41] Both had been educated at Harrow and Oxford and both were baronets. Sir Keith quickly rose to ministerial office, was Secretary of State for Social Services under Edward Heath, 1970-4, and was appointed Industry Secretary in Mrs Thatcher's Government which was elected in May 1979. Sir Henry (who died in December 1976) never attained ministerial office, but was widely regarded as one of the ablest of back-benchers, with an unrivalled grasp of public finance; he involved himself in a wide range of Jewish communal activities, was Chairman of the Anglo-Israel Bank and a governor of the Hebrew University in Jerusalem, and earned praise from all sections of Anglo-Jewry for a masterly speech against a bill to ban *shechita*, introduced in 1956 by his fellow Conservative MP, Robert Crouch.

Until 1970 Sir Henry and Sir Keith remained the only Jewish Conservatives in the House of Commons. Walsall South was not a Jewish constituency but Leeds North-East had a large, though not crucially large, Jewish electorate. Sir Keith could have played for the Jewish vote there, but did not do so. He did not owe his election to Jewish votes and, indeed, though he supported his party's line over Suez, he was rumoured to have expressed reservations about it.[42] Elsewhere, however, in the late 1950s, the Jewish vote became an object of renewed interest among Conservative activists.

The reason was plain to anyone who had kept an eye on patterns of Anglo-Jewish mobility after 1945. The Jewish population of the United Kingdom rose to a peak of around 450,000 in 1950.[43] Since then it has been declining, through emigration (mainly but not only to Israel) and complete assimilation, and in the mid-1960s stood at about 410,000.[44] Today, at the threshold of the 1980s, it is certainly lower still.[45] At the same time over half Anglo-Jewry continues to live (as it has always done) in the London area; in 1970 the proportion was about 68 per cent, or 280,000.[46] Of those Jews who did not live in London in 1970 nearly three-quarters (i.e. over 94,000) were to be found living in Manchester, Leeds, Glasgow, Liverpool, Brighton, Birmingham, and Southend.[47]

So in the quarter-century since the end of the Second World

War the many small provincial Jewish communities of Victorian England fast disappeared, and Anglo-Jewry concentrated itself in a limited number of urban centres. But within
these urban centres, and pre-eminently within the Greater
London area, the Jews moved out of the (often badly war-
damaged) original semi-ghetto areas of settlement, into the
suburbs. Thus the East End of London, which at one time
accounted for two-thirds of London Jewry, now contains less
than a quarter, while the outer London area accounts for nearly
60 per cent. More specifically, the four north-western London
boroughs of Barnet, Brent, Camden, and Harrow account for
an estimated Jewish population of about 107,000 (i.e. over a
quarter of Anglo-Jewry), with another 29,300 living in the
borough of Redbridge, in the north-east.[48] The pattern has
been repeated, albeit on a lesser scale, in other cities. In Leeds
Jews have moved out of the Leylands and Chapeltown into the
newer suburban districts of Moortown and Alwoodley, and
even further afield.[49] In Manchester the suburbs of Crumpsall
and Cheetham Hill, to the north of the city centre, now account
for 15 per cent of Greater Manchester's 35,000 Jews; the district
of Prestwich, in the north-west, contains another 10,500.[50]

The Second World War did of course play its part in this process. But war-time destruction of city centres merely hastened
a trend which was already under way before 1939; in London
many of the synagogues which by 1960 had become those with
the highest membership figures (Golders Green, Edgware,
Hendon, Finchley, Ilford) had in fact been established before
the War, and they provided the framework for ready-made
communities to receive war-time and post-war evacuees.[51]
Jews became more prosperous and naturally wished to climb
further up the social ladder and escape their ghetto antecedents;
just as social emancipation had followed political emancipation,
so economic progress was the prelude to environmental escape.
Professor Ernest Krausz, in his investigation of the Jewish
community of Edgware (part of the Hendon North constituency), has provided some fascinating insights into this process.
Edgware Jewry in the early 1960s was thoroughly working class
in origin, and 53 per cent of Professor Krausz's sample had in
fact been born in London's East End. Yet over 80 per cent
regarded themselves as belonging to the middle class, and only

just over 8 per cent said they belonged to the working class.[52] From the point of view of occupation, moreover, Jewish men in Edgware were to be found predominantly in the professional, managerial, skilled, and self-employed groups of workers, which was the exact opposite of the picture for the general population of the district.[53]

The analysis provided by Professor Krausz has been confirmed by the estimates prepared by Professor S. Prais and Mrs Marlena Schmool of the social-class structure of Anglo-Jewry in 1961:

TABLE I
Estimated Social-Class Distribution of the Live Jewish Population (1961)

Social Class	Population Distributions (Percentage)	
	Jews	General
I Professional	10	4
II Intermediate	34	15
III Skilled	36	49
IV Partly Skilled	10	19
V Unskilled	-	8
Other	8	5

Source: S. J. Prais and M. Schmool, 'The Social-Class Structure of Anglo-Jewry', 1961, *Jewish Journal of Sociology*, xvii (1975), 11.

Here the tendency for British Jews to be found in the higher social classes is very evident. In 1961 over 40 per cent of Anglo-Jewry was located in the upper two social classes, whereas these categories accounted for less than 20 per cent of the general population. The electoral consequences of this trend become clear when it is remembered that, at the time of the 1964 general election which Labour won, three-quarters of the top two social classes supported the Conservative party.[54]

In short, in many of the new parliamentary constituencies in outer London which were created by the Redistribution Acts of 1944 and 1948 (especially Harrow East, Hendon North, Hendon South, Ilford North, Ilford South, Wembley North, and Wanstead and Woodford) and which either became safe Conservative seats or marginals which the Conservatives had an

even chance of winning, Jewish voters were to be found in
increasing numbers during the 1950s. Using the criteria of
class origin and parental background these ought to have been
reliable Labour supporters. But upward social mobility had
weakened their loyalty to Labour, and the behaviour of the
Labour party towards the Palestine problem had in many cases
wrecked it. The Conservatives were placed on the horns of a
dilemma. Ought these voters to be left to drift towards Conservatism in their own good time, or was there some special message, some peculiarly Jewish message, which could be sent out
to them to speed them on? Could the Conservative party, with
its recent history of antipathy towards Jews, afford to send out
such a Jewish message and yet retain its credibility?

At national level the Conservative party decided not to play
the Jewish card. Conservative Central Office did not like obvious and public manifestations of anti-Semitism from constituency parties and genuinely did what it could, as at Chorley,
to stamp out prejudice. But interference with the autonomy of
local parties was never undertaken lightly, and was therefore
reserved only for the most extraordinary situations. In general
local Conservative Associations were left to come to terms with
the Jews as and when they thought fit. As for a specific appeal
to Jewish voters, the calculation seems to have been that any
such appeal, and particularly any promise, would only be a
hostage to fortune, at best embarrassing and at worst a mill-
stone round the neck of a Conservative government. Those
who led the Conservative party at the time of Suez were not
friends of Israel, and the mood in the party as a whole, if it was
anti-Egyptian, was certainly not pro-Israeli. Conservative
Government and back-bench spokesmen alike were very careful to stress this point.[55]

In any case, during the 1950s the party did not need the
Jewish vote. The extensive boundary alterations of 1948 make it
impossible now to quantify the impact which Bevin's Palestine
policy had on Jewish support for Labour at the 1950 general
election compared with 1945. But the profound disenchant-
ment (to put it no higher) with which Jewish voters viewed the
Labour party was there for all to see, to say nothing of the
socio-economic and demographic changes already affecting
Anglo-Jewry. The defeat of the staunchly orthodox and much

respected Jewish communal leader Dr Homa, who had stood as
Labour candidate in Hendon South in 1951 and 1955, seemed
to indicate that the new affluent Jewish suburbanites (the constituency included the Golders Green and Hendon synagogues)
would enter the Conservative camp of their own accord and
without prompting. Furthermore, now that Israel was an accomplished fact the Jewish upper middle classes made their
peace with the Zionist movement, a reconciliation made easier
by the fact that, for most British Jews, political or practical
Zionism was rapidly replaced by cheque-book Zionism. The
Anglo-Jewish Association proclaimed a new policy of 'unqualified good will' towards the Jewish State.[56] To be a Zionist was
no longer unpatriotic; on the contrary, to be a Zionist and a
Conservative was becoming perfectly natural. And what was
particularly pleasing from the Conservative party's point of
view was the way in which Jewish businessmen, many of them
from working-class backgrounds, now gave their support to the
Conservative cause.[57]

So, with the Conservative party going from strength to
strength at successive general elections in the 1950s there really
did not seem to be any special need to woo Jewish voters. But
as the Government of Harold Macmillan began to run into
deep economic and political trouble in the summer of 1961 the
opinion polls showed, for the first time in over two years, a
Labour lead over the Conservatives. This lead the Conservatives were unable fully to reverse, and they were eventually
voted out of office—albeit narrowly—in the general election of
October 1964. In these difficult circumstances for the party the
possibilities of the Jewish vote were re-examined. Again,
nationally the party was silent. But locally groups of Jewish
members of the Conservative party were encouraged to can-
vass their co-religionists and, almost imperceptibly, the anti-
Egyptian stand of the Eden government in 1956 was presented
as unswerving support for Israel.

The private papers of Samuel Landman (1884-1967), now
deposited in the Central Zionist Archives in Jerusalem, contain
a great deal of documentary evidence relating to this process in
the East Willesden constituency, the scene of Maurice Orbach's
defeat in 1959. Landman, brother-in-law of Sir Leon Simon,
and at one time Secretary of the World Zionist Organization's

London Bureau and later a follower of Jabotinsky, lived in the
constituency and had helped bring about the Conservative
victory there.[58] The newly elected Conservative MP, Trevor
Skeet, proved a good friend to Jewish interests; on 1 August
1962, for instance, he and Tom Iremonger, Conservative MP
for Ilford North, introduced a bill to amend the 1936 Public
Order Act, following the Nazi rally in Trafalgar Square the
previous July. But Landman's major interest, set out in a
memorandum (headed 'Attracting Jewish Votes at the next
General Election') which he sent to Conservative Central Office
in November 1962, was 'to enrol British Jews into the ranks of
the Conservative Party and to popularise Conservative principles among Jewish voters in preparation for the General Election'.[59] In 1961 Landman had appeared at the Conservative
party conference at Brighton 'as a representative of Conservative Jewish Zionists'.[60] In January 1962, with 'the whole-
hearted support' of Mr Skeet, Landman formed 'The East
Willesden Conservative Zionist Association'.[61] His eventual
aim was to establish a network of such associations and, from
them, promote a National Association of Conservative Zionists.

In Willesden itself the idea earned much praise.[62] It also enjoyed the support of Zionist bodies. Landman's Association
received, by his own admission, fifty dollars a month from an
unspecified source in New York and about one hundred
pounds a year from the Jewish Agency in London.[63] By the end
of July 1962 Landman felt able to advise Trevor Skeet 'that
steps should be taken now to strengthen your position at the
elections and that your efforts in connection with the Trafalgar
Square rally [the Nazi rally which Skeet had tried to have
banned] provided an excellent starting point'; Landman
suggested that the next step should be an approach to prominent speakers, such as the Conservative peer Lord Mancroft,
then a director of Great Universal Stores Ltd., and Sir Henry
d'Avigdor Goldsmid. 'All these letters and initiatives', Landman told Skeet, would be 'to your advantage among your
Jewish voters at the election, and that is what I have in mind.'[64]

But it was precisely at this point, when the Willesden venture
looked as if it just might expand into something bigger, as
Landman hoped, that the Jewish grandees in the Conservative

party decided to veto the project. On 1 October 1962 Lord Mancroft wrote to Landman as follows:

I have thought this matter over again very carefully and I have also now had an opportunity of discussing it with my Chairman [of Great Universal Stores], Sir Isaac Wolfson, and with two or three ... Jewish members of our organisation who are ... supporters of the Conservative party.

They are all, to put it mildly, a little uneasy about this ... they feel that there is a serious risk of the problem of a Jewish vote raising its ugly head if too blatant a connection is made between the Zionists and Conservatives in a place like Willesden.[65]

What was meant by 'the problem of a Jewish vote raising its ugly head'? In a letter to me, Lord Mancroft has explained that, in his view, 'If you have a "Jewish Vote", there will be many who feel that Jews should only be heard on Jewish affairs & [*sic*] should keep silent when Ships or Shoes or Sealing-wax are under discussion. I believe that a Jewish vote is an aid to anti-Semitism.'[66]

And it may indeed have been that, in the charged atmosphere of 1962, it was felt better that Landman's plan should be put on one side, at least for the present. 1962 was not a good year for Anglo-Jewry, and it was a particularly bad year for Jewish Conservatives. In March the Government had lost the Orpington by-election to the Liberals; Peter Goldman, the Conservative candidate, was a Jewish convert to Christianity, and it was subsequently alleged in some quarters that this fact had contributed to his defeat.[67] The continued immigration of coloured workers, mainly from the West Indies, had given new life to a tiny but vocal group of British Nazis whose Trafalgar Square meeting held in July the Conservative Government had refused to ban. Instead, the response of the Government was to bring in the 1962 Commonwealth Immigrants Act.

In Jewish Conservative circles, therefore, the idea of promoting, just at that time, a nation-wide electoral machine to pull in Jewish votes for the party did not sound such a good idea. Landman was *not* told to cease his efforts locally. Indeed, Lord Mancroft had assured him that 'I will certainly honour my promise to you to try and do as much as I can *behind the scenes* by way of speakers and general propaganda *privately* to help your cause.'[68] The message to the veteran English Zionist seems to have been that publicly the Conservative party would not allow itself to be identified with his efforts and that, for their part, moneyed Jewish Conservatives would not support him to any great extent, but that privately he would receive some help and encouragement and that, provided these conditions were understood, his local initiative to win votes for the party would be welcomed.

In the event, Landman's efforts did not prevent East Willesden from being recaptured by Labour in October 1964.[69] At about that time the East Willesden Conservative Zionist Association appears to have been wound up. Yet the pattern set by the Conservative and Jewish-Conservative response to events in East Willesden has remained, to be followed again whenever it has seemed advantageous; that is, nationally the Conservative party has no policy on the Jewish vote one way or the other (though it is careful, like other parties, to keep well-known Arab apologists away from Jewish audiences), but if local candidates or MPs wish to make a bid for the Jewish vote, or if local Jewish Conservatives wish to help the party in this way, they are free to do so.

Conservative MPs who sit for constituencies with sizeable Jewish electorates know, moreover, that they will be expected to behave in certain ways on certain issues, and those in marginal seats may suffer if this expected behaviour is not forthcoming. Thus of the sixteen Conservative MPs who defied a two-line whip and voted against the Conservative Government's embargo on arms shipments to Israel during the Yom Kippur war (18 October 1973), no less than six sat for marginal seats where the Jewish vote mattered to a greater or lesser extent.[70] Only two of the nine Jewish Conservative MPs returned in 1970 voted with the Government.[71] And two non-Jewish Conservative MPs, A. E. Cooper at Ilford South and A. G. B. Haselhurst at Middleton and Prestwich, who only abstained in this division, both lost their seats in the general election of February 1974 in circumstances which strongly suggest that Jewish voters took revenge upon them in the polling-booths.[72]

The February 1974 general election projected the Jewish

vote into the newspaper headlines with a force which smothered all attempts by the Board of Deputies to argue that a Jewish vote did not exist. The renewal of armed conflict in the Middle East four months previously was itself a sufficient guarantee that Jewish voters would be looking more carefully than usual at the credentials of the parliamentary candidates. The Zionist Federation had issued a list (*Why did they ignore Israel?*) of every MP who abstained or voted with the Government on 18 October 1973. The list was given wide publicity and a covering letter, from Public Relations Committee chairman Eric Moonman, urged that MPs whose names were on the list be contacted to account for their behaviour. 'If your MP voted for the Alec Douglas-Home line', Moonman advised, 'you should also add that his action has considerably distressed a number of his constituents ... a so-called even-handed policy will always harm Israel.' 'We are', the letter ended, 'making a precise record of parliamentary voting and attitudes.'

Although carefully phrased in non-party-political language, the Zionist Federation's letter, and the campaign it inaugurated, was bound to affect Conservative MPs more than others. Almost at once the campaign had been put to the test. The occasion was the Hove by-election, held on 8 November 1973. Hove had been held by the Conservative in 1970 with a majority of over 18,000. The Jewish electorate was said to be around 5,000, mostly Conservative. Normally, therefore, the Jewish vote in Hove would not have been crucial for a Conservative candidate. But in the autumn of 1973 Conservative fortunes were at a low ebb and the Liberals were in the ascendant. It was evident that the Liberal challenge at Hove was going to be a strong one, and all three main parties recognized that the Jewish vote was bound to figure as an important element in the contest.[73] Local Conservatives attempted to attack the Liberal candidate, Des Wilson, by referring to the pro-Arab sympathies of some sections of the Young Liberals. Jewish Liberals retaliated by producing statements in support of Israel made by Liberal leader Jeremy Thorpe. The local Jewish leadership, apparently in an effort to 'defuse' the situation, and play down the role of the Jewish vote, sent a deputation to the main candidates to find out just what they thought about the Middle East.[74] On polling day the Conservative candidate, Tim Sainsbury

(who had written to Alec Douglas-Home asking that the arms
embargo be lifted) scraped home with a majority of 4,846 over
Des Wilson, in second place.

No one can be sure what part the Jewish vote actually played
in this drama. Chaim Raphael, of Sussex University, believed
that the Jews, convinced by the assurances of support for
Israel which they received from Tim Sainsbury, returned to the
Conservative fold.[75] Perhaps they did. The importance of
Hove, however, lay in the fact that it demonstrated that there
was a Jewish vote to be fought for and, even more importantly,
that candidates of the major parties believed the Jewish vote
was *worth* fighting for. The increasingly marginal political
situation in the United Kingdom at that time, resulting in the
stalemate general election of February 1974, meant, inevitably, that Jewish voters would be assiduously cultivated at
the hustings. At Ilford North Tom Iremonger campaigned
vigorously among his Jewish electors, both on the issue of
Israel and on that of Soviet Jewry, and indulged in some forthright advertising in the *Redbridge Extra*, a locally distributed
supplement of the *Jewish Chronicle*.[76] Thus, in a seat made
highly marginal by boundary changes, Iremonger was able to
hold off (until the general election of October 1974) a very
strong challenge from Jewish Labour candidate Mrs Milly
Miller.

But the most remarkable example of attention to Jewish
voters was provided at Hendon North, where Jews accounted
for 15,000 of the constituency's 50,000 electors. John Gorst,
the Conservative MP first elected there in 1970, had then had a
majority of 3,179. John Gorst is not Jewish, but had kept in-
close touch with his Jewish constituents, and voted against the
Government's arms embargo in October 1973. When the
February 1974 election was announced he pulled off a local *coup*
by obtaining the public support of the Reverend Saul Amias, the
outspoken and extrovert minister of the Edgware United Synagogue, a self-confessed socialist and former Aldermaston mar-
cher. Reverend Amias announced in the local press that he was
not merely going to vote for Gorst on polling day; he had agreed
to sign Gorst's nomination papers.[77]

So the Middle East became an issue—perhaps, given the
marginality of the seat, *the* issue, in the Hendon North con-

test.[78] In a poll which I carried out in the constituency at that time, involving a sample of 150 Jewish voters, nearly 16 per cent of those who had not voted Conservative in 1970 indicated that they would now do so because of John Gorst's anti-Government stand on the Middle East.[79] And when the votes were counted Gorst retained his seat with his majority only slightly reduced to 2,612, though he had predicted for himself a majority of 1,350. The boundary revisions brought into effect in February 1974 make any direct comparison with the previous general election particularly difficult. But the authors of the February 1974 Nuffield election study were able to do this, in many cases, by recalculating the 1970 results within the new boundaries. Their figures show that the swing against John Gorst in February 1974 was only 1.1 per cent, whereas the anti-Conservative swing in Greater London as a whole was 2.2 per cent. In Finchley, where Margaret Thatcher (who, as a member of the Government, had supported the October 1973 arms embargo) had come under heavy pressure from Jewish voters, the anti-Conservative swing was 3.2 per cent, and at Leeds North-East Sir Keith Joseph, another Government minister, suffered a swing against him of 6.1 per cent compared with a 1.7 per cent swing against the Conservatives throughout that city.[80]

Jewish support was therefore a crucial element in John Gorst's February victory; without it he would have had considerable difficulty in retaining his seat. But in the second general election of 1974 in the following October Jewish support was absolutely vital. At that election, in which Reverend Amias spoke in support of Gorst from the pulpit on the sabbath before polling[81], the proportion of Jewish voters declaring a definite intention of supporting Gorst actually rose from 59.1 per cent to 68.3 per cent.[82] Although Gorst's majority was reduced to 1,750, the swing against him was only 0.8 per cent, the lowest anti-Conservative swing in any of the constituencies in the borough of Barnet and, again, lower than the swing against the Conservatives in Greater London as a whole (1.9 per cent).

So it was that in the mid-1970s, as a result of economic, social, and demographic changes within Anglo-Jewry, and of alterations in parliamentary constituency boundaries, several

MPs, mostly Conservative, became prisoners of their Jewish voters: John Gorst at Hendon North; Geoffrey Finsberg at Hampstead; Tom Iremonger and Milly Miller (Labour) at Ilford North; Tim Sainsbury at Hove; J. Callaghan (Labour) at Middleton and Prestwich; and, most intriguing of all, Margaret Thatcher at Finchley. In October 1974 Mrs Thatcher retained her seat with a majority reduced to 3,911; she was elected Conservative leader in February 1975, so becoming the first major party leader to sit for a constituency where the Jewish vote (then roughly 8,700, or 16 per cent of the electorate) was crucial.[83]

This unique circumstance did not of itself alter the general approach of the Conservative party towards Jewish voters; as before, the matter was left primarily to the discretion of local constituency Associations. But the political impasse resulting from the two general elections of 1974 (the Labour Government's three-seat overall majority, gained in October 1974, virtually disappeared when Labour lost the West Woolwich by-election the following June) seems to have concentrated the minds of the party leaders on winning seats by appealing to local and sectional as well as national interests. As far as the Jews were concerned, there was a feeling within the Conservative party that the comfortable relationship built up with suburban Jewish communities over the past two decades had been, perhaps unavoidably, damaged by the policy of Edward Heath and Foreign Secretary Alec Douglas-Home during the Yom Kippur war, and that it was expedient that the relationship be repaired.

The repair took several forms. Mrs Thatcher, as party leader, continued to accept invitations to speak to Jewish audiences in her constituency, but her carefully phrased remarks, especially about Israel, had added force and authority, and they were of course widely reported in the local and the Jewish press, as they were doubtless intended to be. At the end of November 1975, for instance, Mrs Thatcher was guest of honour at the annual dinner of the Finchley and Hampstead Garden Suburb branch of the Association of Jewish Ex-Servicemen and Women. She used this opportunity to deny publicly that there had been any change in Conservative policy on the Middle East, following a parliamentary statement by

Reginald Maudling (then chief Conservative spokesman on foreign affairs) in which he had stated that the party favoured a separate Palestinian country and that the Palestine Liberation Organization should be recognized as the official mouthpiece of the Palestinian Arabs. Maudling's statement had angered Anglo-Jewry in general and Finchley Jewry in particular; at the ex-servicemen's dinner one speaker bluntly reminded the Conservative leader of her dependence upon Jewish votes.[84] On a subsequent visit to Syria, in January 1976, Mrs Thatcher went out of her way to attack the Palestine Liberation Organization for its terrorist activities.[85]

At the parliamentary level the 'Conservative Friends of Israel' was formed at the end of 1974 by Michael Fidler who had been President of the Board of Deputies from 1967 to 1973 and Conservative MP for Bury and Radcliffe from 1970 to October 1974. The aim of the group was to enlist the support of Conservative MPs and peers in the cause of the Jewish State, and to demonstrate the strength of support for Israel within the party. Michael Fidler became its Director, the first President was the Duke of Devonshire, and Lord Avon (formerly Sir Anthony Eden) consented to act as Patron.[86] Mrs Thatcher was an early adherent of this new Conservative group.

In the spring of 1978, however, a situation arose which demanded much more than polite words or parliamentary window-displays. The untimely death of Milly Miller in October 1977 created a by-election at Ilford North, and the Conservatives were determined to win it back. With the tide of public opinion running strongly in the Conservatives' favour this might have seemed almost a foregone conclusion. But the situation was not straightforward. Although Mrs Miller had snatched the seat from Tom Iremonger in October 1974 by a mere 778 votes, the Conservative poll (19,843 votes) had been exactly as in the previous February. It was true that, between February and October, the Liberal vote had dropped by a third; but Labour party workers felt, and local Conservatives agreed, that because of her Jewish identity and commitment, Mrs Miller had brought to her side several hundred Jewish voters who might otherwise have abstained, and that it was this which had brought her victory.[87] Labour's candidate for the by-election, Mrs Tessa Jowell, was not Jewish. But Tom Iremonger had fallen out with the local Conservative Association, which did not readopt him but chose instead Vivian Bendall, a thirty-nine-year-old surveyor and valuer. Iremonger announced that he would contest the seat as an Independent Conservative; his personal standing, especially among Jewish voters, was high, and there was no telling how deeply he would cut into the Conservative vote. And, as if to make matters worse for the Conservatives, the National Front announced that they too would be contesting the seat.

Both Labour and Conservative parties saw the Jewish vote as crucial, as it had been in the previous general election. Mrs Jowell announced at the end of January 1978 that she had become a member of the Labour Friends of Israel.[88] Mr Iremonger alleged that one reason why he had not been readopted was his vote against the Heath Government in October 1973.[89] But the campaign was heavy with racial tension. In a television interview in January Mrs Thatcher had warned that Britain might become 'swamped' by peoples who lacked 'fundamental British characteristics', unless immigration laws were tightened. Then the National Front descended on the constituency (where coloured immigrants formed only 3 per cent of the population) and a march by them, planned for 25 February, was banned by the Metropolitan Police Commissioner. Five days previously Sir Keith Joseph, then a senior member of the Conservative Shadow Cabinet, had come to Ilford North to deliver a remarkable speech:

> There is a limit to the number of people from different cultures that this country can digest. We ignore this at our peril, everyone's peril. Therefore I say that the electors of Ilford North, including the Jews—who are just like everyone else, as the saying goes, only more so—have good reason for supporting Margaret Thatcher and the Conservative Party on immigration.[90]

This attempt to enlist the support of the constituency's 6,000 or so Jewish voters[91] was applauded by the Conservative party, especially by Jewish Conservatives[92], but condemned by many others within Anglo-Jewry, from the President of the Board of Deputies downwards, on two counts: firstly, that, since all British Jews are, or are descended from, immigrants, it was unethical—even immoral, for a Jew to support immigration control, or at least tighter immigration control; and secondly, that Sir Keith was trying to activate the Jewish vote, perhaps even to create a Jewish vote, in the Conservative interest.[93] 'To appeal to Jewish electors to vote, as Jews, for the vague Conservative proposals for stricter immigration control, as Sir Keith has incautiously done,' the *Jewish Chronicle* warned, 'goes against the whole tradition of independent Jewish citizenship in Britain.'[94]

But in fact, for better or worse, Mrs Thatcher had correctly judged the mood of the country and Sir Keith had correctly judged the mood of the Jewish electors of Ilford. A poll conducted by Independent Television News at Ilford North showed that almost half of those voters who switched from Labour to Conservative were influenced by the immigration question.[95] During the 1970s Jewish voters had become increasingly alarmed at the spectacle of a renewed growth of racist and Nazi parties in Britain, feeding on the prejudice of the host population towards New Commonwealth immigrants. Mrs Thatcher's policy on this question seemed to offer the best hope of containing both the immigrants and the National Front; Sir Keith's speech had indeed touched a raw nerve.[96] Yet the response was the one he had hoped for. The Conservatives won back Ilford North on a swing of 6.9 per cent, but among Jewish voters there the swing to the Conservatives was a massive 11.2 per cent.[97]

Controversy over the rectitude of Sir Keith's intervention still continues within the Jewish community. Curiously, however, in spite of all the newspaper comment, within and beyond Anglo-Jewry, which his speech provoked, its historical significance was universally ignored by the pundits. It was the first time, in over fifty years, that a leading Conservative politician, more or less officially, had appealed to Jewish voters to support the party on a major policy issue and had secured a positive response.

9. Present Perspectives

The suggestion that there might be 'a Jewish vote' in Great Britain is one which has always been officially discounted by the Board of Deputies of British Jews and by other leading opinion-makers in Anglo-Jewry. 'The whole idea of Jewish political emancipation was based on equality between Jews and other citizens', a *Jewish Chronicle* correspondent wrote in 1951, 'to establish a Jewish vote would mean to reverse that principle, to the service of which the first generation of Jewish MPs devoted all their talents.'[1] On the face of it the argument here—and it is one which has recurred throughout Anglo-Jewish history over the past hundred or so years—is that the organization of provocation, however unintentional, of a bloc vote of the Jewish electors in this country would confer or (just as bad) appear to confer upon them a political influence, or leverage, which the Gentile citizens are supposed not to possess; this in turn, it is argued, would generate a backlash against Anglo-Jewry and would thus be counter-productive.

Since the re-establishment of the Jewish State a further strand has been added to this argument. It arises from the charge often made by anti-Zionists, that British Jews have a 'dual loyalty'. In 1969 Mr Michael Adams, director of the Council for the Advancement of Arab-British Understanding, was reported as having questioned the loyalty of Anglo-Jewry.[2] In December 1972 during a Commons debate on the Middle East the Arab apologist and Labour MP Andrew Faulds declared: 'It is time some of our colleagues on both sides of the House forgot their dual loyalty and another Parliament. They are representatives here and not in the Knesset ... it is undeniable', he continued, 'that many MPs have what I can only term a dual loyalty, which is to another nation and another nation's interests.'[3] Two years later the 'Committee for Justice in the Middle East' inserted a whole-page advertisement in *The Times*: 'Every year', the advertisement alleged, 'millions of pounds of untaxed money under the charities act end up in Israel to support the Zionist movement ... Shouldn't British Money Remain in Britain; to Build more homes, to Improve Social Services, to Help Pensioners?'[4]

The implication behind such remarks as these, that British Jews somehow lack patriotism because of their commitment to Israel, is one which of course is strongly resented. But the charge becomes harder to rebut when organizations or individuals (by no means only Jewish organizations or individuals) try to persuade Jewish voters to cast their votes in terms of their loyalty to Israel.[5] Should such appeals meet with even partial success, as they have done from time to time, the accusation of 'dual loyalty' would seem to have been justified. It was perhaps not entirely coincidental that, on the occasion of the first British general election after the end of the Palestine Mandate, the *Jewish Chronicle* declared, in a leading article brimming with self-righteousness, that British Jews would 'cast their votes as individuals, and will support the Party of their choice, not on the basis of communal interest, but in accordance with their view of the great issues and policies affecting Britain's well-being'.[6] A week later the paper announced that in future no election advertisements 'of any kind' would be accepted for publication'; this decision, it explained, was in 'the best interests' of the community.[7]

At subsequent general elections the same disapprobation of any suggestion that there might be a recognizable Jewish vote in Great Britain has been very evident.[8] On the eve of the February 1974 poll the Board of Deputies advised communal leaders to tell inquirers that 'to all intents and purposes, a "Jewish Vote" does not exist in this country'. Sir Keith Joseph's intervention in the Ilford North by-election, which was described in Chapter 8, above, was condemned partly because it attempted to 'whip up' a Jewish vote. Geoffrey Paul, the present editor of the *Jewish Chronicle*, argued at the time that 'There is no such thing in Britain as a Jewish vote and it will be a wretched day if ever one emerges.'[9] Lord Fisher of Camden, then President of the Board of Deputies, wrote: 'Sir Keith's outburst is not helpful and I say again, and so do all my colleagues—and so does the Jewish community—that there is *no* "Jewish vote" as such. To continue to suggest this is not true and only gives comfort to our detractors.'[10]

Even more damning was the pronouncement of Maurice Unterman, rabbi of the prestigious Marble Arch synagogue, who condemned the invocation of 'an Anglo-Jewish vote' as the fabrication of 'an unwholesome façade' and the postulation of 'a

libellous fallacy'.[11] And when, a year later, Geoffrey Paul inaugurated a new policy on the acceptance of advertisements for
the 1979 general, municipal, and European Parliament elections, the following conditions were laid down:

1. The advertising must be of the same general nature as is likely to
   appear in the National Press and must make no specific appeal to
   Jews nor deal with what may reasonably be regarded as special
   Jewish interests.
2. The advertising must not refer to particular candidates or individuals.
3. The other political parties should be informed when an advertisement is accepted from any political party, giving them the opportunity of taking similar spaces.
4. The advertiser must be a legal political party.[12]

Here, therefore, the premier newspaper catering for Anglo-
Jewry specifically forbids political parties from addressing
themselves, through its pages, to 'what may reasonably be
regarded' as the special interests of the community; yet these
special interests are presumably those with which the *Jewish
Chronicle* concerns itself every week of the year. Such reactions
do indeed smack of 'protesting too much'. They ignore historical
and political realities, and they fly in the face of human nature.
But the fact that they continue to be displayed shows how strong
the vision remains, at least in the top echelons of Anglo-Jewry, of
a community totally integrated with the existing political structure and politically indistinguishable within it.

There is some circumstantial evidence to justify such a stand-
point. The three major parties can all boast 'Friends of Israel'
offshoots. There is no political party of any importance in Great
Britain which does not admit Jews as members. The general
election of February 1974 saw a record number of Jewish MPs
returned (46), including, for the first time since 1935, a Jewish
Liberal MP.[13] The number of Jewish Conservative MPs has also
reached record levels (12 in February 1974, and 11 in 1979).
There are Jewish members of Plaid Cymru[14], the Scottish
National Party[15], and even of the National Front.[16]

It is also true, and has always been true, that however impres-
sive the number of Jewish MPs may appear on paper, the Jewish
lobby in Parliament is much less monolithic in reality. Among

Jewish Labour MPs of recent years are to be found some who take little or no part in promoting Israel's cause at Westminster, others who are contemptuous of the Jewish establishment in Britain—especially the Board of Deputies, yet others who are openly critical of Jewish religious orthodoxy, and one (Robert Sheldon) who actually voted in favour of a 1968 bill to interfere with *shechita*.[17] The behaviour of Jewish Labour MPs at the time of Suez has already been noted. In 1973 two Jewish Conservative MPs (Robert Adley and Sir Keith Joseph) voted in favour of the arms embargo during the Yom Kippur War.[18] On 9 April 1975 at the end of the debate on the Labour government's White Paper approving the re-negotiated terms of Britain's membership of the European Economic Community, 15 Jewish Labour MPs voted with the Government, and 14 against.[19] A month earlier the nation, and Anglo-Jewry, had been told of the unedifying spectacle which occurred in the House of Commons when one Jewish MP, Mr Nigel Lawson (Conservative, Blaby), struck another Jewish MP, Mr Stanley Clinton Davis (Labour, Hackney Central), across the face with his order paper.[20]

More recently Mrs Sally Oppenheim, Conservative MP for Gloucester, admitted that she did not feel 'any relationship with Jews on the other side of the House. Not even moderates.' 'They all make me ashamed', she said of her Labour co-religionists, 'There's no kinship with them. None at all.'[21] And it is worth noting that even on ethical issues which are not subject to the restraints of party politics, Jewish MPs show no unanimity of thought. When Mr Eldon Griffiths introduced a motion in the Commons, in July 1979, to restore capital punishment, 18 Jewish Labour MPs voted against it, and 1 voted in its favour, while it was supported by 6 Jewish Conservative MPs but opposed by 4 others. There is indeed a great deal of truth in the assertion that most Jewish MPs consider themselves to be politicians who happen to be Jewish rather than Jewish politicians.[22] Jewish power in Parliament, though real, is thus not nearly as substantial as numbers might suggest, and certainly has much less impact than anti-Zionists and anti-Semites would like the public to believe.

Only rarely has the political complexion of the Jewish lobby in Parliament mirrored that of Anglo-Jewry at large. At the four general elections of the 1970s a total of 165 Jewish MPs have been returned, of which 120 (i.e. nearly three-quarters) have been Labour, and only 42 (i.e. just over one-quarter) Conservative. Among Jewish voters, however, the pattern of political partisanship has been very different.

The drift to the right among Jewish voters in London has been dramatically reflected in a programme of surveys of Jewish voting intentions which I have carried out since 1974. At each of the general elections in 1974 a poll was undertaken of a sample of Jewish voters in Hendon North; in February 1974 the voters were also asked about their votes in the general election of 1970.[23] The results of the Hendon North surveys and (for comparative purposes) the actual distribution of all votes in the constituency at these three general elections are given in Table II.

TABLE II

Hendon North: Jewish Samples and Constituency Results, 1970-4

Election	Percentage of votes promised or given		
	Conservative	Labour	Liberal
1970			
Jewish sample[a] (N = 150)	55.1	26.5	18.4
All voters	49.3	40.7	10.0
1974 (Feb.)			
Jewish sample[b] (N = 150)	59.1	15.9	25.0
All voters	42.6	36.2	21.2
1974 (Oct.)			
Jewish sample[b] (N = 178)	68.3	21.9	9.8
All voters	44.4	39.7	15.9

[a] Jewish percentages are based on those who voted.
[b] Jewish percentages are based on those who stated an intention to vote.

At each election the proportion of Jews supporting the Conservative party was larger than support for the party generally in the constituency on polling day, and Jewish support for Labour was consistently lower.[24] What is more, the 'ethnic differential' —the difference between the actual result and Jewish support for each candidate—grew during this period, in the case of support for the Conservative party, from 5.8 per cent in 1970 to a massive 23.9 per cent in October 1974. It is almost as if the Jewish voters in Hendon North consciously compensated for the fall in the popularity of the Conservative party over the five years in question in order to help John Gorst retain the seat.

Table III charts in similar fashion the behaviour of the Jewish electorate in Ilford North at the general election of October 1974, the by-election of March 1978, and the general election of May 1979.[25]

TABLE III
Ilford North: Jewish Samples and Constituency Results, 1974-9

Election	Percentage of votes promised or given			
	Conservative	Labour	Liberal	Other
1974 (Oct.)				
Jewish sample[a]	46.6	44.8	8.6	-
(N = 143)				
All voters	40.9	42.5	16.6	-
1978				
Jewish sample[b]	59.3	35.2	5.5	0.0
(N = 143)				
All voters	50.4	38.0	5.0	4.7
1979				
Jewish sample[b]	61.2	34.7	4.1	0.0
(N = 143)				
All voters	51.3	37.3	8.9	2.5

[a] Jewish percentages are based on those who voted.
[b] Jewish percentages are based on those who stated an intention to vote.

In Ilford North the ethnic differential is not as wide as in Hendon North. In October 1974 there was slightly more support for Labour among the Jewish voters than within the Ilford North electorate as a whole: the result, no doubt, of Milly Miller's personal pull on the Jewish vote. But more Jews supported the Conservative party than supported Labour. At the by-election this Conservative advantage grew, and at the 1979 general

election the ethnic differential, in the case of the Conservative
candidate, amounted to 9.9 per cent in his favour; only a third of
Jewish voters in Ilford North supported Labour. Whereas the
swing to the Conservatives among all voters in Ilford North from
October 1974 to May 1979 was 7.8 per cent, among the Jewish
voters it was 12.4 per cent. At Hendon North the swing between
the two elections in 1974 was 0.8 per cent to Labour; but among
the Jewish voters it was 1.6 per cent towards the Conservative
candidate.

It may be objected that such results are only to be expected
from such constituencies. At the London borough-council elections of May 1978, of the five wards in Hendon North only two,
Colindale and Burnt Oak, returned Labour councillors; the
other three wards, Edgware, Mill Hill, and Hale, all returned
Conservatives. Yet it is precisely in Edgware, Mill Hill, and
Hale that the Jews of Hendon North are to be found and in
which all the synagogues of the constituency are located. In
Ilford North those wards with the highest proportion of Jewish
electors (Barkingside 25.3 per cent; Aldburgh 13.5 per cent;
Fairlop 8.0 per cent; Seven Kings 7.0 per cent) all return Conservative councillors; in those wards returning Labour councillors (Clementswood and Hainault) the Jewish electorate
amounts to less than 2.0 per cent.[26] Between them, Hendon
North and Ilford North account for over 21,000 of the United
Kingdom's 300,000 Jewish electors; they are Conservative
partly because so many Jews live in them.

Local-election results provide further evidence of this trend.
There are at present four inner London boroughs where Jews
form over 5 per cent of the population, and four outer boroughs.
In Table IV the number of 'Jewish' wards in each of the boroughs
has been estimated (from survey data, personal knowledge, and
the siting of synagogues) and the number of councillors returned
for these wards in the May 1978 borough elections is shown in
the right-hand columns; the overall state of the parties in the
boroughs is shown in the left-hand columns.

It will be seen that in the four inner London boroughs the
Jewish wards account for just over one-third of the total number
of wards and return just over a quarter of the total number of
Labour councillors, but well over half of the Conservative councillors. In the four outer boroughs the Jewish wards form just

TABLE IV
Results in the Jewish Wards of Eight London Boroughs, May 1978

	All wards				Jewish wards			
	Number of wards	Number of Councillors			Number of wards	Number of Councillors		
		Labour	Con- serv- ative	Other		Labour	Con- serv- ative	Other
Inner London								
Camden	26	33	26	0	6	0	16	0
Hackney	23	59	1	0	11	30	1	0
Tower Hamlets	19	43	0	7	5	9	0	4
Westminster	23	19	39	2	8	0	20	0
Total	91	154	66	9	30	39	37	4
Outer London								
Barnet	20	10	49	1	11	0	33	0
Brent	31	39	27	0	17	19	17	0
Harrow	21	12	46	5	5	3	12	0
Redbridge	20	13	50	0	14	7	35	0
Total	92	74	172	6	47	29	97	0

over half the total; they return just over one-third of the total number of Labour councillors but over half the Conservative councillors.

It must be conceded at once that it is always dangerous to engage in 'cross-level reference', that is, to infer the partisanship of any group of voters from the election results in a much larger aggregate (a constituency, say, or a ward) of which they form only a part. Thus in many of the Hackney wards Jews and coloured immigrants live side by side, so that much of the Labour vote could conceivably have come from the latter rather than from the former. Nor do the figures (especially in view of poor turn-out at local elections) reveal anything about attitudes of Jewish voters to the Liberal party. These factors, however, would tend to understate, rather than exaggerate, Jewish support for Liberal and Conservative candidates.

It is no part of my intention to predict what might happen to the Jewish vote in the future. But the London borough statistics, taken together with the Hendon North and Ilford North surveys, and with other quantitative as well as qualitative evidence, suggests that Jewish Labour voters are becoming fewer in relation to Jewish Conservatives. A survey of Sheffield Jewry undertaken by the Research Unit of the Board of Deputies in the mid-1970s revealed that 66 per cent of Jewish men in Sheffield belonged to the professional, managerial, supervisory, and skilled non-manual occupational classes, whereas in the city as a whole only 28 per cent of the male earners were to be found in these groups.[27] A more recent survey (1978) of the Jewish population of the London borough of Redbridge shows that 66 per cent of the Jewish men there also belong to the higher occupational categories, though for all economically active males in the borough the figure is only 50 per cent.[28] So the drift into the middle classes which was noted in the last chapter and the over-representation of Jews in the upper social categories has continued apace, with obvious and demonstrable political consequences; for at the general election of May 1979 over half the voters in these classes nationally supported the Conservative party.[29]

At the moment there are still important concentrations of Jewish Labour supporters, particularly in inner London. A survey of 130 Jewish voters in the Hackney North and Stoke Newington constituency in 1979 yielded the results shown in Table V.[30]

TABLE V
Hackney North and Stoke Newington: Jewish Sample and Constituency
Result, May 1979

	Percentage of votes given				
	Conservative	Labour	Liberal	National Front	Communist
Jewish sample[a] (N = 130)	36.4	49.1	12.7	1.8	-
All voters	33.2	51.7	10.6	3.0	1.5

[a] Jewish percentages are based on those who voted.

Here it will be seen that, even in such a working-class area, Jewish support for Labour was lower than among all voters, and that Jewish support for the Conservative and Liberal candidates was a few per cent higher; the National Front attracted some Jewish support, but the Communist party none at all among those voters surveyed. Moreover, it is important to remember that Hackney, like other areas (Newham and Tower Hamlets) into which the old Jewish East End has been absorbed, is an area of declining Jewish population; in 1974 the Jewish populations of the boroughs of Hackney, Newham, and Tower Hamlets combined was estimated to be only 37,400.[31] The young Jews have moved away, leaving their parents and grandparents to maintain the institutions of Jewish communal life as best they can. These are still Jewish Labour strongholds, but most of the Jewish Labour voters there are middle-aged and old with no children living nearby to whom they might transmit their own political culture.[32]

Over two-thirds of London Jewry (184,200 out of 259,100) now live in the outer London boroughs, and the four outer boroughs cited in Table IV account for 68 per cent (125,800) of this outer London total. Even within the Labour strongholds in inner London pockets of Conservatism are to be found which turn out to be Jewish, such as Hackney's ultra-orthodox communities located in Stoke Newington and Stamford Hill.[33] In the May 1978 local elections there in the Springfield ward Mr Josef Lobenstein won the only Conservative seat on an otherwise entirely Labour-controlled council; Mr Lobenstein, a staunchly

orthodox Jew and a leading member of both the Union of Orthodox Hebrew Congregations and the Agudas Israel movement of
Great Britain, is held in high esteem by Hackney's ultra-orthodox Jews, and he obtained 204 and 229 votes more than his two
unsuccessful Conservative running-mates in the ward.[34]

This move to the right within the Jewish electorate has devel-
oped at the same time as 'a slow but discernible erosion of sympathy with Israel in the Labour Party'.[35] Harold Wilson's
personal devotion to Israel, and his close friendship with the
Israeli Premier, Golda Meir, was certainly appreciated in
Jewish circles. But the policy towards Israel pursued by the
Labour Governments over which Wilson presided seemed to
run on a different track. Certainly, ever since the Labour
Government's ambivalent attitude at the time of the June 1967
Arab-Israeli War, Jewish Labour MPs have had a hard time of it
explaining the vagaries of Labour's Middle East policy to their
co-religionists. Nor has their task been made any easier by the
presence of a vociferous pro-Arab lobby within the parliamentary Labour party. Ian Mikardo, then Labour party Chairman,
addressing a Zionist Federation forum in June 1974, had to
admit that between thirty and fifty Labour MPs were pro-Arab,
and he added that the group included 'a few nut-cases'.[36] Many
within the Labour movement now see Israel as 'an occupying
power' run by 'a coalition of technocrats, religious zealots and
narrow nationalists, in contrast to the socialist pioneers of the left
who for so long dominated Israeli politics'.[37]

It is true, of course, that pro-Arabists are to be found in the
Conservative party as well, and that the Liberal party suffers in
Jewish eyes because of the anti-Israeli sentiments of many
Young Liberals.[38] After the 1967 war many Liberals discovered
in the Palestinian Arabs a cause to which they could conveni-
ently attach themselves now that the former British colonial
territories had been granted independence and that support for
Moscow in the wake of the Soviet crack-down in eastern Europe
was suspect to say the least. There can be little doubt that the
July 1974 defection of the noted Arab apologist Christopher
(now Lord) Mayhew from Labour to the Liberal Party had a
decidedly negative impact upon Jewish Liberal support, and
was a major factor in the sharp drop in that support at Hendon
North in October 1974 as compared with the previous February

(see Table I).[39] Given, however, that all three main parties contain their pro-Arab factions, Jewish electors find little to choose between them on this score. At general elections Poale Zion is still to be found campaigning faithfully for the Labour party; but the emotional appeal falls on stony ground, and the continued appearance of Poale Zion delegates at Labour party conferences (especially now that the Labour Alignment's thirty-year-old monopoly of power in Israel has been broken) is really an accident of history rather than an expression of modern Anglo-Jewish commitment.

The movement of the Jewish electorate towards the right has had other repercussions too. At one end of the political spectrum support for the Communist party has all but disappeared. As noted in Chapter 7, this support reached its apogee with the election of Phil Piratin as Communist MP for Stepney in 1945. Piratin's success was followed by others at borough-council level in November 1945, when the party won ten seats, and at the London County Council elections in March 1946 Jack Gaster was one of the two successful Communist party candidates in the Mile End division.[40] Some further local by-election successes followed in 1947 and 1948, but even as these victories were being celebrated the Jewish love affair with communism was beginning to sour on both sides.

Although Soviet Russia had voted for the re-establishment of the Jewish state, Stalin's paranoid anti-Semitism, and the dictates of Soviet strategy in the Middle East, soon led him to denounce the Zionist movement as a tool of British imperialism. In Britain Harry Pollitt blindly followed this lead: the State of Israel, he charged, was 'a pawn of the USA'.[41] What little news there was of the situation of Russian Jewry in the late 1940s and early 1950s was not encouraging; by 1956 even the *Daily Worker* had to admit, in answer to a letter of enquiry from Professor Hyman Levy and others, that the charges of anti-Semitic persecution in Russia were 'essentially correct'.[42] The following year Levy went to the USSR to investigate anti-Semitism there; he reported to the Easter Congress of the British Communist party in 1957 that the visit 'shook me to my foundations'.[43]

Revelations about the state of Russian Jewry inevitably eroded Anglo-Jewish support for communism. Jews were prominent in the mass defections from the party at the time of the Russian invasion of Hungary in 1956. But it was the increasingly hostile attitude of the Soviet Union to Zionism, culminating in the Middle East crisis of 1967, when the USSR and her allies broke off diplomatic relations with Israel, which marked the watershed in relations between the Communist party and British Jews. Leading Jewish intellectuals in the party either left or, like Professor Levy, were expelled. At the grass roots the peculiar political atmosphere of the 1930s and 1940s, which had forged real links between the Communist party and working-class Jews in London's East End, gradually disappeared as the East End itself, and Stepney in particular, lost its Jewish identity. Phil Piratin proved to be a good constituency MP. But his 1945 victory, achieved in an electorate of only 16,132 and on a turn-out low even by English standards (66.1 per cent as against a turn-out in England of 73.4 per cent), was not repeated in 1950, when he lost the seat to Labour and polled only 12.5 per cent of the votes—a lower percentage than that of the Conservative candidate, who came second. Although the Communist party has contested the Stepney seat at every general election since then, it has never managed even to save its deposit; in 1979 its share of the poll fell to less than 2 per cent, and was lower than that of the National Front.

At borough-council level the party was more successful, retaining a few seats in the borough of Stepney and its successor, the Greater London borough of Tower Hamlets, in the 1950s and 1960s, mainly on the strength of the local popularity of Jewish Communist candidates such as Solly Kaye and Max Levitas. In the 1970s, however, even such modest successes have eluded party workers. Within the British Communist party Jews—or, as they would prefer to have themselves described, 'persons of Jewish origin'—continue to play a significant role. As late at 1965 the *Jewish Chronicle* estimated that Jews constituted 10 per cent of the party membership.[44] But the enthusiastic mass following which the party once had among Jewish voters has now well and truly disappeared. The only Jewish candidate whom the party put up in the 1979 general election, Monty Goldman at Hackney North, came bottom of the poll. More significantly, the 1979 Hackney North sample (see Table V) yielded not a single Jewish supporter of communism.[45] Young Jews who regard the Labour party as too moderate do not generally join the Communist party, but attach themselves instead to one or other of a variety of New Left groups, such as the Workers' Revolutionary Party or the Socialist Workers' Party. And within the Anglo-Jewish electorate as a whole support for such parties is negligible.

On the extreme right, however, over the past decade there has been evidence of a tendency for some Jews to support, and even to join, the National Front. This is particularly so in certain socially-deprived areas of inner London, where the fabric of Jewish life is visibly crumbling as black immigrants have moved into areas where Jews once lived in large numbers. Relations between blacks and Jews vary a great deal. They are often very good, but can deteriorate remarkably quickly. 'I have found the feeling', one West Indian in Haringey told a *Jewish Chronicle* reporter, 'that the Jews are usually shrewd manipulators in their own self-interest'; West Indians feel, rightly or wrongly, that they are charged more by Jewish money-lenders, are exploited by Jewish employers, and have to pay high rents to Jewish land-lords for substandard accommodation.[46]

It may well be that (as was the case at the turn of the century) many of the allegations made by New Commonwealth immi-grants against Jews are not well founded. The fact is that, whether from ignorance or malevolence or, as with some Muslim immigrants, anti-Zionism, prejudice against Jews has taken root within the coloured communities established in Britain. It is also a fact that some Jews have met prejudice with prejudice. They, or their parents or grandparents, made their way in this country without the benefit of the race relations 'industry', and they have little sympathy with calls from black immigrant leaders for tougher anti-discrimination legislation. In Ealing, for instance, Indian workers feel that 'Jews of Polish origin who are an élite with reactionary ideas ... hold definite Tory party views. They give the impression that they do not want to associate with the worries of the coloured people at local level.'[47]

Moreover, such impressions are reinforced by statements made by Jews and from within the Jewish community. In April 1977 Brian Gordon, a teacher at Edgware Synagogue Hebrew Classes, Vice-Chairman of Young Herut, and Conservative candidate in a local council by-election in Barnet, was reported as having told a meeting of Edgware Conservatives that immigration should be halted because 'Britain could no longer be the "dustbin" of the world'.[48] Some months later the *Jewish Tribune*, the newspaper of the ultra-orthodox Agudas Israel organization, ran an editorial, in Yiddish, which criticized Jewish Labour MP Greville Janner for coming to the defence of Britain's black community:

An identification of the Jewish public with the Black community [the editorial declared], such as Mr Janner and his friends are doing, is a sure way of increasing the hatred against Jews from the whole community.

To show sympathy to the Black community may be a principle, but is this principle so pure and important that it is worth jeopardising the security of the Jewish public?[49]

In March 1978, in a letter to the *Jewish Chronicle*, David Sassoon, headmaster of the Hillel House [Jewish] school, Brondesbury Park, London, wrote: 'As head of a primary school, I find it very disturbing to hear Jewish parents, who only a couple of generations ago were themselves immigrants, refusing to agree to send their children to this or that school simply on the grounds that they don't want their children to mix with those of coloured immigrants.'[50]

More recently in a study of fifty Jewish residents in central Hackney Dr Yona Ginzberg found that many of her respondents, though they realized that the deterioration of the area had begun before the period of black immigration, none the less 'attributed the deterioration ... mainly to the presence of black people'. The Hackney Jews disapproved of the life-style of the blacks; they were apparently convinced that most crimes in the area were committed by blacks; and they resented welfare payments to black immigrants. Dr Ginzberg also found that 'most of the Jewish people interviewed expressed some anti-black sentiments which occasionally echoed the arguments voiced by the National Front'.[51]

Most Jews who feel thus inclined seem to have sought refuge in the Conservative party. But some have gone even further to the right. They feel that the problems associated with the coloured immigrants may cause a backlash against them, as Jews, from their Gentile neighbours. Therefore they are anxious to be seen as not sustaining the coloured community, and they argue that the best way of demonstrating this, and of showing their British patriotism, is by supporting the National Front.

How extensive is this support? There are grounds for believing that in Hackney, where the phenomena is most widespread, it is of significant proportions, in that it is not confined to a few individuals, but is in numbers large enough to be indicative of a trend. In October 1978, in answer to an inquiry from the *Jewish Chronicle*, I estimated that there were then 300 to 400 'potential' Jewish votes for the National Front in the Hackney area.[52] I based this estimate on aggregate analysis of the October 1974 general-election results in Hackney, and the May 1978 local borough-council elections; such analysis suggested that in the mid-1970s the Front enjoyed the support of about 3.25 per cent of all voters in Hackney. Applied to the Jewish electorate of the borough (20,000 or so in 1978), such a percentage yielded about 450 Jewish votes for the Front. Clearly, however, the actual number of Jews who supported the Front was less than this, if only because allowance must be made for a 'repugnance' factor; of Dr Ginzberg's fifty interviewees, one identified with the National Front, but indicated 'he could not vote for them because they were anti-Semitic'.[53] Thus I concluded that the number of potential Jewish votes for the party was nearer 300 and 400, or between 1.5 and 2.0 per cent of the Jewish voters in the borough. In the May 1979 general election, the National Front vote in contested seats fell by over half, from 2.9 per cent in October 1974 to 1.3 per cent. But in Hackney North the decline was only from 3.8 per cent to 3.0 per cent. The Hackney North Jewish sample (see Table V) shows that the Jewish National Front vote in that constituency represented only 1.8 per cent of all Jewish voters there; if this is true of Hackney as a whole, only about 360 Jews in the borough supported the Front at that election.

A small number of Jews have actually joined the party. One such is Albert Elder, an antiquarian book dealer now living in Eastbourne, who stood for the Front at Hendon South in 1979.[54] Mr Elder describes himself as a 'Jewish racialist' who wants 'to put white people, Jews and Gentiles, first in jobs, housing, welfare and education'.[55] He believes that God was 'the first racist', because he forbade Jews to integrate with Gentiles.

'British Jews will best serve their community', Mr Elder advises, 'by identifying with the generally held views of the British people, rather than identifying themselves with an unwanted wave of Immigrants.'[56]

These views are echoed by another Jewish National Front member, Gerry Viner, who stood for the party in the Wenlock ward of Hackney in 1978.[58] Mr Viner now lives in Stoke Newington; but he hails from Leeds, and was originally a socialist.[58] 'I am a Jew', he declares, 'and proud to be a N.F. member. The Jews have preserved their race for thousands of years because they are racialists. And the N.F. wants to do the same thing— preserve the British race.'[59] Mr Viner admits that some leading members of the Front have made blatantly anti-Jewish statements in the past.[60] But such views, he argues, were products of youthful ignorance and have now been abandoned. He feels perfectly safe in the party, and stresses that it is important that Jews should be seen belonging to it, particularly if the party were to achieve political influence or grow more popular.

But whereas Albert Elder claims to be a Zionist, and was indeed a member of British Herut,[61] Gerry Viner confesses to being 'deeply disturbed by the activities of Zionism, who [*sic*] while they claim to speak on behalf of World Jewry, which they certainly do not, are deeply involved in a multiracial conspiracy designed to destroy the White Race ... This policy can only put the Jewish people in a state of peril.' 'Multiracialism' is defined by Mr Viner as 'a conspiracy of international monopoly capitalism', and he sees Zionists as being part of this plot.[62] He does not recognize any national connotation in being a Jew, which, for him, would appear to imply nothing more than a religious affiliation.

This view of Zionism is shared by Mark Lavine, the son of a Jewish father and a non-Jewish mother, who joined the National Front in 1974, when he was nineteen years of age, and has stood for the Front locally (in the borough of Enfield, where he lives) and at Folkestone in the 1979 general election.[63] So far as he is concerned, Zionism is 'big business' and 'anti-British'. Though he believes Israel has a right to exist, he also supports the idea of a separate Palestinian Arab State. He whole-heartedly endorses National Front policy that all Jewish immigrants who entered the United Kingdom after the passage of the 1948 Nationality

Act should be repatriated, presumably to Israel.[64] He recognizes that if an anti-Semitic party ever came to power in Britain, he (though only of Jewish origin) would not escape persecution, but he is not worried by the Nazi past of some National Front leaders; he believes, with Gerry Viner, that the views they once held were 'youthful indiscretions'.

It is impossible to say for certain how many Jews, or persons of Jewish origin, have joined the National Front. The names of six such persons are known to me, excluding that of Joseph Cohen, who stood for the Front in the Bunhill ward of Islington in May 1978, but whose Jewish identity I have been unable to verify.[65] I am informed that the Board of Deputies 'also knew of a few of these people'.[66] Probably the total number of such persons does not exceed eight or nine. For the Front these members, however few, are first-class propaganda material; their views matter less than the fact of their membership, which is used to try and dispel any notion that the party is anti-Jewish.[67] And if, indeed, the Board of Deputies is right to stress that Jews 'who are politically minded have established themselves within the political party of their choice and apart from exceptional circumstances maintain their party allegiance, *in the same way as non-Jews*', such instances of Jewish membership of the National Front are hardly surprising.[68]

But it is clear that the phenomenon of Jewish involvement in the Front, at whatever level and to whatever degree, is an embarrassment to the Anglo-Jewish establishment. A letter from me, on this subject, published in *The Times* of 30 September 1978, was met with hysterical reactions from leading British Jews; one called me a 'crackpot', and at a subsequent meeting of the Board of Deputies the verbal treatment meted out to me (in my absence) was such that even one gentleman who did not agree with my views on the Anti Nazi League none the less condemned 'the vile and disgusting attacks' made upon me.[69] And the Board officially protested to the BBC when it became known that Albert Elder was to be interviewed on the Radio 4 programme 'The World This Weekend'.[70]

But the National Front has caused Anglo-Jewish leaders further difficulties, quite apart from the political threat which, to a greater or lesser extent, it poses for Anglo-Jewry. It has been stressed frequently in this book that the Anglo-Jewish establishment has always fought against the idea of a Jewish vote and has, except on rare and isolated occasions (as in 1906) used its influence against those who have sought to instruct Jewish voters how they should vote. In an interview with Mme Sabine Roitman on 24 February 1977, Lord Fisher of Camden, perhaps with my own research in mind, said:

Pour nous, les opinions politiques des juifs anglais ne diffèrent pas de celles exprimées par le reste de l'électorat. Il n'est donc pas utile de faire des recherches dans cette direction. Si toutefois elles étaient quand même entreprises, nous les jugerions imprudentes, voire dangereuses. L'opinion publique doit croire en une communauté juive bien intégrée et semblable à ses concitoyens.

Pour les mêmes motifs, il ne peut être question de parler d'un vote juif.[71]

Logically, therefore, the leadership of Anglo-Jewry should stand aloof from the National Front and, especially at elections, say nothing about it. Obviously, however, given the racist policies of the Front and the known views about Jews held by some of its leading members, a policy of 'splendid isolation' is absurd. In fact the Board of Deputies plays an active part in promoting good race relations in Britain, and its Defence Department largely occupies itself with anti-National Front propaganda and research. So the Board cannot be, and is not, neutral where candidates of the Front, and other extreme right-wing parties, are concerned. In 1977, a few days before the county-council elections, Lord Fisher of Camden issued a strongly worded appeal to Anglo-Jewry not to abstain, but to come out and vote for one of the three main parties, in order to reduce the percentage of the poll obtained by National Front and National Party contestants.[72] The Association of Jewish Ex-Servicemen took a half-page advertisement in the *Jewish Chronicle* with the same end in view.[73] The following year, at the time of the English municipal elections, the Chief Rabbi's Office issued the following statement: 'In view of the large number of National Front candidates contesting the Borough Council elections on May 4, the Chief Rabbi asks all ministers to urge congregants to go to the polling booths and exercise their voting rights.'[74] During the May 1979 general-election campaign Lord Fisher, the Jewish Ex-Servicemen, and the Chief Rabbi again appealed to the Jewish public to vote rather than abstain.[75] The Ex-Servicemen and the Board of Deputies once more issued thousands of leaflets which, if they did not actually tell voters to vote against the Front, none the less made their meaning very plain. Martin Savitt, then Chairman of the Board's Jewish Defence and Group Relations Committee, declared explicitly 'We have to defeat the National Front at the General Election.'[76] The Board produced an 'anti-NF kit' which was sent to 325 local newspaper editors and many parliamentary candidates; the kit was stated 'to have been effective in producing the generally low-profile reporting of NF candidates in the press'.[77] What is more, the *Jewish Chronicle*, in a leading article entitled 'How to vote', declared: 'Any vote cast for one of the established parties is a vote against the Front and, in this sense alone, might it be said that Jews are not only obliged to vote but have a vested collective interest, with the rest of civilised society in this country of ours, in exercising their franchise.'[78] In short, a Jewish anti-National Front vote was officially encouraged, on grounds upon which there was a wide measure of agreement within Anglo-Jewry.[79]

And if against the National Front, why not on other matters? Even as late as the 1920s it was quite usual for Jewish ministers of religion to issue statements in support of parliamentary candidates.[80] The practice then ceased, doubtless because of fears of an anti-Semitic reaction. In 1974, although rabbis of synagogues in, or adjacent to, Hendon North were none too happy about Reverend Amias's *démarche* there (some feared, wrongly, that it might provoke anti-Semitism; others felt that it was not 'the right thing' for a Jewish religious leader to do), most of them none the less thought the use of the Jewish vote to support the parliamentary friends of Israel was perfectly in order, even desirable, and one rabbi, A. S. Chaitowitz, of Stanmore United Synagogue, went further, declaring that though he would not at that time use the pulpit to urge support for any political party, he was prepared to admit that circumstances (which he did not specify) could arise in which he might have to change his view.[81]

The following year Rabbi Chaitowitz publicly condemned the Labour Government's inclusion in its Finance bill of a clause which, he claimed, 'will bring disaster to charities already suffering from the effects of inflation'.[82] In May 1975 Rabbi Dow

Marmur, of the North-Western Reform Synagogue, Golders Green, preached a sermon urging his congregants to vote 'Yes' in the Common Market referendum, because of 'the menace of Soviet Communism'.[83] At the same time the *Jewish Chronicle* ran a leading article also urging, for a variety of reasons, a 'Yes' vote from Anglo-Jewry.[84] In 1979 the Board of Deputies, in addition to urging an anti-National Front vote, also circulated individual Deputies with a list of eighty-six 'key seats', in which it recommended approaches to all candidates of the main political parties 'to ascertain their views on Middle East matters'.[85] And, following the 1979 general election, the Reverend L. Tann, of the Sutton synagogue, urged Anglo-Jewry to think carefully before supporting proportional representation, for, he argued, such a system would be of benefit to the National Front and the Socialist Workers' Party.[86]

Mrs Thatcher's Government has also been the target of Jewish electoral pressure, because of its attitude towards the role of the Palestine Liberation Organization in a comprehensive Middle East peace settlement. Following a statement made in March 1980 by Lord Carrington, the Conservative Foreign Secretary, that the PLO was not 'a terrorist organization', and must be brought into a peace settlement, a series of synagogue meetings in north-west London resulted in the Jewish vote being openly flaunted as a weapon against the Government, and specifically against the Prime Minister. At Hendon the Reverend Leslie Hardman urged his audience—'especially those in Mrs Thatcher's constituency'—to write to their MPs 'telling them you cannot vote for a Conservative Party adopting the present stand' on the Middle East.[87] At Edgware the Reverend Saul Amias declared 'If Mrs Thatcher meets with the terrorists, she must know that, north-west of Baker Street, there are many voters in Barnet who will think twice about re-electing her.'[88] In Finchley itself the Conservative MP Hugh Fraser, chairman of the Conservative Friends of Israel, assured a meeting of over 1,000 Jewish voters that Mrs Thatcher 'understands the anxiety of the Jewish community in London'.[89]

One result of these protest meetings was that the Prime Minister wrote to the *Hendon Times*, and to Rabbi B. J. Gelles, of the Finchley synagogue, defending her Administration's policy and condemning 'the PLO's links with terrorism'.[90] At the same time thirty Conservative members of Barnet Borough Council signed a statement reaffirming their support for the State of Israel and deprecating any attempt by the British Government to recognize the PLO until it radically alters its policy towards the Jewish State.[91] At Hendon North John Gorst called Lord Carrington's policy 'lamentable and misguided', and declared that he would vote against 'a policy of surrender to violence'.[92]

Since 1974, therefore, in a variety of ways and on many different grounds, the Jewish voters of Great Britain have been exhorted, both by political parties and by communal leaders, to approach political affairs, and hence to exercise their franchises, in a 'Jewish' way; in a way, that is, which would reflect and serve their interests not just as British citizens but as Jewish citizens. The indications are that such promptings have not gone unheeded. Nor is there any good reason why such appeals should not be made. If Jews in the United Kingdom really do enjoy political equality, it follows that they must be as free to vote, and to organize their votes, as anyone else.

Certainly the idea of a Jewish vote, so often repudiated by Anglo-Jewish leaders, is none the less recognized by many, within and beyond Anglo-Jewry, as a legitimate means of political expression. British Jews do not vote, and have never voted, in an entirely uniform way. Jews have supported and joined all the major and minor political parties to be found in modern British history. At the same time it is undeniable that during periods of critical importance for Jews, and especially when Anglo-Jewry has had to grapple with issues which, in its view, have touched the roots of its own, and world Jewry's, existence and survival, the norms of class and economic self-interest have been discarded in favour of a specific and unashamedly Jewish approach to British politics.

Far from being totally assimilated within British political culture, Jewish voters in Britain have always been capable of independent political behaviour, sometimes in marked contrast to national or regional trends. It is this capability, coupled with the territorial concentration of Anglo-Jewish voters in a few, often politically marginal, urban localities, which has made the concept of a Jewish vote a political reality. Nor should those who study British politics be surprised at the discovery of such a phenomenon. Far from being a contradiction of the emancipation won over a hundred years ago, the continued existence of a Jewish vote in this country is, surely, emancipation's natural corollary.

Appendix

Jewish Performance at Parliamentary Elections 1859-1979

Although Jewish MPs have figured frequently in this book, it has not been concerned centrally with the attitudes and behaviour of these MPs, except in so far as they have illustrated the influences upon, and influence of, Jewish voters. None the less for reference purposes the reader might wish to have a list of the numbers of professing Jews elected to Parliament; the list is based on figures given in the *Jewish Chronicle, Jewish World*, and *Jewish Yearbook*, supplemented by personal knowledge.

The number of Jews standing for election to the House of Commons, and the number elected, rose to record levels in the 1960s and 1970s. This has caused worry and embarrassment in some Jewish quarters. A speaker in a Jewish 'Brains Trust' organized on the eve of the 1964 general election 'thought that there were too many Jewish candidates'.[1] When the number of Jewish MPs rose to a record 46 in 1974, Jewish Conservative MP Malcolm Rifkind asked whether this also was 'too many', especially in view of the fact that there were no coloured MPs.[2] In conversation with me in March 1975 Mr Rifkind said he felt that if the number of Jewish MPs significantly increased to, say, 80, an 'ugly situation' would arise.

Not much has been written about Jewish MPs, and the subject still awaits definitive study. Those who wish to pursue it further should read the useful University of Essex MA Thesis, entitled 'Jewish M.P.s', written by Gary Zimmerman in 1976.

Readers might also wish to know that three Jews, all Conservatives, (D. Prag, M. Seligman, and F. Tuckman), were returned from Great Britain in the first direct elections to the European Assembly, in June 1979.

TABLE A.1
Professing Jews Elected to Parliament

Year of Election	Jewish Candidates Standing	Elected[a]	Con[b]	Jewish MPs[a] Lib	Lab	Others	Percentage of House of Commons
1859	3	3(1)	0	3(1)	0	0	0.002
1865	7	6(2)	0	6(2)	0	0	0.9
1868	9	6(2)	0	6(2)	0	0	0.9
1874	7	5	1	4	0	0	0.8
1880	13	5	1	4	0	0	0.8
1885	18	8(1)	3	5(1)	0	0	1.2
1886	9	7(2)	4	3(2)	0	0	1.0
1892	11	7	4	3	0	0	1.0
1895	18	8(5)	7(4)	1(1)	0	0	1.2
1900	23	10(3)	7(1)	3(2)	0	0	1.5
1906	32	16	4	12	0	0	2.4
1910 (Jan)	32	15	7	8	0	0	2.2
1910 (Dec)	37	16(2)	7(2)	9	0	0	2.4
1918	22	11(1)	7(1)	4	0	0	1.6
1922	30	11	6	4	1	0	1.8
1923	25	13	5	6	2	0	2.1
1924	36	14	9	3	2	0	2.3
1929	48	17	6	5	6[c]	0	2.8
1931	32	16(1)	9(1)	7[d]	0(1)[e]	0	2.6
1935	44	16(1)	8	4[d]	4	0(1)[y]	2.6
1945	59	28(1)	0	0	26(1)	2[g]	4.4

1950	67	23	0	0	23	0	3.7
1951	43	17	0	0	17	0	2.7
1955	57	18(1)	1(1)	0	17	0	2.9
1959	67	22(2)	2	0	20(2)	0	3.5
1964	86	36	2	0	34	0	5.7
1966	86	40	2	0	38	0	6.3
1970	84	40(2)	9	0(1)	31(1)	0	6.3
1974 (Feb)	101	46	12	1	33	0	7.2
1974 (Oct)	91	46	10	1	35	0	7.2
1979	74	33	11	1	21[h]	0	5.2

[a] Number of MPs elected at by-elections subsequent to any general election is shown in round brackets.
[b] Includes Liberal Unionist MPs from 1886.
[c] Of whom one was Dr Marion Phillips, the first Jewish woman MP.
[d] Includes two National Liberal MPs.
[e] Defection of Harry Nathan from the Liberal party.
[f] Independent Conservative.
[g] Independent Conservative and Communist.
[h] At the time of writing (Dec. 1981), three Jewish Labour MPs have defected to the Social Democratic party (D. Ginsburg, E. Lyons, and N. Sandelson).

1. The Politics of Pre-Emancipation Jewry

1. This paragraph is based on C. Roth, *A History of the Jews in England* (2nd edn., Oxford, 1949), and P. Hyams, 'The Jewish Minority in Medieval England, 1066-1290' (Paper presented to the Past and Present Annual Conference, 4 July 1973).
2. Roth, *History*, 145-72, and C. Roth, 'The Resettlement of the Jews in England in 1656', in V. D. Lipman (ed.), *Three Centuries of Anglo-Jewish History* (London, 1961), 1-21. See also D. S. Katz, *Philo-Semitism and the Readmission of the Jews to England 1603-1655* (Oxford, 1982).
3. W. S. Samuel, 'Sir William Davidson, Royalist (1616-1689), and the Jews', *Transactions of the Jewish Historical Society of England*, xiv (1935-9), 59-60.
4. A. Hyamson, *A History of the Jews in England* (London, 1908), 189.
5. L. D. Barnett (trans.), *El Libro de los Acuerdos* (Oxford, 1931), 53-5.
6. E. R. Samuel, 'The First Fifty Years', in Lipman, *Three Centuries*, 39.
7. Roth, *History*, 206-7.
8. This account of the Naturalization Bill is based on Roth, *History*, 211-21, and T. W. Perry, *Public Opinion, Propaganda and Politics in Eighteenth-Century England. A Study of the Jew Bill of 1753* (Cambridge, Mass., 1962), *passim*.
9. A print of October 1753, attacking the Naturalization Act, shows Samson Gideon offering bribes to Newcastle and Pelham: Perry, 9.
10. *Jackson's Oxford Journal*, quoted in R. J. Robson, *The Oxfordshire Election of 1754* (Oxford, 1949), 88.
11. J. B. Owen, *The Eighteenth Century 1714-1815* (London, 1974), 74-5.
12. Roth, *History*, 285.
13. Ibid. 213; Barnet, *El Libro*, 50.
14. Roth, *History*, 222-3.
15. Ibid. 225-8.
16. Ibid. 233.
17. Ibid. 235.
18. Ibid. 236; C. H. L. Emanuel, *A Century and a Half of Jewish History Extracted from the Minute Books of the London Committee of Deputies of the British Jews* (London, 1910), 9. For a few instances of Jewish democratic radicals, see T. M. Endelman, *The Jews of Georgian England 1714-1830* (Philadelphia, 1979), 276.
19. P. H. Emden, 'The Brothers Goldsmid and the Financing of the Napoleonic Wars', *Transactions of the Jewish Historical Society of England*, xiv (1935-9), 225-46.
20. Liverpool Poll Book of 1832, in the Institute of Historical Research, London. See also Endelman, 113.
21. C. Roth, *Anglo-Jewish Letters (1858-1917)* (London, 1938), 246-7.
22. The association of the Younger Pitt with Toryism is reflected in T. E. Kebbel's famous *History of Toryism from the Accession of Mr Pitt to Power in 1783 to the Death of Lord Beaconsfield in 1881* (London, 1886).
23. E. M. Tomlinson, *A History of the Minories* (London, 1922), 310.
24. M. J. Landa, 'Kitty Villareal, the Da Costas and Samson Gideon', *Transactions of the Jewish Historical Society of England*, xiii (1932-5), 285.
25. Lopes was a supporter of Pitt, and later of Lord Liverpool; the remaining three were all Whigs. I am grateful to Dr David Fisher of the Institute of Historical Research for broadening my knowledge of these MPs.

2. The Jewish Vote is Born

1. See Roth, *History*, 248-63; V. D. Lipman, 'The Age of Emancipation, 1815-1880', in Lipman, *Three Centuries*, 77-81; U. R. Q. Henriques, 'The Jewish Emancipation Controversy in Nineteenth Century Britain', *Past and Present* No. 40 (July 1968), 126-46; I. Finestein, 'Anglo-Jewish Opinion During the Struggle for Emancipation (1828-1858)', *Transactions of the Jewish Historical Society of England*, xx (1959-61), 113-43; P. Pinsker, 'English Opinion and Jewish Emancipation (1830-1860)', *Jewish Social Studies*, xiv (1952), 51-94; M. C. N. Salbstein, 'The Emancipation of the Jews in Britain, with particular reference to the Debate concerning the admission of the Jews to Parliament, 1828-1860' (University of London Ph.D. thesis, 1975).

2. H. Mayhew, *London Labour and the London Poor* (4 vols., London, 1861-2; Cass reprint, 1967), ii. 126-7.

3. Bill Williams, *The Making of Manchester Jewry 1740-1875* (Manchester, 1976), 129 and 193.

4. Peel Papers, British Library, Additional MS 40560, fol. 126: Goldsmid to Peel, 18 Feb. 1845; the Reform memorandum is in Add. MS 40612, fols. 163-4.

5. L. D. Barnett (trans.), *El Libro de los Acuerdos* (Oxford, 1931), 53-5.

6. Finestein, 116-17; see also U. R. Q. Henriques, *Religious Toleration in England 1787-1833* (London, 1961), 182-3. It was the opinion of Elim d'Avigdor, I. L. Goldsmid's grandson, that Montefiore had deliberately refused his support in the early efforts to achieve emancipation because 'he feared that political emancipation wd. lead the Jews to religious latitudinarianism': Lucien Wolf Archives, Mocatta Library, University College London, file B20 GOL: Elim d'Avigdor to Wolf, no date.

7. Pinsker, 65 and 69.

8. *Pall Mall Gazette*, 24 Nov. 1885, 11.

9. *Jewish Chronicle* (cited hereafter as *J. C.*), 17 July 1908, 25.

10. *Northern Star*, 13 Nov. 1847, 8, quoted in E. Silberner, 'British Socialism and the Jews', *Historica Judaica*, xiv (1952), 34. James Bronterre O'Brien referred to 'Jews and jobbers' in the Chartist Convention on 12 Feb. 1839: A. Plummer, 'The Place of Bronterre O'Brien in the Working-Class Movement', *Economic History Review*, ii (1929-30), 72.

11. W. E. Gladstone, *The State in its Relations with the Church* (London, 1838), 218-35.

12. Henriques, *Religious Toleration*, 190.

13. L. Abrahams, 'Sir I. L. Goldsmid and the Admission of the Jews of England to Parliament', *Transactions of the Jewish Historical Society of England*, iv (1899-1901), 124 and 169.

14. Henriques, *Religious Toleration*, 191.

15. J. Picciotto, *Sketches of Anglo-Jewish History* (ed. I. Finestein, London, 1956), 383; Henriques, *Religious Toleration*, 186-7.

16. Roth, *History*, 249-50; Abrahams, 159.

17. Abrahams, 161.

18. Picciotto, 383.

19. *Mirror of Parliament*, 29 April 1830, 1423, cited in Henriques, *Religious Toleration*, 189. On Levy, see Endelman, 279.

20. Salomons, elected as the first Ashkenazi President of the Board of Deputies in October 1838, resigned less than a month later, probably because he objected to the exclusion of Reform Jews and found that the policy of the Board in this matter hampered his political work: A. M. Hyamson, *David Salomons* (London, 1939), 36.

21. Grey to Goldsmid, 6 Feb. 1834, printed in Abrahams, 169. Grey had made a similar refusal in June 1832: Salbstein, 313.

22. L. Loewe (ed.), *Diaries of Sir Moses and Lady Montefiore* (2 vols., London, 1890), i. 93-4.

23. *Parliamentary Debates*, 3rd series, xxxv (1836), col. 874, 3 August 1836.

24. F. H. Goldsmid, *The Arguments advanced against the Enfranchisement of the Jews, considered in a Series of Letters* (London, 1831), 3-4.

25. Abrahams, 175-6.

26. Salbstein, 324-5, 347-8.

27. Lord George Bentinck was of the opinion that 600 Jews had voted for Russell in 1841: *Parliamentary Debates*, 3rd series, xcv, cols. 1332-3, 17 Dec. 1847. I doubt whether there were that many Jewish voters in the constituency at that time. An examination of the City of London electoral registers (in the Guildhall Library), with particular reference to those voters with Jewish ethnic names, suggests that in the late 1840s about 350 Jews were on the register, 270 of them in the Aldgate, Billingsgate, Portsoken, and Tower wards; a decade later these wards contained 370 Jewish electors, and the total Jewish electorate of the constituency was then about 500. In 1847 the City had 20,057 registered electors, and in 1857 only 19,115.

28. B. Disraeli, *Coningsby* (Everyman edn., London, 1959), 207.

29. *J. C.*, 25 Dec. 1846, 49.

30. A Jewish Association for the Removal of Civil and Religious Disabilities issued an address to the electors of the City in Rothschild's favour: Picciotto, 392.

31. See Bentinck's speech of Dec. 1847, cited in note 27 above.

32. Of the 25 MPs (excluding Rothschild) who represented the constituencies in which four-fifths of Anglo-Jewry lived (the City of London, Finsbury, Greenwich, Lambeth, Marylebone, Southwark, Tower Hamlets, Westminster, Middlesex, Birmingham, Liverpool, and Manchester), 23 supported the resolution: *Parliamentary Debates*, 3rd series, xcv, cols. 1397-1400, 17 Dec. 1847.

33. *Parliamentary Debates*, 3rd series, xcvi, cols. 536-40, 11 Feb. 1848 (second reading); xcviii, cols. 667-70, 4 May 1848 (third reading).

34. Bentinck to Croker, 29 Sept. 1847, in L. J. Jennings (ed.), *The Croker Papers* (3 vols., London, 1885), iii. 138. Bentinck added (ibid., 139) 'I am sure Peel is, and so was Lord Lyndhurst, in favour of the Jews. No doubt it was this knowledge made Lord John [Russell] identify himself with Rothschild.' The Jewish vote was also in evidence in provincial centres. At Birmingham the Jewish vote was 'in a great measure' responsible for the defeat of the previous MP, Richard Spooner, a declared opponent of Jewish emancipation: *J. C.*, 6 Aug. 1847, 214-15.

35. *J. C.*, 21 Jan. 1848, 400; the article is appropriately headed 'Better Late than Never'!

36. *Morning Advertiser*, 4 March 1851, 2.

37. The Oath of Abjuration, prescribed by statute in 1701, was aimed at the Stuart claim to the throne; by the mid-nineteenth century it was a complete anachronism.

38. *J. C.*, 22 June 1855, 213.

39. Ibid., 27 March 1857, 947-8.

40. Ibid., 3 April 1857, 959.

41. *Plymouth and Devonport Journal*, 2 April 1857, 6; Collier and White were returned with majorities of 545 and 484 respectively. The total population of Plymouth at that time was 52,221, and the Jewish population, in 1850, was between 200 and 250: V. D. Lipman, *Social History of the Jews in England 1850-1950* (London, 1954), 19.

42. *J. C.*, 27 March 1857, 950; 3 April 1857, 957.
43. Ibid., 27 March 1857, 948. See also the report of the meeting of Jewish electors and non-electors in Tower Hamlets, ibid., 7 May 1852, 242-3.
44. *J. C.*, 8 May 1857, 996-7; 22 May 1857, 1014-15; 12 June 1857, 1038.
45. *Parliamentary Debates*, 3rd series, cl, cols. 1138-93, 31 May 1858.
46. The poll books referred to here are in the Institute of Historical Research; identification of Jewish voters is by ethnic name.
47. I am indebted to my friend Bill Williams, of the Manchester Polytechnic Institute of Advanced Studies, for the information concerning Manchester and Salford, which is based on his own work on Manchester Jewry. The Birmingham statistics come from *Birmingham Jewry 1749-1914* (Birmingham Jewish History Research Group, 1980), 25.
48. I. Finestein, 'Forcing the Pace of the Law', *J. C.*, 8 Nov. 1857, 9.
49. *J. C.*, 31 Oct. 1924, 10; 19 Oct. 1951, 13; see also C. Bermant, *The Cousinhood* (London, 1971), 99. There is one vote by Montefiore recorded, in 1852; when faced with a choice between a Peelite and a Conservative anti-emancipationist, he voted for the former: East Kent Poll Book, 1852, in the Guildhall Library. In 1846 he wrote to Peel asking to be created a baronet; the request was granted by return of post: Peel Papers, British Library Add. MS 40594, fols. 259-61. There is absolutely nothing in Sir Moses's life to suggest that he was ever a Liberal in matters of domestic politics.
50. *J. C.*, 27 May 1859, 5.
51. Ibid., 11 Aug. 1865, 5.
52. Ibid., 16 Jan. 1880, 6.
53. It is also noteworthy that the first Viscount Samuel's father, Edwin (1823-77) was also a Conservative: Viscount Samuel, *Memoirs* (London, 1945), 3.
54. Finestein, *Transactions of the Jewish Historical Society of England*, xx (1959-61), 127.
55. *J. C.*, 8 Feb. 1861, 4.

3. The Eclipse of Jewish Liberalism

1. He did, however, use his influence with the Government during the passage of the Bill to establish voting by secret ballot, in 1872; orthodox Jews were allowed to have their votes marked by the returning officer in the event of a Saturday poll. This concession had been sought by the Board of Deputies, but a great number of orthodox Jews repudiated it, no doubt on the grounds that not only were they not permitted to write on the sabbath, but neither were they permitted (save in the case of danger to life) to request anyone else to do the writing for them. The concession had the further effect of making public (or, at least, less secret) the votes of those Jews who actually took advantage of it: *J. C.*, 10 May 1872, 81; 18 May 1894, 11; 13 July 1894, 9. Saturday polls were popular in the nineteenth and early twentieth centuries; the last general election to be held on a Saturday was that of 14 December 1918.
2. *J. C.*, 3 Sept. 1858, 302. In 1868 Jews formed about 0.2 per cent of the population, but nearly 1 per cent of the House of Commons: see Appendix.
3. Isaac's mother hailed from Margate, his father from Poole, and he was born in Chatham in 1823. He and his elder brother were chief army contractors to the Confederate Government during the American Civil War. In 1869 he took the lease of a colliery in Nottingham, but as an MP he made little political impact, and in 1880 was defeated in a campaign marred by anti-Semitism. In 1885 he offered himself for election at Clerkenwell, but was again defeated, and he died in penury in a bed-sitting-room in South Hampstead in 1903. He was a founder of

the Bayswater synagogue and a life member of the Council of the United Synagogue. See M. Caplan, 'Tory's First Jewish MP', *J. C.*, 1 March 1974, 9.

4. The vote was taken in the early hours of Saturday 28 April: *J. C.*, 4 May 1866, 5; *Parliamentary Debates*, 3rd series, clxxxiii, cols. 152-4.

5. On Jessel, see A. L. Goodhart, *Five Jewish Lawyers of the Common Law* (Oxford, 1949), 16-23.

6. Hyamson, *David Salomons*, 88-9; *J. C.*, 25 Aug. 1871, 6.

7. D. W. Marks and A. Löwy, *Memoir of Sir Francis Henry Goldsmid* (2nd edn., London, 1882), *passim.*

8. On Simon (1818-97) see *J. C.*, 2 July 1897, 21-5; *Dewsbury Reporter*, 3 July 1897, 5; *Dictionary of National Biography*. On the Cork affair see *The Times*, 13 March 1888, 10, and L. Hyman, *The Jews of Ireland* (Jerusalem, 1972), 219-21. On the Holborn by-election see *J. C.*, 30 Nov. 1888; 9 and 21 Dec. 1888, 7. Simon was knighted in 1886.

9. *Standard*, 3 Aug. 1868, 4.

10. *J. C.*, 27 Jan. 1860, 5.

11. Ibid., 11 Aug. 1865, 5.

12. *Standard*, 3 Aug. 1868, 4.

13. *J. C.*, 21 Aug. 1868, 5.

14. Ibid., 4 Aug. 1865, 4.

15. Ibid., 15 Feb. 1867, 4.

16. On Michael Henry, see C. Roth, *The Jewish Chronicle 1841-1941* (London, 1949), 81-2.

17. *J. C.*, 13 Sept. 1872, 329.

18. Ibid., 9 Aug. 1872, 262; the total number of MPs in the Commons at that time was actually 658.

19. Ibid., 6 Feb. 1874, 752; 12 Oct. 1900, 6.

20. Ibid., 11 Aug. 1865, 5; see also Henry de Worms, quoted in ibid., 13 Feb. 1880, 8.

21. Ibid., 7 Aug. 1868, 2; 23 Oct. 1868, 7.

22. Ibid., 16 Oct. 1868, 5.

23. Ibid., 24 July 1868, 5; 21 Aug. 1868, 2 and 4; 20 Nov. 1868, 5. Rothschild had also wounded orthodox feelings by attending an election meeting on the festival of Tabernacles; he was re-elected, unopposed, at a by-election the following February (1869) but lost the seat, finally, in 1874, and died in 1879.

24. R. T. Shannon, *Gladstone and the Bulgarian Agitation 1876* (London, 1963), 198-9.

25. *The Times*, 23 Dec. 1879, 6.

26. *Daily News*, 13 Oct. 1876, 6; Green also wrote a similar letter to *The Times*, 14 Oct. 1876, 11.

27. Shannon, 127-8; the seat was retained by the Conservatives. For a discussion of the Rothschild influence in Buckinghamshire, where the family owned several great estates, see H. Pelling, *Social Geography of British Elections 1885-1910* (London, 1967), 119.

28. *J. C.*, 1 Dec. 1876, 55; 8 Dec. 1876, 570; 15 Dec. 1876, 583; 22 Dec. 1876, 599.

29. Ibid., 29 Dec. 1876, 619.

30. L. Wolf, *Sir Moses Montefiore* (London, 1884), 271-3.

31. *J. C.*, 20 Oct. 1876, 458.

32. J. Cang, 'Anglo-Jewry and the Berlin Congress', *J. C.*, 22 Jan. 1954, 15.

33. Count Corti, *The Reign of the House of Rothschild* (trans. B and B. Lunn, London, 1928), 449.

34. Cang, loc.cit.

35. P. Goodman, *Moses Montefiore* (Philadelphia, 1925), 221.

36. Shannon, 200-1; R. Blake, *Disraeli* (London, 1966), 604-7; C. Holmes, *Anti-*

Semitism in British Society 1876-1939 (London, 1979), 10-12 and 31; *J. C.*, 7 Oct. 1881, 6.

37. *J. C.*, 30 Jan. 1874, 730. Gladstone later admitted that he had been misled: *The Times*, 24 Dec. 1879, 6, letter from 'Politicus'.

38. *J. C.*, 13 Oct. 1876, 438.

39. Ibid., 3 Nov. 1876, 486.

40. Marks and Löwy, 136.

41. *J. C.*, 24 Jan. 1879, 4; 7 Feb. 1879; 4.

42. On the change of allegiance by Jews in the City of London, see ibid., 19 Aug. 1881, 9.

43. Ibid., 27 Oct. 1876, 469; 19 Dec. 1876, 6 and 10.

44. *The Times*, 22 Dec. 1879, 8. Gladstone's refusal to act on behalf of Romanian Jewry was conveyed in a letter from him to the Manchester Liberal Association, printed in ibid., 20 Dec. 1879, 11.

45. As was his Liberal colleague, Arthur Cohen; see Dilke Papers, British Library Add. MS 43880, fols. 142-3: Cohen to Sir Charles Dilke, 7 March 1882.

46. Gladstone Papers, British Library Add. MS44474, fols. 103-4: Simon to Gladstone, 29 Jan. 1881.

47. Ibid., fols. 133-4: Simon to Gladstone, 5 Feb. 1882.

48. In his reply to Simon in the House of Commons, Gladstone had made it clear that the Government would not make any official representations in a matter 'purely internal and under the control of another Government': *Parliamentary Debates*, 3rd series, ccclxvi, col. 244, 9 Feb. 1882.

49. Gladstone Papers, British Library Add. MS 44462, fols. 253-4: telegrams from Cohen to Gladstone, 23 March 1880.

50. *J. C.*, 7 Dec. 1888, 7.

51. Ibid., 1 July 1887, 7; the quotation is from a letter dated 8 Feb. 1874.

52. Ibid., 30 Oct. 1885, 8.

53. Dilke Papers, British Library Add. MS 43913, fol. 90: Ferdinand de Rothschild to Dilke, 14 Jan. 1885.

54. *J. C.*, 30 March 1894, 7: letter from the Liberal MP H. S. Leon. Thus the politically ambitious and essentially materialistic Jew of Lancaster Gate, Reuben Sachs, the central figure of Amy Levy's novel of the same name, published by Macmillan in 1888, naturally became a Conservative MP.

55. *J. C.*, 13 March 1885, 11.

56. Ibid., 30 Nov. 1888, 9.

57. Ibid., 12 July 1895, 9.

58. C. Roth, 'Britain's Three Chief Rabbis', in L. Jung (ed.), *Jewish Leaders (1750-1940)* (New York, 1953), 484; *J. C.*, 21 July 1911, 22.

59. *The Times*, 7 Jan. 1898, 6.

60. *J. C.*, 14 Jan. 1898, 7. The letter also caused a sensation in Jewish circles, for it appeared to demonstrate that the Adlers preferred a non-Jew to a Jew in Parliament!

61. *The Times*, 8 Jan. 1898, 6.

62. *J. C.*, 10 Nov. 1899, 1.

63. Israel Finestein thought so: I. Finestein, 'The New Community 1880-1918', in Lipman, *Three Centuries*, 111. Those of my readers who are familiar with my article 'Not Quite British: The Political Attitudes of Anglo-Jewry', in I. Crewe (ed.), *British Political Sociology Yearbook, Volume 2. The Politics of Race* (London, 1975), 190, will know that I, too, inclined to this view; more detailed examination of the evidence has led me to modify this opinion.

64. *J. C.*, 13 Nov. 1885, 10.

65. Ibid., 2 July 1886, 9.

66. *Eastern Post*, 9 July 1892, 5; *East London Observer*, 20 July 1895, 6.
67. *East London Observer*, loc.cit.
68. Thus in September 1900 J. de Haas, Honorary Secretary of the English Zionist Federation, had to confess to Theodor Herzl that, from an electoral point of view, Zionist influence in Whitechapel was not great, because 'so many of our friends are not naturalized': Central Zionist Archives, Jerusalem, Records of the Central Zionist Office, Vienna: Z1, file 243: de Haas to Herzl, 27 Sept. 1900.
69. Pelling, *Social Geography*, 42 and 44.
70. *East London Observer*, 20 July 1895, 6. My own calculation of the number of Jewish electors in the constituency at the turn of the century, based on the occurrence of Jewish ethnic names in the 1900 electoral register, is remarkably close to this estimate: about 1,550.
71. A copy of his 1885 election address, in Yiddish, is in the Local Collection of the Tower Hamlets Central Library, Stepney, file 321.5.
72. *Eastern Post*, 9 July 1892, 5.
73. *East London Observer*, 6 July 1895, 5; 20 July 1895, 6; *Reynolds's Newspaper*, 14 July 1895, 1.
74. My own estimate of the number of Jewish voters in St. George's is somewhat higher, at about 350, or roughly 10 per cent of the 1900 electorate of the constituency.
75. *East London Observer*, 22 Sept. 1900, 3; 25 Sept. 1900, 3.
76. *J. C.*, 12 Oct. 1900, 7.
77. Ibid.
78. Ibid., 28 Sept. 1900, 5.
79. *East London Observer*, 11 June 1892, 4; *Eastern Post*, 18 June 1892, 2.

4. The Socialists Arrive

1. I am of course excluding from this account the activities of German *émigrés*, such as Karl Marx, who might well have been of Jewish origin but who repudiated their ethnic roots and had no contact with Anglo-Jewry.
2. M. Beer, *Fifty Years of International Socialism* (London, 1935), 104.
3. Lipman, *Social History*, 76-7.
4. H. Pollins, 'Anglo-Jewish Trade Unions, 1870-1914' (Paper delivered to the Jewish Historical Society of England, 16 March 1977).
5. E. Tcherikower (ed.), *The Early Jewish Labour Movement in the United States* (trans. A. Antonovsky, New York, 1961), 181-2.
6. P. Elman, 'The Beginnings of the Jewish Trade Union Movement in England', *Transactions of the Jewish Historical Society of England*, xvii (1951-2), 58-9. There is a detailed account of the meeting in W. J. Fishman, *East End Jewish Radicals 1875-1914* (London, 1975), 114-17, based, however, on Lieberman's own one-sided report. See also L. P. Gartner, *The Jewish Immigrant in England 1870-1914* (London, 1960), 105.
7. R. Rocker, *The London Years* (trans. J. Leftwich, London, 1956), 121; Fishman, *East End Jewish Radicals*, 131. On Lieberman and the Hebrew Socialist Union generally, see the work in Yiddish by E. Tcherikower, *Der Onhayb Fun Der Yiddisher Sotsialistisher Bavegung (Liebermans Tekufeh)* ['The Beginning of the Jewish Socialist Movement (Lieberman's Period)'] (Warsaw, 1929) where in cols. 533-94 the minute book of the Union is printed in full. See also N. Levin, *Jewish Socialist Movements, 1871-1917* (London, 1978), 40-5.
8. *J. C.*, 8 Sept. 1876, 364.
9. Gartner, *The Jewish Immigrant*, 106.

10. Rocker, *The London Years*, 118.
11. Ibid. 120.
12. Quoted in Tcherikower, *The Early Jewish Labour Movement*, 185.
13. L. Kochan, 'Jews on the Move', *Listener*, 27 May 1971, 677; two million Jews settled in the USA.
14. Roth, *History*, 267; *J. C.*, 2 Feb. 1883, 10-11.
15. Lipman, *Social History*, 103.
16. Lipman, in Lipman, *Three Centuries*, 85.
17. Quoted in Gartner, 25.
18. B. Homa, *A Fortress in Anglo-Jewry* (London, 1953), 192 and *passim*; Gartner, 209-14.
19. D. Miller, 'Traditionalism and Estrangement', in P. Longworth (ed.), *Confrontations with Judaism* (London, 1967), 201.
20. E. Mendelsohn, *Class Struggle in the Pale: The Formative Years of the Jewish Workers' Movement in Tsarist Russia* (Cambridge, 1970), 22.
21. Ibid. 110-11.
22. A. L. Patkin, *The Origins of the Russian-Jewish Labour Movement* (Melbourne, 1947), 138.
23. The Bund could not, however, make up its mind how far it was prepared to go down the assimilationist path, and at the second Russian Social-Democratic Party conference, in London in 1903, it left the party when its plan of organization based upon the principle of a federation of national parties was rejected: Patkin, op. cit., 189. It re-entered the party at the Unity Convention in Stockholm in April 1906: O. I. Janowsky, *The Jews and Minority Rights (1898-1919)* (New York, 1933), 37-40. The Bund was not finally dissolved until 1949: *J. C.*, 28 Jan. 1949, 10.
24. Janowsky, 42-6; Levin, 411.
25. Mendelsohn, 106.
26. Patkin, 17.
27. Mendelsohn, 109.
28. For a résumé of its contents see Fishman, 140-51.
29. Ibid. 150.
30. Rocker, 123; A. Frumkin, *In Friling Fun Yidischen Sozialism* [Yiddish: 'In the Springtime of Jewish Socialism'] (New York, 1940), 35-75, deals with the history of the *Arbeter Fraint*, of which Frumkin became editor.
31. Tcherikower, *The Early Jewish Labour Movement*, 188.
32. *Arbeter Fraint*, No. 3, 1885, quoted in Tcherikower, *The Early Jewish Labour Movement*, 188.
33. Silberner, 38.
34. *J. C.*, 13 Oct. 1905, 28.
35. Silberner, 40-1. On 'rich-Jew anti-Semitism' at the time of the Boer War see Holmes, *Anti-Semitism in British Society*, 66-70.
36. Tcherikower, *The Early Jewish Labour Movement*, 191. See also the speech of Lewis Lyons to the Chief Rabbi, *J. C.*, 18 Nov. 1892, 10.
37. Quoted in Tcherikower, *The Early Jewish Labour Movement*, 194.
38. Gartner, 132.
39. Ibid. 132-3; Levin, 132.
40. *J. C.*, 25 March 1932, 12.
41. Gartner, 117.
42. Ibid. 118.
43. *J. C.*, 25 Feb. 1887, 7.
44. Gartner, 114-15; Fishman, 155-7.
45. *J. C.*, 21 Oct. 1887, 7.

46.   J. E. Blank, *The Minutes of the Federation of Synagogues. A Twenty-Five Years' Review* (London, 1912), 20. See also the circular issued by the Federation on 20 Nov. 1889, quoting from a letter written by Montagu to Blank on 6 Nov.: Tower Hamlets Central Library, Stepney, Local Collection, file 230.7.

47.   C. Holmes, 'The Leeds Jewish Tailors' Strikes of 1885 and 1888', *Yorkshire Archaeological Journal*, vol. 45 (1973), 158.

48.   J. Buckman, 'The Economic and Social History of Alien Immigration to Leeds, 1880-1914' (University of Strathclyde Ph. D. Thesis, 1968), 26-7.

49.   Ibid. 247-8.

50.   Ibid. 256-7.

51.   Ibid. 261-73; Holmes, *Yorkshire Archaeological Journal*, 161-4; H. Burgin, *Die Geschichte fun der Idisher Arbayter Bavegung in America Russland un England* [Yiddish: 'The History of the Jewish Labour Movement in America, Russia, and England'] (New York, 1915), 57-62.

52.   Sweeney was secretary of the Tailors' Trade Society in Leeds in 1888.

53.   Buckman, 258-60.

54.   *Arbeter Fraint*, 18 Jan. 1889, quoted in Buckman, 282.

55.   Buckman, 291-2.

56.   Holmes, *Yorkshire Archaeological Journal*, 165; Buckman, 322.

57.   Buckman, 343-6.

58.   Rocker, *The London Years*, 130, called him 'an opportunist'.

59.   Tcherikower, *The Early Jewish Labour Movement*, 196-7.

60.   In November 1890 Montagu used his influence with the Chief Rabbi to suppress a meeting called in Mile End, by the Berner Street Club, to protest against the persecution of Jews in Russia. 'It was thought that Dr Adler was hostile to the meeting', a local paper explained, 'because the club had been most serviceable in organising trade unions amongst the Jewish workers, a matter which is inimical to the interests of the wealthy portion of the [Jewish] community': *East London Advertiser*, 15 Nov. 1890, in the Tower Hamlets Central Library, Stepney, Local Collection, file 430. See also Adler's sermons preached in German in the East End in May 1892 and October 1895: *J. C.*, 27 May 1892, 9 and 1 Nov. 1895, 16-17.

61.   Gartner, 124.

62.   *J. C.*, 6 Sept. 1889, 4.

63.   Ibid., 4 Oct. 1889, 7-8.

64.   Gartner, 126.

65.   *Arbeter Fraint*, 16 Dec. 1892, quoted in Gartner, op.cit. 130-1.

66.   On Rocker see Fishman, 229-309, and Rocker, *The London Years, passim.*

67.   Fishman, 277, 281-2, 294-300; J. Lestchinsky, *Der Idisher Arbayter (in London)* [Yiddish: 'The Jewish Worker (in London)'] (Vilna, 1907), 23-8.

68.   Fishman, 301.

69.   Ibid. 302.

70.   Gartner, 139-40; Buckman, 245 and 340.

71.   Lestchinsky, 31-2; Gartner, 141.

72.   *J. C.*, 6 Nov. 1903, 33.

73.   Ibid., 26 Feb. 1904, 30.

74.   S. Levenberg, *The Jews and Palestine. A Study in Labour Zionism* (London, 1945), 126-7.

75.   S. Brodetsky, *Memoirs* (London, 1960), 32.

5. The Alien Makes His Mark

1.   The reports of the two Select Committees are summarized in Lipman, *Social History*, 135-7.
2.   *J. C.*, 31 July 1891, 11; and see B. Gainer, *The Alien Invasion* (London, 1972), 61-2.
3.   Dr Gainer reckons that the higher-than-average Conservative share of the poll in East End boroughs at the general elections of 1886, 1895, 1900, and 1906 'reflected anti-alienism': Gainer, 59.
4.   *Parliamentary Debates*, 4th series, viii, col. 1210, 11 Feb. 1893.
5.   On Liberal attitudes generally see J. A. Garrard, *The English and Immigration 1880-1910* (London, 1971), 85-102.
6.   Gartner, 47.
7.   M. J. Landa, *The Alien Problem and its Remedy* (London, 1911), 188-9.
8.   Bethnal Green South-West and Hoxton were Conservative gains.
9.   *East London Observer*, 2 Oct. 1900, 3; 6 Oct. 1900, 5.
10. *Daily News*, 28 Sept. 1900, 5; *J. C.*, 28 Sept. 1900, 15.
11. *J. C.*, 28 Sept. 1900, 5; Gainer, 67-73.
12. Holmes, *Anti-Semitism in British Society*, 89-97.
13. *J. C.*, 30 Aug. 1901, 18.
14. Garrard, 191-2.
15. *J. C.*, 19 Jan. 1900, 15.
16. *Cornish Echo*, 28 Sept. 1900, 8; see also Cohen's attack on the Falmouth Liberals in *J. C.*, 26 Oct. 1900, 6.
17. Among the Liberal MPs who supported the League was Sydney Buxton, MP for Poplar; see C. Bermant, *Point of Arrival A Study of London's East End* (London, 1975), 145.
18. *East London Observer*, 18 Jan. 1902, 2; other Jewish MPs who supported restrictions on immigration were Louis Sinclair (Conservative, Romford) and Benjamin Cohen (Conservative, Islington): *J. C.*, 13 Nov. 1903, 27; Gartner, 55.
19. The report of the Royal Commission is summarized in Lipman, *Social History*, 139-41.
20. *J. C.*, 6 May 1904, 19.
21. Ibid., 27 May 1904, 10; the deputation was led by Lord Rothschild.
22. O. K. Rabinowicz, *Winston Churchill on Jewish Problems* (London, 1956), 37, 50-3; and see Gainer, 146.
23. *J. C.*, 2 Dec. 1904, 12. For a full account of Churchill's wrecking tactics see Gainer, 188-90.
24. *J. C.*, 15 July 1904, 20; and see Rabinowicz, 56-9.
25. Laski to Churchill, 14 July 1904, printed in R. S. Churchill, *Winston S. Churchill*, vol. II, *Companion*, part I, *1901-1907* (London, 1969), 357.
26. *Parliamentary Debates*, 4th series, cxlv, col. 734, 2 May 1905.
27. On Straus see *J. C.*, 22 Feb. 1907, 18.
28. *East London Observer*, 26 Aug. 1905, 7. From an examination of Jewish ethnic names in the Mile End electoral registers, I estimate that between 1900 and 1906 the registered Jewish electors of the constituency increased from 6 to over 8 per cent (about 450 voters) of the total electorate which, however, fell from 5,915 to 5,419 between these dates.
29. *J. C.*, 13 Jan. 1905, 10.
30. *Eastern Post*, 14 Jan. 1905, 5.
31. *East London Observer*, 14 Jan. 1905, 5.
32. *J. C.*, 5 May 1905, 25.
33. Ibid., 24. Of the 12 Jewish MPs then in the House, 4 (3 Unionists and 1 Liberal)

abstained, 4 (all Unionists) supported the bill, and 4 (1 Unionist and 3 Liberals) voted against it.

34. *J. C.*, 12 May 1905, 13.
35. Ibid., 26 May 1905, 12 and 18; 2 June 1905, 4; 9 June 1905, 7 and 9; 16 June 1905, 25; 23 June 1905, 25.
36. Ibid., 26 May 1905, 27: speech of Sir William Walrond, MP, Conservative Chief Whip 1900-2.
37. *J. C.*, 21 July 1905, 12.
38. Chief Rabbi Adler later wrote to Herbert Bentwich, a founder of the English Zionist Federation and one of Herzl's earliest English supporters, that 'we [Anglo-Jewry] must frankly agree, that we do not desire to admit criminals, and that there is force in the argument against the admission of those [Jews] mentally or physically afflicted': Herbert Bentwich Papers, Central Zionist Archives, A100, file 7a: Adler to Bentwich, 1 April 1906.
39. *J. C.*, 8 Dec. 1905, 11.
40. Garrard, 46.
41. *J. C.*, 19 May 1905, 7; 26 May 1905, 16-17.
42. Between 1900 and 1905 the number of naturalization certificates issued rose by 18 per cent: *Parliamentary Papers* 1901, lxiv (194) and 1906, xcvi (93).
43. *J. C.*, 9 June 1905, 18: letter from M. Sidney of Bermondsey. At Whitechapel, for instance, the total electorate fell from 5,004 to 4,279 between the elections of 1900 and 1906, but I estimate that the Jewish proportion rose from about 31 per cent to about 34 per cent. In 1910, by which time the total electorate had dropped still further—to 3,986, the Jewish proportion was certainly at least 35 per cent. In the neighbouring St. George's constituency, the Jewish proportion of the total electorate rose from about 10 per cent to over 15 per cent between 1900 and 1906. For Mile End, see note 28 above.
44. *J. C.*, 9 June 1905, 18.
45. *Eastern Post*, 6 Jan. 1906, supplement, 2; 13 Jan. 1906, 8. Balfour's Government had resigned in December 1905, but the general election was not held until January 1906.
46. *East London Advertiser*, 13 Jan. 1906, 5; *J. C.*, 19 Jan. 1906, 10.
47. *J. C.*, 12 Jan. 1906, 19; 26 Jan. 1906, 27; *East London Observer*, 6 Jan. 1906, 5.
48. Pelling, *Social Geography*, 43.
49. The most important being Mile End, which Straus won by 178 votes. He later claimed that the constituency contained about 500 Jewish voters, but presumably some of these had already supported him at the by-election in 1905: *J. C.*, 22 Feb. 1907, 18; and see note 28 above.
50. *J. C.*, 19 Jan. 1906, 9; Garrard, 122.
51. Pelling, *Social Geography*, 293. For a survey of the Jewish vote in the constituency see E. E. Burgess, 'The Soul of the Leeds Ghetto', *Yorkshire Evening News*, 4 Feb. 1925, 4. The total electorate in Leeds Central in 1906 was 8,893.
52. Gaster Papers, Mocatta Library, University College London: Gaster to Winston Churchill, 26 Feb. 1906.
53. *J. C.*, 26 Jan. 1906, 19; 2 Feb. 1906, 20-21; 9 Feb. 1906, 19; 16 Feb. 1906, 21; *Leeds and Yorkshire Mercury*, 3 Jan. 1906, 6; 5 Jan. 1906, 5; 6 Jan. 1906, 5; 8 Jan. 1906, 6; 10 Jan. 1906, 5.
54. A. K. Russell, *Liberal Landslide—The General Election of 1906* (London, 1973), 194.
55. *J. C.*, 19 Jan. 1906, 27.
56. Garrard, 105.
57. *J. C.*, 25 Oct. 1907, 7; 13 Dec. 1907, 14; 17 Jan. 1908, 7-8.
58. Ibid., 17 July 1908, 8.

59. Ibid., 17 Jan. 1908, 7.
60. Garrard, 126.
61. *J. C.*, 24 April 1908, 7.
62. Ibid., 7 Nov. 1902, 15-16; 4 May 1906, 7; 18 May 1906, 7; 3 Aug. 1906, 6-7; 27 Nov. 1908, 14.
63. See the useful discussion in M. Beloff, 'Lucien Wolf and the Anglo-Russian Entente 1907-1914', *The Intellectual in Politics* (London, 1970), 111-42.
64. *J. C.*, 2 Aug. 1907, 8; 9 Aug. 1907, 8. At its March 1907 conference at Carlisle the Social-Democratic Federation had condemned further pogroms in Russia; this resolution was proposed by Henry Alexander, a member of the Willesden branch of the movement and the representative of Brondesbury synagogue at the Board of Deputies: Ibid., 5 April 1907, 19.
65. Speech by D. L. Alexander, reported in *J. C.*, 14 Dec. 1906, 16.
66. Ibid., 23 Nov. 1906, 17.
67. *J. C.*, 10 Dec. 1909, 5.
68. *J. C.*, 24 Jan. 1908, 18.
69. Ibid., 24 April 1908, 10.
70. Ibid. 11.
71. Ibid., 1 May 1908, 14.
72. *Manchester Guardian*, 16 April 1908, 7.
73. *Manchester Courier*, 16 April 1908, 7; *J. C.*, 17 April, 11.
74. *J. C.*, 1 May 1908, 13.
75. Ibid., 24 April 1908, 11.
76. Ibid., 12 April 1907, 12: letter from Moses Baritz of Cheetham, who declared 'I belong to a branch of the Social-Democratic Federation of which the members—with two exceptions—are all Jews.' See also *Manchester Guardian*, 17 April 1908, 7.
77. *Manchester Guardian*, 23 April 1908, 10; *J. C.*, 1 May 1908, 13. A week before polling the *J. C.* had to announce that the Government had definitely refused to reduce the naturalization fee: *J. C.*, 17 April 1908, 5.
78. *J. C.*, 1 May 1908, 13.
79. Ibid.
80. Garrard, 129 note 1.
81. *J. C.*, 22 May 1908, 17; the number of Jewish voters was probably nearer 1,000.
82. R. S. Churchill, *Winston S. Churchill*, vol. II (London, 1967), 257.
83. *J.C.*, 1 May 1908, 14.
84. Churchill himself laid most of the blame upon the Irish Catholics; his son stressed the desertion of Unionist Free Traders: R. S. Churchill, *Winston S. Churchill*, vol. II, 260.
85. For some evidence of Conservative switchers, see *Manchester Courier*, 16 April 1908, 8.
86. *J. C.*, 15 May 1908, 13.
87. Ibid., 1 May 1908, 15.
88. Ibid., 29 May 1908, 7; 13 May 1910, 14; 10 June 1910, 25; Garrard, 130.
89. *J. C.*, 21 Jan. 1910, 16.
90. On the 1910 elections in North-West Manchester see P. F. Clarke, *Lancashire and the New Liberalism* (Cambridge, 1971), 259-60, 300. The Liberals lost the seat again at a by-election in 1912. On that occasion Nathan Laski refused to use his influence with the Jewish voters, on the grounds that the Government had not lowered the naturalization fee; a manifesto, signed by the Revd H. Levin and fifty other Jewish electors, explained why, for the same reason, they intended to switch sides and vote Conservative. Stuart Samuel was brought into the constituency to try to redress the balance, but to no avail; it was estimated that

half of the Jewish vote went to the victorious Conservative candidate: Sir Stuart
Montagu Samuel Press Cuttings Book 1911-20, pp. 24-5, House of Lords
Record Office Historical Collection 97; see also *J. C.*, 9 Aug. 1912, 18.

91. *J. C.*, 17 Dec. 1909, 17; 21 Jan. 1910, 11.
92. Lipman, *Social History*, 169; both Mile End and North Hackney were retained by
     the Conservatives in December 1910.
93. *The Times*, 18 Dec. 1909, 8. The previous day, in a speech to Nonconformists at
     the Queen's Hall, Lloyd George had referred to 'those Philistines, who are not
     all uncircumcized': ibid., 17 Dec., 6.
94. *J. C.*, 7 Jan. 1910, 16; Belloc won the seat by 316 votes.
95. *The Times*, 10 Jan. 1910, 11.
96. *J. C.*, 14 Jan. 1910, 26.
97. Ibid., 31 Dec. 1909, 18.
98. Ibid., 7 Jan. 1910, 15.
99. *Commons Debates*, 5th series, i. col. 976, 25 Feb. 1909.
100. Ibid., xix. col. 1320, 20 July 1910.
101. Garrard, 133.
102. *J. C.*, 14 Jan. 1910, 9.

6. The Zionist Dimension

1. *J. C.*, 18 Sept. 1908, 7. Irish Nationalist MPs were fervent in their support of
    Jews, both in Britain and Russia, and over the question of Zionism. Michael
    Davitt, the founder of the Land League, had visited Palestine, and supported
    Zionist policies; in 1903, three years before his death, he travelled to Russia as
    special correspondent of Hearst newspapers, to investigate the Kishinev
    pogrom, and the book he subsequently wrote, *Within the Pale*, was 'an eloquent
    plea for Zionism': F. Sheehy-Skeffington, *Michael Davitt* (London, 1967), 127,
    185-6. For Davitt's support of the Jews of Limerick during the local Catholic
    'boycott' of them in 1904, see Emanuel, 160-1. For Samuel Montagu's support
    (including financial) of Parnell, see L. H. Montagu, *Samuel Montagu First Baron
    Swaythling* [London, 1913], 74. For John Redmond's support of the Balfour
    Declaration, see *J. C.*, 7 Dec. 1917, 14.
2. *J. C.*, 10 Sept. 1909, 14; Jewish Conservatives in the city attempted a counter-
    organization, though less formally: ibid.
3. I. Abrahams (ed.), *The Literary Remains of the Rev. Simeon Singer* (London, 1908),
    209-15.
4. *J. C.*, 29 Oct. 1909, 27; 5 Nov. 1909, 27.
5. Ibid., 8 Nov. 1912, 12.
6. Ibid., 28 Feb. 1913, 29; 16 May 1913, 18; 23 May 1913, 19; 26 June 1914, 44.
    The League sported a Hebrew banner declaring 'It is the joy of the righteous to
    do justice.' See also M. Wohlgelernter, *Israel Zangwill* (New York, 1964), 212-18.
7. *J. C.*, 14 March 1913, 28.
8. Ibid., 17 Oct. 1913, 10.
9. Ibid., 5 June 1914, 25.
10. Emanuel, 181: 'Steps were successfully taken to impede the formation of a
    Jewish Political Club in a provincial city.'
11. *J. C.*, 7 July 1911, 3; 14 July 1911, 17-19; 28 July 1911, 11; 24 Nov. 1911, 16.
    The offending clauses were dropped so far as London, West Ham, and parts of
    Leeds, Liverpool, and Manchester were concerned.
12. Ibid., 27 Oct. 1911, 16-17.
13. Sir Stuart Montagu Samuel Press Cuttings Book 1911-20, pp. 6-7, 9: House of

Lords Record Office Historical Collection 97; R. S. Churchill, *Winston S. Churchill*, vol. II, *Companion*, part 2, *1907-1911* (London, 1969), 1260-1: Stuart Samuel to W. S. Churchill, 26 June 1911.

14.   *J. C.*, 20 Oct. 1899, 17; 3 Nov. 1899, 17; 10 Nov. 1899, 13.

15.   *J. C.*, 25 May 1900, 11. The *J. C.* (23 March 1900, 17) claimed that over 600 Jews were serving at the front.

16.   A. Newman, *Chief Rabbi Dr Joseph H. Hertz* (London, 1973), 6; P. Paneth, *Guardian of the Law The Chief Rabbi, Dr J. H. Hertz* [London, 1943], 7.

17.   *J. C.*, 7 Aug. 1914, 5; Roth, *The Jewish Chronicle*, facing p. 105. Greenberg suspended publication of the *Darkest Russia* supplement, which had chronicled the pogroms there.

18.   *J. C.*, 14 Aug. 1914, 14.

19.   B. A. Kosmin and N. Grizzard, *The Jewish Dead in the Great War as an Indicator for Anglo-Jewish Demography and Class Stratification in 1914* (Board of Deputies mimeo., London, 1974), 2.

20.   *J. C.*, 17 March 1916, 23. See also S. G. Bayme, 'Jewish Leadership and Anti-Semitism in Britain, 1898-1918' (Columbia University Ph. D. thesis, 1977), 25.

21.   *J. C.*, 1 Oct. 1915, 6.

22.   N. Bentwich, 'The Social Transformation of Anglo-Jewry 1883-1960', *Jewish Journal of Sociology*, vol. 2 (1960), 16.

23.   L. Stein, *The Balfour Declaration* (London, 1961), 489.

24.   The fullest treatment of this episode is in Holmes, *Anti-Semitism in British Society*, 126-31; see also Bermant, *Point of Arrival*, 222-30.

25.   Lipman, *Social History*, 157-9, 164.

26.   *J. C.*, 17 Dec. 1920, 25; by then *Poale Zion* membership in Britain was about 1,000: *Encyclopaedia Judaica*.

27.   Those who wish to pursue this subject should consult D. Vital, *The Origins of Zionism* (Oxford, 1975), W. Laqueur, *A History of Zionism* (London, 1972), and Stein.

28.   Samuel Montagu was one of the first *Hovovei* Zionists in England: J. Fraenkel, 'Lucien Wolf and Theodor Herzl', *Transactions of the Jewish Historical Society of England*, xx (1959-61), 175.

29.   The term 'Zionism' was coined by Nathan Birnbaum in his journal *Selbsteman-zipation*, published in Vienna on 1 April 1890: see *Encyclopaedia Judaica* and Vital, 222-3.

30.   M. Lowenthal (trans. and ed.), *The Diaries of Theodor Herzl* (London, 1958), 81, 24 Nov. 1895.

31.   Lloyd George Papers, House of Lords Record Office, C/25/14/1: Memo by Edwin Montagu, 16 March 1915.

32.   On this see H. Sacher, *Jewish Emancipation: The Contract Myth* (London, 1917), *passim.*

33.   C. Russell and H. S. Lewis, *The Jew in London* (London, 1900), 107; and see Lowenthal, 361-7, for Rothschild's unsuccessful opposition to Herzl giving evidence to the Royal Commission on Alien Immigration. See also Laqueur, 119.

34.   *J. C.*, 16 July 1897, 13. Adler added that the idea of a Jewish State 'might lead people to think that we Jews are not fired with ardent loyalty for the country in which it is our lot to be placed'. See also H. M. Adler, *Religious versus Political Zionism* (London, 1898), *passim.*

35.   Laqueur, 157.

36.   *J. C.*, 6 Aug. 1897, 11; see also Vital, 305-8.

37.   *J. C.*, 7 Oct. 1898, 12.

38.   Ibid., 27 Jan. 1899, 12-13.

39. Bermant, *The Cousinhood*, 243.
40. *J. C.*, 21 July 1905, 16.
41. Central Zionist Archives, Records of the Central Zionist Office, Vienna, Z1, file 236: Joseph Cowen (a founder of the English Zionist Federation) to Herzl, 28 Sept. 1900; J. de Haas to Herzl, 27 Sept. 1900.
42. *English Zionist Federation. General Election, 1900. Opinions of Parliamentary Candidates on Zionism* (London, 1900), 2. [copy in Central Zionist Archives, Jerusalem]
43. *J. C.*, 12 Jan. 1906, 19.
44. Ibid., 28 Sept. 1900, -10. The dilemma in Whitechapel was such that many Zionists apparently abstained: *East London Observer*, 22 Sept. 1900, 3; *Daily News*, 28 Sept. 1900, 5.
45. *J. C.*, 12 Oct. 1900, 8.
46. C. Weizmann, *Trial and Error* (London, 1949), 124.
47. 'Israel Zangwill', in *Encyclopaedia Judaica*; and see M. Simon (ed.), *Speeches Articles and Letters of Israel Zangwill* (London, 1937), 232. The Jewish Territorial Organization was wound up in 1925, a year before Zangwill's death.
48. On this episode see M. M. Weisgal (general editor), *The Letters and Papers of Chaim Weizmann* (London, 1968-), vol. I, series A, 401: Weizmann to Vera Chatzman, 16 Sept. 1902; vol. II, series A, 28-9 and 69: Weizmann to Evans-Gordon, 24 Nov. and 8 Dec. 1902.
49. Ibid., vol. III, series A, 313-4: Weizmann to M. Ussishkin, 3 Aug. 1904.
50. Weizmann remained sympathetic to Evans-Gordon, of whom he wrote apologetically in *Trial and Error*, 118-19.
51. On these events see Weizmann, 125-33.
52. Quoted in Stein, 147. See also *The Letters and Papers of Chaim Weizmann*, vol. IV, series A, 19: Weizmann to Vera Chatzman, 28 Jan. 1905.
53. Rabinowicz, 36.
54. David Wolffsohn Papers, Central Zionist Archives, W. 59 III: Weizmann to Wolffsohn, 28 Dec. 1905; this letter is also printed in *The Letters and Papers of Chaim Weizmann*, vol. IV, series A, 215-16.
55. Stein, 150-1; Rabinowicz, 188-91.
56. Weizmann, 142.
57. Stein, 151; B. E. C. Dugdale, *Arthur Balfour*, i (London, 1936), 433.
58. *Letters and Papers of Chaim Weizmann*, vol. IV, series A, 219: Weizmann to Vera Chatzman, 9 Jan. 1906. This letter is the only contemporary record of the conversation; its very short account of what took place none the less differs considerably from Weizmann's later recollection, recorded in *Trial and Error*, 142-5. In his memoirs Weizmann referred to this as his 'first meeting' with Balfour; but we know that it was his second.
59. Stein, 153-4.
60. Weizmann's own approach to British politics remains shrouded in mystery. In a letter which he wrote to Baron Edmond de Rothschild, in Paris, on 23 Dec. 1931, he repudiated the suggestion that he belonged to the 'extreme Left', but at the same time he spoke sympathetically of socialism, and condemned Vladimir Jabotinsky's right-wing Zionist Revisionist movement as 'Jewish Fascism': *Letters and Papers of Chaim Weizmann*, vol. XV, series A, 234-5. When approached for his support by Henry Graham White, an independent candidate in the Combined English Universities by-election in 1946, Weizmann refused, saying that he had 'so far made it an inviolable rule...not to give public support to any political party or candidate': ibid., vol. XXII, series A, 9: Weizmann to White, 1 Feb. 1946.
61. Stein, 103-7, 131, 137. Samuel became a Zionist after reading *Der Judenstaat*: Fraenkel, loc.cit. 168; and see J. Bowle, *Viscount Samuel* (London, 1957), 170-8.

62. Levenberg, 204-5.
63. Ibid. 205-6.
64. *J. C.*, 7 Jan. 1916, 16-18.
65. Laqueur, 158.
66. L. G. Montefiore, 'Anglo-Jewry at the Cross-roads', *Jewish Review*, v (1914), 132.
67. *J. C.*, 26 March 1909, 22; 17 July 1914, 16.
68. Ibid., 23 April 1909, 11.
69. In 1918 Hertz became president of the newly formed British section of the religious Zionist *Mizrachi* movement, which was not affiliated to the English Zionist Federation: P. Goodman, *Zionism in England: English Zionist Federation 1899-1929* (London, 1929), 44-5.
70. The phrase quoted is taken from R. N. Salaman's perceptive Lucien Wolf Memorial Lecture, *Whither Lucien Wolf's Anglo-Jewish Community?*, published by the Jewish Historical Society of England in 1953, p.19. As Salaman pointed out a large proportion of the Deputies represented provincial communities they never saw; it may be added that some represented communities or organizations which hardly existed, except on paper; these were the truly 'rotten boroughs', and some observers would claim that they have not yet been eliminated.
71. The Conjoint, consisting of fourteen persons, had been formed in 1878, and was recognized by the Foreign Office 'as having full authority to speak in the name and on behalf of Anglo-Jewry': *J. C.*, 26 Feb. 1915, 17: and see Stein, 172-5.
72. *J. C.*, 15 Jan. 1915, 11-13; 22 Jan. 1915, 13.
73. Weizmann, 200; and see Fraenkel, 179-81.
74. Wolf to N. Sokolow, 15 July 1915, quoted in Weizmann, 201.
75. *J. C.*, 26 Feb. 1915, 16-17; 26 March 1915, 17; 22 Oct. 1915, 9.
76. These moves were greatly accelerated by the almost unanimous decision of the Board, in June 1915, to do absolutely nothing to challenge the Government's decision to intern Jewish 'enemy aliens': ibid., 18 June 1915, 12; 25 June 1915, 13; 2 July 1915, 15.
77. Ibid., 28 Jan. 1916, 18.
78. Ibid., 7 April 1916, 16.
79. Ibid., 27 Oct. 1916, 16.
80. Laqueur, 193.
81. *The Times*, 24 May 1917, 5.
82. *J. C.*, 25 May 1917, 5.
83. Ibid., 16 March 1917, 7; this attack was highly reminiscent of one which had appeared anonymously in the *Fortnightly Review* the previous November: *J. C.*, 3 Nov. 1916, 9-10.
84. *J. C.*, 25 May 1917, 5-6.
85. Ibid., 15 June 1917, 10 and 13.
86. *The Times*, 28 May 1917, 5.
87. *J. C.*, 22 June 1917, 14-19; 20 July 1917, 5. The Conjoint was however, superseded by a new 'Joint Foreign Committee' which survived until the definitive Zionist conquest of the Board of Deputies in 1943.
88. Moreover, even a year after the revolution, Harry Sacher—the famous Manchester Zionist and a member of the editorial board of the *Manchester Guardian*—was declaring to Simon Marks, chairman of Marks and Spencer Ltd., that it was becoming urgent 'to carry through and organise all Zionist forces on the Board of Deputies': Central Zionist Archives, Papers of the Zionist Organization, London, Z4 file 120: Sacher to Marks, 12 April 1918.
89. *J. C.*, 22 June 1917, 5.
90. Of the 56 deputies who voted in favour of the vote of censure, 42 represented pro-

vincial congregations: *J. C.*, 29 June 1917, 14. Nathan Laski, who became the new treasurer following these events, was the first provincial deputy to be elected to the position of an honorary officer of the Board.

91.   *J. C.*, 27 June 1919, 17. The events of 1917 are admirably treated in S. A. Cohen, 'The Conquest of a Community? The Zionists and the Board of Deputies in 1917', *Jewish Journal of Sociology*, xix (1977), 157-84.

92.   Weizmann, 256-62; the final version of the Declaration differed in two important respects from the Zionist draft: it referred to the establishment in Palestine of *a* rather than *the* National Home for the Jewish people, and it referred to the civic and religious rights of the existing non-Jewish communities there. On Montagu generally see S. D. Waley, *Edwin Montagu* (London, 1964), especially 139-41.

93.   F. Owen, *Tempestuous Journey* (London, 1954), 427; Bermant, *The Cousinhood*, 258-61.

94.   *J. C.*, 16 Nov. 1917, 5-6; and see L. Magnus, *Old Lamps for New. An Apologia for the League of British Jews* (London, 1918), *passim*.

95.   *J. C.*, 8 Feb. 1918, 9.

96.   Ibid., 7 Dec. 1917, 13.

97.   Ibid., 22 March 1918, 15-16; 21 March 1919, 9.

98.   Ibid., 28 May 1926, 15: annual meeting; attendance six persons.

99.   Ibid., 2 Jan. 1920, 22; 30 June 1922, vi-vii.

100. Ibid., 21 Feb. 1919, 9: speech of Laurie Magnus at a League meeting.

101. Ibid., 24 Jan. 1919, 5; *Morning Post*, 8 April 1919, 6. The policy of the *Post* is discussed at length in Holmes, *Anti-Semitism in British Society*, 141-2, 147-51.

102. *Morning Post*, 23 April 1919, 6; *J. C.*, 2 May 1919, 14 and 21.

103. *J. C.*, 24 Feb. 1922, 7.

104. Ibid., 3 Nov. 1922, 15.

105. Ibid., 10 Nov. 1922, 7.

106. Ibid., 17 Nov. 1922, 7.

107. *Morning Post* of 9 Nov. 1922, quoted in *J. C.*, 10 Nov. 1922, 12.

108. *Bradford Daily Argus* of 6 Nov. 1922, quoted in *J. C.*, 10 Nov. 1922, 12.

109. *J. C.*, 24 Nov. 1922, 8 and 9. For an earlier diatribe along the same lines see *Morning Post*, 10 July 1917, 6.

110   *J. C.*, 16 March 1923, 9; 29 June 1923, 11.

111. Ibid., 7 July 1922, 26-30; 3 Nov. 1922, 15.

112. Ibid., 12 May 1922, 24; 23 June 1922, 13-14.

113. Mond, who 'married out', cared nothing for Judaism or Zionism until a visit to Palestine, in 1921, awakened emotions deep within him, and he declared 'I do not consider myself as an Englishman. I am a Palestinian ... my heart is in Eretz-Israel.' He became President of the English Zionist Federation. Elected first as a Liberal MP in 1906, Mond joined the Conservatives twenty years later through his opposition to land nationalization: H. Bolitho, *Alfred Mond First Lord Melchett* (London, 1933), 368-70.

114. *J. C.*, 3 Jan. 1919, 7; 1 July 1921, 30.

115. Ibid., 3 Nov. 1922, 16. In the final months of his Administration Lloyd George was subject to attacks in the Conservative press because of his circle of Jewish friends: Lloyd George Papers, House of Lords Record Office, F/4/6/11: Beaverbrook to Lloyd George, 30 March 1922; F/4/6/12: Lloyd George to Beaverbrook (telephone message), 31 March 1922.

116. *J. C.*, 3 Nov. 1922, 15.

117. Holmes, *Anti-Semitism in British Society*, 127-9, 136-7.

118. *J. C.*, 10 Nov. 1922, 13-14: letter from S. Kaplansky of Poale Zion; between 1919 and 1921 Kaplansky had been a member of the Zionist Executive in London, and from 1929 to 1931 he lived in London as an emissary of Poale Zion to the British Labour party.

119. *J. C.*, 17 Feb. 1922, 26. The British Labour movement had addressed an appeal to the San Remo Conference, in 1921, supporting the implementation of the Balfour Declaration: Levenberg, 206-7.
120. *J. C.*, 3 Nov. 1922, 16; Central Zionist Archives, London files of the Zionist Organization, Z4, file 1845 I: memo of 1922 headed 'Propaganda Among Non-Jews. General Election.'
121. My examination of Jewish ethnic names in the Whitechapel electoral registers for 1922 suggests that of the constituency's total registered electors (just over 24,000), at least half were Jewish.
122. *J. C.*, 10 Nov. 1922, 12; 17 Nov. 1922, 12. The result was: Labour, 6,367 votes; Liberal, 5,839; Conservative, 3,502.
123. Ibid., 1 Aug. 1919, 7; for the identification of the pseudonym see Roth, *The Jewish Chronicle*, 136-7.
124. Central Zionist Archives, Papers of S. Kaplansky, A137, file 49: poster, in English and Yiddish, put out by Poale Zion for the 1923 general election. See also *J. C.*, 30 Nov. 1923, 8: letters from Sir Herbert Jessel (Conservative and Jewish), Viscount Gladstone (Liberal) and Poale Zion.
125. *J. C.*, 14 Dec. 1923, 5; 25 Jan. 1924, 7.
126. Levenberg, 207, referring to a speech in the Commons on 25 Feb. 1924.
127. *J. C.*, 17 Oct. 1924, 10. A similar donation was made by Baron in 1929: *Daily Telegraph*, 10 May 1929, 13. Baron was knighted by Ramsay MacDonald during the second Labour Government.

7. Love Affair With the Left

1. *J. C.*, 30 Nov. 1923, 5.
2. Ibid., 24 Oct. 1924, 7.
3. Ibid., 14 Nov. 1930, 23.
4. Ibid., 13 Feb. 1925, 20, 23-4.
5. Ibid., 2 April 1926, 12.
6. Ibid., 12 Feb. 1926, 10; 19 Feb. 1926, 7 and 15. One Gateshead correspondent referred to the proposed *yeshiva* as 'a hare-brained scheme'; but in 1929 it went ahead, and is now the most prestigious institution of its kind in Europe.
7. Ibid., 21 Nov. 1924, 16; the Jewish electors represented just over 4 per cent of the constituency's 36,332 registered voters.
8. Ibid., 3 Dec. 1926, 10.
9. Ibid., 20 Nov. 1925, 13-14.
10. Ibid., 29 Oct. 1926, 26; there is a file of papers concerning the committee, 1928-30, in Central Zionist Archives, F13, file 56 III.
11. *J. C.*, 10 June 1927, 12; 25 Nov. 1927, 18.
12. Ibid., 25 Nov. 1927, 18.
13. Ibid., 3 May 1935, 10.
14. H. L. Smith (ed.), *The New Survey of London Life and Labour*, vi (London, 1934), 22.
15. *J. C.*, 24 Oct. 1930, 27; 7 Nov. 1930, 22; 14 Nov. 1930, 22.
16. Ibid., 24 Oct. 1930, 27; 14 Nov. 1930, 23; 21 Nov. 1930, 32; 28 Nov. 1930, 16.
17. Ibid., 7 Nov. 1930, 6.
18. Ibid., 28 Nov. 1930, 8 and 16.
19. The term 'swing' is used here, and throughout this work, in the conventional sense, as a measure of one party's percentage gain in votes cast against another's percentage loss, based upon the total number of valid votes cast for all parties.
20. *Commons' Debates*, 5th series, vol. 248, cols. 751-7, 13 Feb. 1931.

21.   S. Brodetsky, *Memoirs* (London, 1960), 140; Brodetsky wrongly dates the by-election at 1929, and wrongly states that the reason for it was the death of the 'Liberal' MP. Brodetsky himself had been a Liberal, but changed parties during the First World War: ibid., 44.

22.   Just how much support from Jews was forthcoming for the 'New Party' is problematic. Probably a few Jews were attracted to it, as were a few socialists, like John Strachey, and we know, from the private papers of Philip Guedalla, chairman of the Press and Information Committee of the Board of Deputies, 1925-35, that one of the members of Mosley's January Club was Sir Philip Magnus, a founder-member of the League of British Jews; indeed, in a letter written to Guedalla on 25 Oct. 1934, Magnus admitted that he was 'not quite the only one of my faith who was a member of the Club': Central Zionist Archives, Papers of Philip Guedalla, A159, file 3. By 1934 Jews were being refused membership of the New Party's successor, the British Union of Fascists and, according to Colin Cross, 'the few Jews who had joined in the early days, including "Kid" Lewis, had been frozen out': C. Cross, *The Fascists in Britain* (London, 1961), 102. On the January Club see R. Griffiths, *Fellow Travellers of the Right* (London, 1980), 49-53.
      But it is worth noting that in February 1937, at the time of the London County Council elections, the *J. C.*, then edited by Ivan Greenberg (Leopold's son), thought it worth while to devote two pages to urging Jews not to vote for fascist candidates: *J. C.*, 26 Feb. 1937, 17-18. The late John M. Shaftesley, who was at that time assistant editor of the paper, informed me in December 1978 that, in his view, this article is 'reliable'; it must be assumed, therefore, that it was prompted by information which had come into the *J. C.*'s possession.

23.   Lloyd George Papers, House of Lords Record Office, G/26/1/34: typescript minute from Jones, 27 Nov. 1930. I can find no trace, in local newspapers or the national press, of the projected speech ever having been made; but the Liberal leader did send Janner a letter of support, which devoted some space to Liberal approval of the Mandate: *The Times*, 1 Dec. 1930, 9.

24.   Brodetsky, 140.

25.   Neville Laski Papers, Mocatta Library, University College London, AJ33/90: typescript note by Laski, 14 Oct. 1936, 7.

26.   *J. C.*, 30 June 1933, 42; 8 Dec. 1933, 11; 19 July 1935, 19. On the work of the Parliamentary Palestine Committee see B. Janner, 'Zionism in Parliament', in P. Goodman (ed.), *The Jewish National Home* (London, 1943), 106-10. As Prime Minister of the National Government, 1931-5, Ramsay MacDonald failed 'to utter one *public* word of disapproval of the Nazi Government's anti-Jewish campaign': *J. C.*, 19 Nov. 1937, 11.

27.   *J. C.*, 17 Feb. 1933, 27; 7 May 1937, 11. On Nathan see H. Montgomery Hyde, *Strong for Service. The Life of Lord Nathan of Churt* (London, 1968); in 1928 Nathan had unsuccessfully contested the Whitechapel seat, and had brazenly appealed to the Jews there to vote for him on ethnic lines; in a straight fight with Gosling he lost heavily, by nearly 3,000 votes. He was raised to the peerage in 1940.

28.   *J. C.*, 14 March 1930, 25; 7 Nov. 1930, 21. I am grateful to Mr Moshe Rosetté, of Tel Aviv, for affording me his recollections of Marcus.

29.   *J. C.*, 3 July 1931, 16.

30.   Ibid., 12 March 1937, 24.

31.   I. Montagu, *The Youngest Son* (London, 1970), 115-18, 338.

32.   C. C. Aronsfeld, 'Communists in British Jewry: A Zionist Socialist Analysis', *Jewish Monthly*, i (1947), 33. Gaster had been a member of the Independent Labour Party and a leader of the so-called 'Revolutionary Policy Committee' within it: H. Pelling, *The British Communist Party* (London, 1975), 77.

33. Aronsfeld, 33.
34. Pelling, *The British Communist Party*, 56-7, 85.
35. Buckman, 394.
36. Neville Laski Papers, Mocatta Library, University College London, AJ33/90: typescript note by Laski, 14 Oct. 1936.
37. G. C. Lebzelter, *Political Anti-Semitism in England 1918-1939* (London, 1978), 147-9.
38. *J. C.*, 19 May 1939, 18.
39. S. Bunt, *Jewish Youth Work in Britain* (London, 1975), 22-3.
40. P. Piratin, *Our Flag Stays Red* (new edn., London, 1978), 20: Samuels, 35. The Jewish Labour Council actively campaigned on behalf of the Labour party: *J. C.*, 17 May 1929, 22; 24 May 1929, 16.
41. Lebzelter, 139-41; Holmes, *Anti-Semitism in British Society*, 193.
42. Piratin, 33-49.
43. B. Litvinoff, *A Peculiar People* (London, 1969), 158. The comparison with support for the Communist party from devout Roman Catholics in Italy at the present time is worth stressing. Mr Piratin, in conversation with me in December 1978, stated that about 2 per cent of the British Battalion which fought in the Spanish Civil War was Jewish.
44. Interview in November 1978 with a former official of the Stepney Communist party.
45. Aronsfeld, 31. The paper ceased publication in December 1956.
46. Piratin, then thirty-eight years of age and the son of a *Chassid* from Vitebsk, had joined the party as a result of the fascist demonstration at Olympia, London, in June 1934: Piratin, op. cit. 5. My examination of the Mile End electoral register suggests that in 1945 Jews accounted for about one-third (roughly 5,400) of the registered electorate.
47. Aronsfeld, 32.
48. Pelling, *The British Communist Party*, 192, gives the membership of the party as 55,138 in 1943; 45,435 in 1945; and 42,123 in 1946.
49. Mr Piratin informs me that in the 1930s the Stepney Communist party was about 900 strong.
50. In Whitechapel in 1930 it would have amounted to about 1,100, and in 1931 to about 1,300; that is, Jewish voters accounted for about half Pollitt's total vote.
51. This accords with Mr Piratin's own estimate of his Jewish support at that time.
52. In 1947 the research unit of the Jewish Fellowship conducted a wide-ranging survey of 40,000 Jews; 22.5 per cent of the respondents identified themselves as Conservative supporters, 33.1 per cent as Liberals, 32.9 per cent as Labour supporters or 'socialists', and 2.3 per cent as Communists. The Communist percentage would yield a total Jewish Communist vote of nearly 8,000. But the number of respondents who answered the question dealing with party preference amounted to less than 8 per cent of those to whom questionnaires were sent; because of this very low response rate (8.5 per cent for the survey as a whole) the findings of the poll must be treated with scepticism: *J. C.*, 2 Sept. 1949, 9.
53. For the activities of Jewish Conservatives in the Liverpool Exchange by-election of 1933 see *J. C.*, 27 Jan. 1933, 8; in this contest Sydney Silverman reduced the Conservative majority from 13,144 to 2,786. For the activities of Jewish Conservatives in Hackney see ibid., 11 May 1934, 10 and 23; 18 May 1934, 10. And for the attempts by Jewish Conservatives to sway Jewish voters in the West Ham by-election of 1934 see ibid., 11 May 1934, 38.
54. This statement is based on interviews with Jews who ceased supporting the Liberal party in the 1930s.
55. *J. C.*, 12 Jan. 1940, 14; S. J. Goldsmith, *Twenty 20th Century Jews* (New York, 1962), 58-64. In 1951 Hore-Belisha became the first Sephardi peer.

56. R. R. James, *The British Revolution: British Politics 1880-1939* (London, 1978), 526-7; and see Owen, 736-7, for Lloyd George's adulatory article on Hitler in the *Daily Express* in September 1936. Even Jews were not wholly immune from this sort of approach. In November 1937 Herbert Samuel, a supporter of the Government's foreign policy, wrote that he regarded Hitler 'as a man with a conscience … he was not a man who would do what he knew to be a crime as Napoleon would have': Bowle, 309. C. G. Montefiore had already sought to explain the rise of Nazism partly as a reaction to Zionism: L. Cohen, *Some Recollections of Claude Goldsmid Montefiore 1858-1938* (London, 1940), 253.

57. A. Sharf, *The British Press and Jews under Nazi Rule* (London, 1964), 161.

58. Ibid. 168.

59. Ibid. 155.

60. Cross, 94-108.

61. O. Mosley, *My Life* (London, 1970), 343; Cross, 118; *J. C.*, 6 July 1934, 8. See also R. Churchill, 'The Press', *Spectator,* 27 Dec. 1963, 846.

62. A. J. Sherman, *Island Refuge. Britain and the Refugees from the Third Reich, 1933-1939* (London, 1973), 217; M. George, *The Hollow Men* (London, 1967), 142, 149-52.

63. Neville Laski Papers, Mocatta Library, University College London, AJ33/158: typescript memo headed 'The Jewish Defence Committee', written by its secretary, Sidney Salomon, some time after the end of the Second World War, p. 14.

64. *The Times,* 12 March 1955, 9; *J. C.*, 1 June 1945, 5. Ramsay did not stand for Parliament in 1945, and died ten years later.

65. Another anti-Semitic Conservative MP was Edward Doran, who sat for North Tottenham from 1931 to 1935: Lebzelter, 31. Dr Lebzelter states that Doran was 'dismissed by his constituency after he had publicly attacked the Jews'; in fact Doran stood for the Conservatives in 1935, but was defeated by Labour.

66. *Gloucestershire Echo,* 9 June 1937, 3 (election speech by Lipson); *J. C.*, 25 June 1937, 12; 15 Feb. 1946, 15; 18 March 1966, 8. Lipson's majority in the by-election was 339.

67. In 1945 his majority was 4,986.

68. Sherman, 30.

69. *J. C.*, 20 Oct. 1933, 35; 24 Jan. 1936, 13.

70. There is a file of material on the Boycott Council in the papers of Philip Guedalla, Central Zionist Archives, A159, file 3. The Council's inauguration, and its repudiation by the Board of Deputies, is chronicled in the newspaper collection of the Kibbutz Lohamei Hagetaot, 'Nazi Rule 1933', vols. 38 and 39.

71. *J. C.*, 20 Oct. 1933, 35.

72. Ibid., 28 Sept. 1934, 8.

73. Ibid., 20 Jan. 1939, 29; Sherman, 219.

74. *J. C.,* 11 May 1934, 8.

75. Salomon, 'The Jewish Defence Committee', p. 8, in Neville Laski Papers, Mocatta Library, University College London, AJ33/158.

76. Ibid. The British Union of Fascists was proscribed by the Government at the end of May 1940. An example of one of the Defence Committee's election leaflets, issued for the Leeds North-East by-election on 13 March 1940, is to be found at the end of Salomon's memo. It reads: 'Facism means Peace for Hitler!! A Concentration Camp for You!! Who so base as would be a bondsman? Vote Against the Fascist candidate.'

77. S. Salomon, *The Jews of Britain* (London, 1938), *passim.*

78. Salomon, 'The Jewish Defence Committee', pp. 22-3, in Neville Laski Papers, AJ33/158. As far as I am aware this agreement no longer exists. The Board of Deputies does, however, maintain close contact with leading executives in both

the BBC and Independent Television, and I am informed that funds from the
Board's Charitable Trust help to provide a specialist part-time producer and a
researcher for BBC Radio London's programme 'You Don't Have To Be
Jewish'. Mr J. F. Wilkinson, secretary of the BBC, to whom I am indebted for
this information, has stressed that 'such assistance is provided on the strict
understanding that editorial control remains with the station concerned': letter
from Mr Wilkinson to me, 18 Aug. 1979.

79. Neville Laski Papers, Mocatta Library, University College London, AJ33/155:
typescript 'Note of an interview with Mr Maurice [*sic*] Myer Regarding Proposed Loan', 22 Nov. 1940, signed by Myer and Liverman.

80. Neville Laski Papers, AJ33/154: Myer to Liverman, 5 Dec. 1940, acknowledging receipt of the loan.

81. Salomon, *The Jews of Britain,* 39.

82. Bloch contested the seat in 1929, 1931, and 1935. In 1929 the Labour majority
was over 16,000, and in 1935 over 17,000; but in 1931, with a Communist intervention, it fell to 8,014. The Jewish population of Glasgow in the 1920s and
1930s was between 12,000 and 13,000, of whom a large number lived in the Gorbals constituency; I estimate, from the incidence of Jewish ethnic names, that
there were about 3,500 registered Jewish electors in the Gorbals in the 1930s, forming just over 7 per cent of the total electorate.

83. No Labour party conference was held in 1938.

84. S. Levenberg, *The Jews and Palestine,* 198-9.

85. Ibid. 209.

86. Ibid. 130; Dr Levenberg, born in Russia in 1907, came to England in 1936; he
was, and has remained, a leading figure in the British Labour Zionist movement, and is now (1981) president of Poale Zion.

87. Ibid. 199.

88. After Kristallnacht the British Government announced that immediate admission of Jews to the United Kingdom would be limited to children to be trained for
re-emigration; anything more, the Government declared, would encourage 'the
making of a definite anti-Jewish movement': *The Times,* 22 Nov. 1938, 9.

89. *J. C.,* 26 May 1939, 28; 8 March 1940, 1 and 6.

90. Ibid., 15 Dec. 1944, 1 and 5; Weizmann admitted that this proposal went
beyond the Zionist movement's 'own official programme': Weizmann, 535.

91. *J. C.,* 11 May 1945, 10.

92. Ibid., 1 June 1945, 16: letter from Ian Mikardo.

93. Ibid., 25 May 1945, 1.

94. Ibid., 30 April 1943, 9; 7 May 1943, 5; 9 July 1943, 1; Brodetsky was unopposed
as President, but Sir Robert Waley Cohen, a Vice-President, and not a Zionist,
was defeated.

95. Bunt, 111.

96. Bermant, *The Cousinhood,* 381-2; and see Bunt, 102-10.

97. *J. C.,* 15 June 1945, 7; 27 July 1945, 11.

98. Ibid., 29 June 1945, 1.

99. In addition, one Jew stood unsuccessfully as a National Liberal, and one, also
unsuccessful, ran as an Independent.

100. *J. C.,* 3 Aug. 1945, 10.

8.   Return to the Right

1. *J. C.,* 16 Nov. 1945, 1.
2. The events are chronicled in M. Gilbert, *Exile and Return* (London, 1978),
272-309.

3.   *J. C.,* 4 Feb. 1949, 1. In December 1947 Jon Kimche, then managing editor of the left-wing newspaper *Tribune,* commented that, as General Secretary of the Transport and General Workers' Union, 'Bevin found often that his bitterest opponents in the union were Communists who happened to be Jews, or Jews who happened to be Communists. Either way, the connection became firmly planted in Bevin's mind': J. Kimche, 'Labour's Turnabout on Zionism', *Commentary,* iv. no. 6 (Dec. 1947), 514.

4.   Interview with Moshe Rosetté, Tel Aviv, Feb. 1979.

5.   Central Zionist Archives, F13, file 54: typescript statement on the political work of the Zionist Federation, June 1945; and see generally file 332.

6.   Ibid., file 332: minutes of the meeting of the Zionist Federation's Political Committee, 30 May 1945.

7.   Ibid., file 92: typescript report on the work of Poale Zion, April 1944.

8.   Ibid., file 339: Hammersley to L. Bakstansky, 9 July 1945.

9.   Ibid. file 125: speech by Mikardo to Finchley and Hampstead Garden Suburb Zionist societies, 8 Oct. 1945.

10. E. Samuel, 'Changing Attitudes of British Jews to Israel', *J. C.,* 2 Feb. 1951, 13.

11. Central Zionist Archives, F13, file 292: a file of reports from local Zionist societies, summer 1946.

12. Ibid., file 575: note from Dr Schafler, 10 Oct. 1945.

13. *J. C.,* 26 April 1946, 5: the most prominent of these MPs were Janner, Lipton, and Sydney Silverman.

14. *J. C.,* 14 June 1946, 1.

15. Mr Rosetté informs me that, in his view, such a threat would have been 'irresponsible'.

16. *J. C.,* 8 Aug. 1947, 1. There were serious outbreaks of anti-Jewish rioting in Liverpool, Glasgow, Manchester, London, and elsewhere: S. Temkin, 'Three Centuries of Jewish Life in England, 1656-1956', *American Jewish Yearbook,* vol. 58 (1957), 53; D. Nathan, '1947 The Agony of Anglo-Jewry', *J. C.,* 26 Aug. 1977, 17.

17. Sharf, 203.

18. *J. C.,* 12 March 1948, 12.

19. See, for example, the speeches of Harold Laski and Ian Mikardo at a 'Third Seder' (Passover meal) organized by the Palestine Histadruth Committee in Britain, *J. C.,* 18 April 1947, 8.

20. *J. C.,* 27 Jan. 1950, 1 and 5. See also the report of the first annual dinner of the Cardiff branch of Poale Zion, in ibid., 10 Feb. 1950, 15; here the guests of honour were the Labour MPs David Grenfell, James Callaghan, and George Thomas; Leo Abse presided.

21. *J. C.,* 28 April 1950, 1.

22. See generally H. Thomas, *The Suez Affair* (London, 1966) and A. Nutting, *No End of a Lesson* (London, 1967).

23. L. D. Epstein, *British Politics in the Suez Crisis* (London, 1964), 187.

24. *J. C.,* 9 Nov. 1956, 8; Epstein, 188-9.

25. *J. C.,* 16 Nov. 1956, 1; Shinwell was in the Far East at the time of the 8 Nov. division.

26. The other five Jewish Labour MPs who abstained were Austin Albu (Edmonton), Barnet Janner (Leicester North-West), Leslie Lever (Manchester Ardwick), Moss Turner-Samuels (Gloucester), and David Weitzman (Stoke Newington and Hackney North). For Harold Lever's forthright defence of Israel in Parliament see Epstein, 190.

27. This, for example, was Ian Mikardo's defence of his obedience to the party whip: *J. C.,* 16 Nov. 1956, 1.

28. Epstein, 195; *J. C.*, 16 Nov. 1956, 1; 23 Nov. 1956, 1.
29. Male membership of the Willesden synagogue rose from 281 in 1940 to 748 in 1950; that of Cricklewood from 663 to 742 in the same period. In 1970 male membership of both still stood at over 700: A. Newman, *The United Synagogue 1870-1970* (London, 1977), 218-19.The counting of Jewish ethnic names becomes increasingly hazardous as a method of arriving at a reliable estimate of the size of any Anglo-Jewish electorate after 1945 (if not before), since many Jews anglicized their names as a way of achieving social integration. My examination of the East Willesden electoral register for 1959 suggests that the constituency then contained about 10,000 Jewish voters; the total electorate was 58,865.
30. *J. C.*, 4 May 1979, 23. At a memorial meeting for Orbach at the House of Commons in July 1979 Ian Mikardo declared that Orbach had lost his seat in 1959 following 'the politically illiterate hysteria of the Jewish Press' over his 1954 mission to Egypt: *J. C.*, 27 July 1979, 5.
31. In 1955 Orbach's majority at East Willesden had slumped to 659 votes.
32. Ian Mikardo also lost his seat, at Reading, in 1959, by 3,942 votes; but the Jewish community there was far too small to have influenced the result.
33. The remark was made in the Commons on 3 November 1956, and is quoted by Epstein, 192.
34. Ibid. 194.
35. *J. C.*, 4 Oct. 1957, 1; 8 Nov. 1957, 25. In August 1979 the Labour Friends of Israel included 100 MPs, compared with 40 Labour MPs who were reckoned to be committed pro-Arabists: *J. C.*, 17 Aug. 1979, 36.
36. The phrase was that used by Colonel Sir Wavell Wakefield, the successful Conservative candidate at St. Marylebone: *J. C.*, 29 June 1945, 5.
37. Epstein, 177.
38. *Harrow Observer*, 2 Dec. 1948, 4; A. Ranney, *Pathways to Parliament* (London, 1965), 118, note 27.
39. Ranney, 42-8.
40. Ibid. 117; and see B. Glanville, 'The British Jews', *The Queen*, 1 March 1961, 53. In 1964 the unexpected revival of the Finchley Liberal party was widely ascribed to the alleged exclusion, in 1957, of some local Jews from membership of the Finchley Golf Club, 'which was officered by prominent Conservatives'. The Liberals capitalized on this affair and did well in Jewish wards locally as a result; but this success was not carried over into the general election: D. E. Butler and A. King, *The British General Election of 1964* (London, 1965), 250-2. As late as 1976 one Jewish Conservative MP admitted 'that there was still a degree of anti-Jewishness' in the party: G. Zimmerman, 'Jewish M.P.s' (University of Essex MA thesis, 1976), 4 and 24.
41. *J. C.*, 13 Sept. 1974, 19, which also reported Sir Keith as being a member of the United Synagogue in Chelsea.
42. Epstein, 185.
43. H. Neustatter, 'Demographic and Other Statistical Aspects of Anglo-Jewish Population, 1960-65', in M. Freedman (ed.), *A Minority in Britain* (London, 1955), 76.
44. S. J. Prais and M. Schmool, 'The Size and Structure of the Anglo-Jewish Population, 1960-65', *Jewish Journal of Sociology*, x (1968), 7.
45. In 1975 the Board of Deputies' Research Unit estimated the total Jewish population of the United Kingdom at 408,311: B. A. Kosmin and N. Grizzard, *Geograhical Distribution Estimates of Ethnically Jewish Population of the United Kingdom, 1974* (Board of Deputies, mimeo., London, June 1975), 3.
46. Lipman, *Social History*, 168; S. J. Prais, 'Synagogue Statistics and the Jewish Population of Great Britain 1900-1970', *Jewish Journal of Sociology*, xiv (1972), 217.

47. Prais, 217. In 1974 these seven communities accounted for 93,900 Jews, and London (Greater London area plus the adjacent Home County areas of north Surrey, north-west Kent, south Hertfordshire, and south-west Essex) accounted for 272,000: Kosmin and Grizzard, *Geographical Distribution Estimates,* 2.
48. Kosmin and Grizzard, *Geographical Distribution Estimates,* 4.
49. E. Krausz, *Leeds Jewry* (Cambridge, 1964), 24-5; over half Leeds' 18,000 Jews now live in the Alwoodley-Moortown districts.
50. Kosmin and Grizzard, *Geographical Distribution Estimates,* 5.
51. G. Alderman, *The History of the Hendon Synagogue 1928-1978* (London, 1978), 1-4.
52. E. Krausz, 'A Sociological Field Study of Jewish Suburban Life in Edgware 1962-63 with special reference to Minority Identification' (University of London Ph. D. thesis, 1965), 93 and 103. A few years later a similar pattern of response was found among Jews in Hackney: J. W. Carrier, 'Working Class Jews in Present-Day London: A Sociological Study' (University of London M. Phil. thesis, 1969), 346.
53. Krausz, 'A Sociological Field Study', 67.
54. G. Alderman, *British Elections: Myth and Reality* (London, 1978), 155.
55. Epstein, 176-8.
56. L. Stein, 'Anglo-Jewry and Israel', *Jewish Monthly,* July 1950, 215-22; J. Left-wich, 'Anglo-Jewry and the State of Israel', *Jewish Monthly,* April 1949, 10-21; R. N. Carvalho, 'Has Zionism a Place in Anglo-Jewry?', *Anglo-Jewish Association Quarterly,* March 1959, 1-9; H. Soref, 'Portrait of Anglo-Jewry', *Menorah Journal,* xli (1953), 80.
57. This was reported by Lord Mancroft to have been true of a number of senior executives in Great Universal Stores Ltd.: Samuel Landman Papers, Central Zionist Archives, A216, file 53: Mancroft to Landman, 1 Oct. 1962. In a memorandum (undated but probably June 1962) sent to Lord Mancroft, Landman declared that may well-known British Jews who gave money to the Zionist Federation were Conservatives; among those he mentioned by name was Lord Marks of Broughton, then chairman of Marks and Spencer Ltd., who died in 1964.
58. *J. C.,* 25 Sept. 1959, 11; 21 April 1967, 27.
59. Samuel Landman Papers, Central Zionist Archives, A226, file 53: 'Memorandum for Mr. Selwyn Lloyd', sent 24 Nov. 1962.
60. Ibid., 'Report on the 1961 Conservative Conference by Samuel Landman'.
61. Ibid., *Willesden Chronicle,* 22 March and 13 April 1962; memorandum by Landman for Lord Mancroft, undated but probably June 1962.
62. Ibid: R. J. Cody (Chairman, Willesden Conservative Association) to Landman, undated but probably June or July 1962.
63. Ibid: Landman to Jewish Agency, London, 15 Aug. 1962, suggesting that Mr and Mrs Skeet be invited to Israel; in his memorandum for Lord Mancroft Landman had claimed that Poale Zion in Britain received a subsidy of £2,500 per annum from the Zionist Federation.
64. Ibid: Landman to Skeet, 26 July 1962.
65. Ibid: Mancroft to Landman, 1 Oct. 1962.
66. Mancroft to the author, 24 May 1979. I am grateful to Lord Mancroft for generously allowing me to quote from his correspondence with Samuel Landman and with myself. In November 1981 Lord Mancroft added to his letter to me of May 1979 the following observation: 'A different situation would of course arise should a Government take some action which was palpably & [*sic*] openly contrary to Jewish interests. Then a Jewish vote might well spring to life. But then the same principles would apply to the Catholics.'

67. C. Bermant, *Troubled Eden* (London, 1969), 261. In August 1960 'Cross-bencher', in the *Sunday Express,* had suggested that Goldman, then director of the Political Centre of Conservative Central Office, 'cannot get off the launching pad' to a parliamentary career because of anti-Jewish bias among Conservative Associations in winnable seats: *Sunday Express,* 21 Aug. 1960, 12; *J. C.,* 9 March 1962, 9. See also the letter from Mr Rudolph Stern, *J. C.,* 30 March 1962, 36.

68. Samuel Landman Papers, Central Zionist Archives, A226, file 53: Mancroft to Landman, 1 Oct. 1962. The italics are mine—G. A.

69. The constituency was won back by the Jewish Labour MP Reg Freeson, who held the seat until it was absorbed into the Brent East constituency, a much safer Labour seat, which Mr Freeson still holds, following the boundary changes of February 1974. Mr Skeet, in a letter to me in June 1979, expressed the view that his 1964 defeat by Mr Freeson was due to the New Commonwealth (principally West Indian) immigrant vote, which had grown significantly in the constituency, and which was overwhelmingly Labour. Mr Skeet added that he 'was nevertheless supported by a considerable part of the Jewish vote'; this is undoubtedly true.

70. Andrew Bowden (Brighton Kemptown); Michael Fidler (Bury and Radcliffe); Geoffrey Finsberg (Hampstead); John Gorst (Hendon North); Tom Iremonger (Ilford North); Sir S. J. McAdden (Southend East). At Hampstead Mr Finsberg's share of the poll increased from 43.3 to 44.9 per cent between the two 1974 elections.

71. Sir Keith Joseph and Robert Adley; Mr Adley has since become a Christian *J. C.,* 17 Sept. 1976, 19.

72. G. Alderman, *British Political Sociology Yearbook,* vol. 2, 201.

73. *Brighton Evening Argus,* 18 Oct. 1973, 26.

74. Ibid., 19 Oct. 1973, 11; 23 Oct. 1973, 10. I am grateful to Mr Leslie Glenville, of Hove, for providing me with material relating to Conservative tactics at the time of the by-election.

75. *Jewish Chronicle Colour Magazine,* 24 May 1974, 34-5.

76. *J. C.,* 22 March 1974, 7.

77. On Reverend Amias see ibid., 28 Feb. 1975, 14; on the Jewish group in the Campaign for Nuclear Disarmament see ibid., 16 March 1962, 14, and 15 April 1966, 11.

78. The first paragraph of John Gorst's February 1974 election hand-out read: 'John Gorst is 45. His great-grandfather was a prominent Conservative M.P. during the days of Disraeli. He became the first Chairman of the Conservative Party and also held various Ministerial offices, including that of Solicitor General. Another of John Gorst's relations was Sir Mark Sykes, a leading British Zionist, who played a prominent part in the events leading up to the Balfour Declaration of 1917, which recognised Palestine as a national home for the Jewish people.'

79. Alderman, *British Political Sociology Yearbook,* vol. 2, 202; the methodology of this survey is described in detail on page 210 of this article. Briefly, it involved the haphazard selection of Jewish households, within streets chosen at random, in the Mill Hill, Hale, and Edgware wards of the constituency. Respondents were asked which way they had voted in 1970 and what their voting intention was in 1974; if their party preference had changed, they were invited to give reasons for their new choice. In all 150 Jewish voters were interviewed, but no attempt was made to interview on a quota basis.

80. D. Butler and D. Kavanagh, *The British General Election of February 1974* (London, 1974), 284.

81. *J. C.,* 28 Feb. 1975, 14.

82. These figures are based on the findings of a poll carried out by me in the Hendon North constituency in October 1974. The methodology was similar to that employed in February (see note 79 above) but the sample size was increased to 178.

83. As MP for Stepney, Limehouse, from 1922 to 1950, Clement Attlee had many Jewish voters, but the constituency was so solidly Labour anyway that their support was never crucial to his tenure of the seat.

84. *J. C.*, 21 Nov. 1975, 7 and 12; 5 Dec. 1975, 1; *Hendon Times*, 5 Dec. 1975, 23.

85. *The Times*, 12 Jan. 1976, 6. In Nov. 1976 Maudling was dropped from the Shadow Cabinet, mainly because of disagreements over economic policy. As Prime Minister Mrs. Thatcher did not allow her own constituency relationship with the Zionist movement to affect her political appointments; in May 1979 she appointed Lord Carrington as Foreign Secretary and Sir Ian Gilmour Lord Privy Seal (to be principal foreign affairs spokesman in the Commons); neither is well known as being particularly friendly to Israel (*J. C.*, 18 May 1979, 7 and 20 July 1979, 5). But in October 1981 she attacked the Palestine Liberation Organization as a movement associated with terrorism, and her sacking of Sir Ian Gilmour, though prompted by differences over domestic policy, caused quiet satisfaction in Jewish circles: *J. C.*, 9 Oct. 1981, *The Times*, 29 Oct., 14.

86. *J. C.*, 17 Jan. 1975, 11; 31 Jan. 1975, 6; 17 Oct. 1975, 8; 15 Oct. 1976, 7; 10 Aug. 1979, 6. The total number of Conservative MPs in the Conservative Friends in August 1979 was 135, of whom 10 were members of the Cabinet and 25 were ministers outside the Cabinet.

87. *Guardian*, 23 Sept. 1974, 7; interviews conducted by me with local Conservative and Labour party members in July and September 1974. Mrs Miller was a former Mayor of Stoke Newington, 1957-8, and of Camden, 1967-8; she was an active member, and at one time Chairman, of the North London progressive synagogue, and was also actively interested in several Jewish causes, including Soviet Jewry, the Jewish Welfare Board, and the Labour Friends of Israel.

88. *J. C.*, 27 Jan. 1978, 4.

89. *The Times*, 17 Feb. 1978, 2.

90. *J. C.*, 24 Feb. 1978, 1.

91. This figure is based on the estimate of the Board of Deputies Research Unit; it represents 9.4 per cent of the total electorate of Ilford North at the time of the by-election.

92. Councillor Alfred Sherman's letter to *The Times*, 4 Feb. 1978, 15, seems in my opinion to epitomize the reaction of Jewish Conservatives. The coloured immigrants, he argued, 'have already been given the inestimable privilege of living in one of the fairest, most advanced, decent and open societies in the world ... Surely it is up to them ... to find their own place, or, if they cannot, to make their contribution in their ancestral homes.' Councillor Sherman, who originates from the East End, is reported as having fought for the Communists in the Spanish Civil War. He is now a leader-writer for the *Daily Telegraph*; in 1978 he was described as the 'éminence grise' behind Sir Keith Joseph: *Sunday Times*, 4 June 1978, 6.

93. The debate within Anglo-Jewry on Sir Keith's speech can be followed in the issues of the *J. C.* for 24 Feb. and 3, 10, and 17 March 1978.

94. *J. C.*, 24 Feb. 1978, 22: leading article.

95. *The Times*, 4 March 1978, 15.

96. This was admitted by one of his critics, Mr Bernard Garbacz, President of B'nai B'rith First Lodge of England, who declared that Sir Keith had done 'a great disservice to the [Jewish] community by spotlighting quite unnecessarily a problem facing the Jews of Ilford': *J. C.*, 3 March 1978, 1.

97.   This emerged from a poll I conducted in Ilford North, during the by-election, involving an unstratified sample of 143 Jewish voters selected at random from annotated electoral registers made available to me by the Research Unit of the Board of Deputies; the voters were asked how they had voted in October 1974 and how they intended to vote in March 1978. It should be noted that at this by-election both the National Front candidate and Mr Iremonger lost their deposits.

9. *Present Perspective*

1.   *J. C.*, 19 Oct. 1951, 15.
2.   Ibid., 11 July 1969, 16: report of a BBC 'Panorama' programme.
3.   Ibid., 22 Dec. 1972, 8.
4.   *The Times,* 11 Dec. 1974, 7.
5.   H. Soref, 'Portrait of Anglo-Jewry', *Menorah Journal,* xli (Spring 1953), 82.
6   *J. C.,* 13 Jan. 1950, 12.
7.   Ibid., 20 Jan. 1950, 12; for further official condemnation of the notion of a Jewish vote at that time see ibid., 10 Feb. 1950, 17 (letter from Sir Robert Waley-Cohen) and 17 Feb., 21 (address by Leonard Stein, ex-president of the Anglo-Jewish Association, to the Association of Jewish Refugees in Great Britain).
8.   See, for example, *J. C.,* 25 Sept. 1964, 7 (leading article) and 16 (interview with the Chairman of the Board of Deputies' Defence Committee).
9.   *J. C.,* 24 Feb. 1978, 22.
10.   Ibid., 10 March 1978, 20.
11.   Ibid., 3 March 1978, 16.
12.   I am grateful to Mr Paul for making these conditions available to me.
13.   This was Clement Freud, who won the Isle of Ely for his party at a by-election in July 1973 and who has held the seat ever since. In 1974 Mr Freud contacted the *J. C.* asking not to be included in their list of Jewish MPs. Yet he subsequently admitted that he was 'Jewish by descent but not practising', and he is listed as a Jewish MP in the *Jewish Year Book:* see *Sunday Express,* 27 Oct. 1974, 2; *Jewish Year Book,* 1979, 174.
14.   In July 1974 Dafydd Williams, General Secretary of Plaid Cymru, informed me that he could 'only recall three or four Welsh Jews' whom he had known to be members of the party, and added that, in his view (with which I agree) this reflected the comparative weakness of the Blaid in Cardiff, where most Welsh Jews (2500 out of 3,000) live. In August 1976 Gwynfor Evans, President of Plaid Cymru, made a statement to the *J. C.* in which he said: 'We have never found any sympathy and support for the national aspirations of the Welsh people among the Jewish community. I cannot recall any Welsh Jewish community which has ever identified itself with us.' In a reply I pointed out that on the basis of the October 1974 general-election results in Cardiff (where the Blaid polled only 2.1 per cent of the electorate) the number of Cardiff Jews who supported the party could not have been more than 40: *J. C.,* 27 Aug. 1976, 6; 10 Sept. 1976, 20.
15.   In June 1974 Mrs Winifred Ewing, Scottish National Party MP for Moray and Nairn, informed me that, to her knowledge, some Jewish lawyers were members of the party.
16.   I deal with Jewish involvement in the National Front later on in this chapter. The political preferences of Northern Ireland's 900 or so Jews, located almost entirely in Belfast, remain an enigma. In the past it was commonplace for Northern Irish Jewry to identify with the Unionist party, but that was before the troubles which have plagued the province in recent years. Since 1968, and the fragmentation of

Northern Irish politics, the tendency has been for the Jews to keep out of the conflicts there, a tendency warmly supported by communal leaders (see *J. C.*, 29 Nov. 1974, 9: statement by Harold Ross, Senior Warden of the Belfast Hebrew Congregation). But it is known that a few Jews support the non-sectarian Alliance party. I know of no instance of Northern Irish Jews supporting the mainly Catholic Social Democratic and Labour party or, indeed, any branch of the Republican movement in the province.

17. P. Rose [Labour MP for Blackley, 1964-79], 'The So-Called Jewish Lobby in Parliament', *J. C.*, 29 May 1970, 7; *Hansard,* 10 Dec. 1968, 220.
18. On Robert Adley see Chapter 8, note 71.
19. Of the ten Jewish Conservative MPs then in Parliament, nine voted with the Government and one (Toby Jessel) abstained: *J. C.*, 2 May 1975, 9.
20. The encounter was vividly described in *The Times,* 5 March 1975, 1; it was occasioned by a Government decision to apply the 'guillotine' to the remaining stages of the Finance Bill.
21. In an interview with David Nathan, *J. C.*, 21 Oct. 1977, 21.
22. Zimmerman, 33-9.
23. For a description of the methodology see Chapter 8, notes 79 and 82.
24. Indeed Ivor Crewe, co-director of the British Election Study at the University of Essex, has shown that the party preferences of my Jewish sample in Hendon North in February 1974 were practically identical with those of social classes A and B in a national sample of voters at the same election: I. Crewe, 'The black, brown and green votes', *New Society,* 12 April 1979, 76-8.
25. For a description of the methodology see Chapter 8, note 97; a poll similar to that carried out at the time of the 1978 by-election was undertaken for the May 1979 general election; samples of identical size were used.
26. These percentages are taken from B. A. Kosmin, *Report on the Jewish Population of the London Borough of Redbridge based upon analysis of the 1976 Register of Electors* (mimeo., Board of Deputies, London, Oct. 1976); Clementswood is partly in Ilford North and partly in Ilford South.
27. I have derived these figures from B. A Kosmin, M. Bauer, and N. Grizzard, *Steel City Jews* (London, 1976), 22.
28. This information is based upon the 1971 Census Small Area Statistics and the computer analysis of Redbridge Jewry. I am grateful to Dr Kosmin, Executive Director of the Board of Deputies' Research Unit, and to Dr Lesley Morgan, Senior Computer Programmer at Royal Holloway College, for help in interpreting this data. The Redbridge Jewish Survey constitutes the largest single body of data relating to any Jewish community in the British Isles. See generally B. A. Kosmin and C. Levy, *The Work and Employment of Suburban Jews: The Socio-Economic Findings of the 1978 Redbridge Jewish Survey* (London, 1981).
29. See P. Kellner, 'Not a defeat: a disaster', *New Statesman,* 18 May 1979, 704; the findings of the election-day poll conducted by Independent Television News confirm those of Market and Opinion Research International which Mr Kellner uses.
30. The survey was carried out in September and October 1979; 130 Jewish electors, selected at random from the electoral register, were asked to recall their votes cast the previous May.
31. Kosmin and Grizzard, *Geographical Distribution Estimates,* 4.
32. On the age-structure and demographic characteristics of Hackney Jewry see B. A. Kosmin and N. Grizzard, *Jews in an Inner London Borough* (London) [1975], 13-18. My Hackney sample revealed Jewish support for Labour to be just less than 50 per cent. A survey of Jews still living in Chapeltown, Leeds, carried out for the Board of Deputies in the first half of 1979, and financed by the Social

Science Research Council, showed only 55 per cent of respondents as being Labour supporters: N. Grizzard and P. Raisman, 'Inner City Jews in Leeds', *Jewish Journal of Sociology,* xxii (1980), 31.

33. No precise data exist on the numerical extent of this Consevative commitment. But in a survey of a small number of members of the Hendon Adath Yisroel synagogue (a constituent of the Union of Orthodox Hebrew Congregations, to which most of the ultra-orthodox of Hackney are affiliated), in May and June 1976, Dr Sabine Roitman found that 70 per cent of her respondents identified themselves as Conservative supporters: S. Roitman, 'Les Juifs Anglais de 1966 a 1976—Pratiques, Mentalités, Compartements' (Université des Sciences Humaines Ph. D. thesis, Strasburg, 1978). 220.

34. I am grateful to Mr Lobenstein for having given me his impressions of the politics of the ultra-orthodox and Chassidic communities in Hackney. The intriguing further question raised here is whether and to what extent Jewish voters prefer Jewish candidates. In the Hackney Borough Council elections of May 1974 there was definite evidence that Jewish voters did have such a preference. In the Northfield ward only three of the ten contestants were Jewish. Of the 412 votes cast for the Jewish Liberal candidate, Maurice Owen, 310 were cast on the party line, but many of Owen's other votes were linked with those given to the Communist candidate (Monty Goldman, a Jew) or, to a lesser extent, with those cast for R. B. Coleman, a Conservative candidate and also Jewish. Maurice Owen, fighting in a ward thickly populated with orthodox Jews, personally polled more votes than any other Liberal candidate in the borough, a performance he repeated in 1978. In the Springfield ward (another orthodox Jewish area) Harry Goldstein, a strictly orthodox Jew, was one of the three Jewish Liberal candidates; he polled 89 and 101 votes in excess of his fellow Liberals. And in the New River ward, which also contains many orthodox Jews, Mr Lobenstein polled 901 votes as against 677 and 636 for his fellow Conservative candidates.

These instances, together with Mr Lobenstein's 1978 triumph, suggest that being Jewish, and particularly being an orthodox Jew in an orthodox Jewish area, gives a candidate a limited but distinct and perhaps decisive advantage, at least at local-election level, where Jewish electorates are concerned.

At parliamentary level the situation is less clear. I can find no evidence that Jewish parliamentary candidates have done less well than non-Jews over the past twenty years or so, though some resistance to Jews being chosen as Conservative candidates undoubtedly persists. There are plenty of instances of well-known Jews being defeated in Jewish areas: Barnet Janner at Whitechapel in 1930, for instance, and Dr Bernard Homa (Labour) at Hendon South in 1951 and 1955. But Mrs Miller's success at Ilford North in October 1974 has already been mentioned (see chapter eight), and it is interesting to note that the nearest Labour has ever come to winning Hendon North was in 1966, when the Jewish candidate whom Labour put up, Mr E. Wistrich, polled only 600 votes, or 1.4 per cent of the total poll, less than his Conservative opponent.

35. P. Rose, 'Labour and Israel', *J. C.*, 29 June 1979, 2.

36. *J. C.*, 14 June 1974, 7.

37. Rose, *J. C.*, 29 June 1979, 21.

38. On Young Liberal support for Arab terrorism see ibid., 20 Nov. 1970, 11 and 27 Nov. 1970, 7.

39. See also ibid., 12 July 1974, 7. In 1978 Mr Mayhew and Mr Michael Adams sued the Israeli evening newspaper *Maariv* for libel; this paper had asserted that their book *Publish it not ... The Middle East Cover-Up* (London, 1975), was pervaded by anti-Semitic statements and Nazi-style propaganda. Mr Mayhew and Mr Adams claimed that this had seriously tarnished their reputation in

Britain. The action was brought in Israel, in the justice of whose courts Mr Mayhew declared he had 'full faith', and was rejected, with costs awarded to the defendants: *J. C.*, 10 Aug. 1979, 3. I am grateful to Maurice Owen, a member of the Liberal party in Hackney, and Harold Lightstone, a member of the Hale Ward Liberal Association, Edgware, for having provided me with their impressions of the impact of the Young Liberals and of Mr Mayhew upon Jewish support for the party.

40. See Piratin, 84-6. That Jewish votes contributed to these victories is beyond reasonable doubt. I have met many Jews, including practising orthodox Jews, who have told me that they voted for the Communist party in Stepney in the late 1940s. The actual level of such support is more problematic. In my interview with him in Dec. 1978 Mr Piratin stated that some Jewish voters in the local elections voted for the Communist Jew and/or the Labour Jew; that is, their votes were given on ethnic rather than on party lines. I find this entirely credible.

41. Pelling, *The British Communist Party,* 168.

42. Ibid. 173.

43. Ibid. 179.

44. Quoted in B. Litvinoff, *A Peculiar People* (London, 1969), 158.

45. This does not, of course, mean that there are no such supporters in the constituency; it does mean that they are numerically insignificant.

46. J. Rose, 'Black views on Jews', *J. C.*, 28 Oct. 1977, 8.

47. Ibid: statement by Mr P. S. Khabra, secretary of the Indian Workers' Association of Southall.

48. *J. C.*, 15 April 1977, 9; Young Herut is a branch of the British Herut Movement, which is affiliated to the Herut party of Israel.

49. The Yiddish editorial was reprinted in *West Indian World,* no. 341 (27 Jan.-2 Feb. 1978), 1.

50. *J. C.*, 3 March 1978, 18.

51. Y. Ginzberg, 'Sympathy and resentment. Jews and coloureds in London's East End', *Patterns of Prejudice,* vol. 13, no. 2-3 (March-June 1979), 39-42. See generally L. M. Waldenburg, 'The History of Anglo-Jewish Responses to Immigration and Racial Tension, 1950-70' (University of Sheffield MA (Economics) thesis, 1972), especially Chapter III.

52. *J. C.*, 13 Oct. 1978, 1.

53. Ginzberg, 42.

54. Before moving to Eastbourne Mr Elder lived in Winchmore Hill, north London; at the general election in Hendon South, 1979, he obtained 290 votes, amounting to 0.8 per cent of the poll.

55. *J. C.,* 17 June 1977, 25: letter from Mr Elder; letter from Mr Elder to me, 21 Aug. 1978.

56. A. Elder, 'The Passionate Belief of the Jews in Race', *Spearhead,* Aug. 1978, 20.

57. He obtained 302 votes, about 17 per cent of the poll.

58. In conversation with me in Aug. 1978 Mr Viner confessed to having voted Labour or Communist up to the time he joined the National Front in 1976.

59. *J. C.*, 26 May 1978, 5.

60. In 1969 John Tyndall, later National Front Chairman, was quoted as saying 'The Jew is like a poisonous maggot feeding on a body in an advanced state of decay': *Sunday Times,* 30 March 1969, 2. Martin Webster, later National Activities Organizer of the Front, was the author of an article entitled 'Why I am a Nazi': M. Walker, *The National Front* (London, 1977), 45.

61. Mr Elder was a member of British Herut and was one of their delegates at the Zionist Federation conference in London in Oct. 1975; he informs me that he resigned from Herut after 'some members objected strongly to my being in the

National Front': letter to me, 28 Sept. 1979. In his article in *Spearhead,* Aug. 1978, Mr Elder praises Zionism as 'Jewish racial nationalism'.

62.   Letter from Mr Viner to me, 3 April 1978; interview with him at his Stoke New-ington home, 8 Aug. 1978. This view of Zionism is entirely in keeping with National Front ideology, which sees Zionism as a component of 'the remorseless drive towards Internationalism, that is, towards a total monopoly of political power'; behind this world conspiracy is an international financial élite, 'dominated by persons of a Jewish or pro-Zionist background': *Spearhead,* March 1977, quoted by N. Nugent and R. King, 'Ethnic minorities, scapegoating and the extreme right', in R. Miles and A. Phizacklea (eds.), *Racism and political action in Britain* (London, 1979), 38.

63.   At Folkestone Mr Lavine obtained 478 votes, 1.0 per cent of the poll; he was interviewed by me in July 1979.

64.   This policy was enunciated by P. Kavanagh, National Front candidate in the City of London by-election in 1977; it is party policy that all post-1948 immigrants be repatriated: *J. C.,* 25 Feb. 1977, 9.

65.   Two letters to Mr Cohen have remained unanswered.

66.   Letter to me, 23 Feb. 1978, from a member of the Defence and Group Relations Committee of the Board of Deputies.

67.   See, for instance, the interview of Martin Webster by Michael Freedland in *J. C.,* 27 May 1977, 19, and of John Tyndall by Ian Bradley in *The Times,* 30 Aug. 1977, 10. The Front tries desperately to draw a distinction between Zionism and Jewry, and in recent years has occasionally demonstrated 'grudging admiration' of Jewish talents: Nugent and King, loc. cit. 39-40.

68.   The quotation is from a letter written to me by Mr Abraham Marks, then Secretary of the Board of Deputies, on 1 May 1974; the italics are mine.

69.   I was called a 'crackpot' in a communication from Mr. F. M. Landau, a leading member of the Board of Deputies, 1 Oct. 1978; the reference to the vile and disgusting attacks comes from a letter from Mr M. A. Benjamin in the *J. C.,* 20 Oct. 1978, 20. I should like to stress that, as a Jew and a Zionist, I find the views and policies of the National Front totally abhorrent, and I believe Jewish support for and membership of the Front to be a matter of the deepest regret.

70.   Report of the Jewish Defence and Group Relations Committee, in the Board minutes of 8 Oct. 1978, 8.

71.   Roitman, 218-19. I translate this passage as follows: 'As far as we are concerned, the political views of English Jews are no different from those of the rest of the electorate. So it serves no useful purpose to make inquiries along these lines. If, however, such research was nevertheless carried out, we would deem it to be imprudent, indeed dangerous. Public opinion must believe in a truly integrated Jewish community, no different from its fellow citizens.
        'For the same reasons, there can be no question of speaking of a Jewish vote.'

72.   *J. C.,* 29 April 1977, 20.

73.   Ibid. 7; and see ibid., 22 April 1977, 1 and 4.

74.   Ibid., 28 April 1978, 6.

75.   Ibid., 27 April 1979, 7, 12, and 24.

76.   Board of Deputies minutes of meeting, 29 April 1979, 11-12.

77.   Report of the Jewish Defence and Group Relations Committee, 5 June 1979, 2.

78.   *J. C.,* 20 April 1979, 18.

79.   The official logic used to justify this approach seems to be that it is the duty of British Jews to cast their votes in such a way as to 'help diminish the threat of a Britain in which racialists, bigots and anti-semites are able to exercise power and influence', but that the Board of Deputies, in urging such action, is none the less not involving itself in 'party politics': Board of Deputies minutes of

meeting, 29 April 1979, 6: statement by Lord Fisher of Camden.

80.   See for instance *J. C.*, 18 Aug. 1922, 27 (statement by Gatchell Isaacs, minister of the South Hackney synagogue, in support of the Coalition candidate in the South Hackney by-election); 10 Nov. 1922, 11; 30 Nov. 1923, 10; 24 Oct. 1924, 24 (statements by Dayan H. M. Lazarus, Rabbi Dr Samuel Daiches, and the Reverend S. J. Roco, in support of the Liberal candidate at East Willesden); 24 May 1929, 21 (statement by Dr Gaster in support of the Liberal candidate at North Paddington).

81.   Telephone conversation with me, 14 Feb. 1974.

82.   *J. C.*, 31 Jan. 1975, 8.

83.   *Hendon Times*, 30 May 1975, 1.

84.   *J. C.*, 30 May 1975, 14.

85.   Circular letter from Lord Janner, Chairman of the Board's Israel Committee, 6 April 1979. The 86 'key seats' comprised 25 seats with 'significant Jewish populations', 17 Conservative-held and 16 Labour-held marginals, and 28 seats in which the sitting members were not seeking re-election; a list of suggested questions to candidates was also enclosed.

87.   *The Times*, 18 March 1980, 5; *Hendon Times*, 27 March 1980, 3. On 7 June 1980, in a sermon delivered at the Hendon synagogue, the Reverend Leslie Hardman answered those in the Jewish establishment who deprecated an appeal to the Jewish vote in this matter by asking 'If Mrs Thatcher had it in her power to veto an anti-*Shechita* bill, wouldn't we be right to put pressure on her to do so?'

88.   *Hendon Times*, 17 July 1980, 6.

89.   *J. C.*, 13 June 1980, 6; *Hendon Times*, 16 June, 3.

90.   *Hendon Times*, 3 April 1980, 1; 22 May, 4.

91.   *Ibid.*, 16 June 1980, 1.

92.   *Ibid.*, 17 July 1980, 6; *J. C.*, 18 July, 8. The Edgware Conservative Association Central Branch had previously voted unanimously to condemn the Government for its apparent intention to 'promote within the European Economic Community the idea of a separate Palestinian State within territory presently held by Israel': *J. C.*, 23 May 1980, 8. Later that summer Mr Gorst confessed: 'If the Jewish community in Edgware abstained at the next election I would be in real trouble', *Hendon Times*, 2 October 1980, 2. In August 1981 Mrs Thatcher refused to discuss her Government's Middle East policy at a public meeting of Finchley voters: *Hendon Times*, 20 August 1980, 6. See also I. Bradley, 'A Finchley Problem for Mrs Thatcher', in *The Times*, 29 October 1981, 14.

Appendix

1.   *J. C.*, 23 October 1964, 16.

2.   M. Rifkind, 'How Many is Too Much?', *J. C.*, 20 December 1974, 16.

Index